Architects of Re

C000056561

Walter L. Hixson since 2019 serves as colun
at the *Washington Report on Middle East Affairs*. This is his second book on
the Israel lobby following *Israel's Armor: The Israel Lobby and the First
Generation of the Palestine Conflict*. (Cambridge University Press, 2019) He is
the author of several books focused on the history of US foreign relations,
including *American Foreign Relations: A New Diplomatic History* (Routledge,
2015), *American Settler Colonialism: A History* (2013, Palgrave-Macmillan),
The Myth of American Diplomacy: National Identity and U.S. Foreign Policy (Yale
University Press, 2008). More at www.WalterHixson.com.

This book offers a compelling history of the most powerful lobby acting
on behalf of a foreign government in all of American history. The book
puts to rest any doubt as to whether the Israel lobby has played and
continues to play the crucial role in enabling aggression, the suppression
of Palestinian rights, and the failure to achieve a comprehensive Middle
East peace accord.

Rooted in archival evidence and an abundant secondary literature,
Architects of Repression shows how AIPAC and other Israel affinity groups
deploy propaganda, target campaign contributions, organize
demonstrations, and exert political pressure to manage public opinion—
and, especially, to influence the Congress. The massive foreign aid that the
United States has provided Israel—far more than allocated to any other
country and dispersed on favorable terms reserved for Israel alone--is only
one of many enabling benefits the small Zionist state has received over
many decades from the most powerful nation in the world.

For decades, as the book explains in depth, the Israel lobby has played the
pivotal role as the US enabled Israel's disdain for a negotiated settlement
of the Middle East conflict; its contemptuous dismissal of the plight of
Palestinian refugees; its cultivation of nuclear weapons in defiance of the
global nuclear non-proliferation movement; its profusion of palpably
racist, illegal and destabilizing Jewish-only settlements; its takeover of
Jerusalem, much of the West Bank, and the Golan Heights; and its
ongoing violent aggression, which has victimized Palestinians in the West
Bank and the Gaza Strip as well as neighboring states notably Lebanon. In
more recent years the Israel lobby launched a campaign to criminalize
political engagement and freedom of speech by equating criticism of Israel
with anti-Semitism. Hixson convincingly reveals that there will never be
peace in the Middle East until the monolithic Israel lobby is neutralized.

Architects of Repression:

How Israel and Its Lobby Put Racism, Violence and Injustice at the Center of US Middle East Policy

By Walter L. Hixson

Library of Congress Cataloging-in-Publication Data
Names: Hixson, Walter. L., author.
Title: Architects of repression: how Israel and its lobby put racism, violence and injustice at the center of US Middle East policy/ by Walter L. Hixson.
Description: Washington, D.C.: Institute for Research: Middle Eastern Policy, Inc., 2021 | Includes bibliographical references and index.
Identifiers: LCCN 2021002233 (print) | LCCN 2021002234 (eBook) | 9780982775745 (hardcover) | 9780982775776 (paperback) | ISBN 9780982775783 (kindle edition)
Subjects: LCSH: American Israel Public Affairs Committee. | Lobbying--United States. | Pressure groups--United States. | Arab-Israeli conflict. | Zionism. | Israel--Foreign relations--United States. | United States--Foreign relations--Israel. | Israel--Politics and government--20th century. | Israel--Politics and government--21st century.
Classification: LCC E183.8.I7 H578 2021 (print) | LCC E183.8.I7 (ebook) | DDC 327.5694073--dc23
LC record available at https://lccn.loc.gov/2021002233
LC ebook record available at https://lccn.loc.gov/2021002234

Contents

Introduction:
Explaining the Israel Lobby

On May 14, 2018, Israeli and American dignitaries assembled before a sprawling American Flag to dedicate the relocation of the US Embassy to Jerusalem. The Trump administration's decision to relocate the embassy from Tel Aviv was putting a stamp of approval from the world's most powerful nation on Israel's efforts to establish unilateral authority over the historic city of Jerusalem.

For Muslims and especially for Palestinians, the embassy relocation was the latest in a long series of humiliations that were enabled or openly supported by the United States, Israel's chief benefactor in world affairs. For generations Israel had sought to take control of Jerusalem, a city that is sacred to three religious-traditions: Jewish, Christian, and Muslim. Moreover, East Jerusalem was supposed to be the capital of a long-envisioned but never realized Palestinian state; instead, Israel was claiming the entire holy city as its "eternal capital." Under Trump the United States, which for decades had refrained from recognizing Israel's claim to Jerusalem, was now acknowledging it.

As the stylishly attired American and Israeli dignitaries smiled and mingled with flutes of champagne, only 50 miles away that same day Israeli snipers fired from behind protective shields on unarmed Palestinian protesters on the border of the Gaza Strip. The Israeli Defense Force (IDF) massacred 60 protesters, including six children, and wounded hundreds of others amid horrifying "scenes of smoke, fire, teargas, dust, agony and blood."[1] Among the victims targeted by the Israeli snipers were first responder health care workers, "despite seeing that they were clearly marked as such."[2]

The Gaza protesters posed no threat to the Israeli forces--other than the symbolic one of engaging in the "Great March of Return" to the border of the homeland from which their families had been displaced 70 years earlier. "The demonstrations held in Gaza today came as no surprise," the Israeli human rights group B'Tselem declared. "Israel had plenty of time to come up with alternate approaches for dealing with the protests, apart from firing live ammunition. The fact that live gunfire is once again the sole measure that the Israeli military is using in the field evinces appalling indifference towards human life on the part of senior Israeli government and military officials."[3]

1

Introduction

Meanwhile, back at the embassy dedication the US Ambassador-- Trump's longtime bankruptcy attorney, David Friedman—introduced the Israeli delegation led by Prime Minister Benjamin Netanyahu followed by the American dignitaries, including several members of Congress, and Israel lobby benefactors led by the Las Vegas casino mogul Sheldon Adelson. Sitting next to Netanyahu were Trump's "senior advisers," his son-in-law Jared Kushner and daughter Ivanka.

The two sites, the new embassy and the blood-drenched Gaza border, juxtaposed privilege and deprivation; liberation and occupation; celebration and slaughter. One group of people—overwhelmingly white— were well fed, well groomed, and free to come and go as they pleased. The other group of people, brown-skinned, was confined, deprived of essential resources, denied a national existence--and shot dead when they arose in unarmed protest.

The embassy dedication was a triumph not only for Israel, but also for the Israel lobby, which is the subject of this book. The embassy relocation was the latest in a series of many such triumphs, stretching over many decades, for the pro-Israel lobby in the United States. The lobby has thus played—and continues to play—a crucial role in mobilizing decisive American support for a long history of aggressive and often illegal Israeli actions, which have come at the expense of human rights, racial justice and equality in Palestine.

The Israel lobby lives and breathes to dissemble and distort perceptions of the Israel-Palestine issue in Israel's favor. By so doing it has successfully fueled an American Middle East policy that has for many decades enabled Israeli aggression and injustice. The lobby has contributed powerfully to the failure to achieve peace and—to a much greater extent than has been acknowledged--to the evolution of a disastrous American foreign policy in the Middle East region (West Asia) since World War II.

Despite the centrality of the Israel lobby to the Middle East conflict, with a few notable exceptions scholars and journalists have been reluctant to assess its role—in part because they are certain to be attacked for so doing.[4] While most scholars and university presses steer clear of the controversial subject, the most original work has emanated from a small Washington think tank, the Institute for Research: Middle East Policy (IRmep), which is also the publisher of this book. IRmep's Director Grant F. Smith has produced a series of richly researched studies, beginning with *Foreign Agents* in 2007. More recently Smith published *Big Israel* (2016), an in-depth analysis of the Zionist lobby, and *The Israel Lobby Enters Sate Government* (2019).[5]

By far the most well-known academic study, *The Israel Lobby*, by John Mearsheimer and Stephen Walt, appeared in 2007. To their credit the two eminent political scientists produced a well-researched and boldly critical assessment of the lobby, including its support for the Iraq War that was then raging. Mearsheimer and Walt were bitterly attacked—an attack encouraged, ironically, by the very subject of the book—with critics exaggerating and distorting the Iraq War aspect of the book at the expense of their broader argument on the lobby's deleterious influence on US foreign policy.[6]

Oddly, it has become fashionable even in progressive and radical circles to downplay the influence of the Israel lobby, as if explaining the powerful role that it plays in American Middle East policy entailed subscribing to some sort of naïve or overblown conspiracy theory. Skeptics invariably cite a few anomalous cases in which a lobby campaign failed to achieve its aims in order to make the broader a-historic claim—which goes unsupported by actual research--that such incidents "prove" the lobby is not all that influential.[7] The reality, as this study will conclusively demonstrate, is far different.

Architects of Repression offers a comprehensive, up to date, and evidence-driven historical assessment of the role of the Israel lobby in US politics and foreign policy since World War II. This book puts to rest any doubt as to whether the lobby has played and continues to play a crucial role in enabling Israeli aggression, the suppression of Palestinian rights, and the failure to achieve a comprehensive Middle East peace accord.

Rooted in archival evidence and an abundant secondary literature, the book shows how the lobby *works* by deploying propaganda, targeting campaign contributions, organizing demonstrations, and exerting political pressure to manage public opinion—and, especially, to influence the Congress. *Architects of Repression* thus lays bare the ways and means by which a critical branch at the epicenter of the United States government, and in control of the purse strings, became heavily influenced by a lobby representing the interests of a foreign country. The massive largesse that the United States has provided Israel—far more than allocated to any other country and dispersed on favorable terms reserved for Israel alone--is only one of many enabling benefits the small Zionist state has received over many decades from the most powerful nation in the world.

While the Zionist movement long preceded the creation of Israel, this book homes in on the period since World War II and not on the formative years of Zionist advocacy. The full-blown Israel lobby was forged in the early 1940s and has grown explosively to the present day. That eight decade-period is the focus here, though for those who wish to dig deep into the past the Appendix provides critical analysis of the biblical narrative and the arc of Jewish history. This book does not offer a comparison with other lobbies nor does it examine in depth Israel's domestic politics nor its political system. Neither does it focus on the UK and Western Europe, where the Israel lobby has also been active and consequential. What the book does do is to illuminate the history of the Israel lobby in the United States and its powerful impact on the ground in Palestine and on American Middle East policy as a whole.

What Is the Israel Lobby?

This study embraces the term "lobby" as a widely recognized trope conveying organized and well-funded efforts to wield political influence to advance a self-interested cause. Lobbies are not neutral or objective, they instead raise large amounts of money in order to mobilize information and advocacy in their own behalf and to combat other sources of knowledge that might counter or work against their interests.

While the purpose of a lobby is fairly straightforward, the Israel lobby itself is much more complex. The Israel lobby is not a single, monolithic entity. Rather it is a multi-faceted grouping of ideas, individuals and organizations united by the commitment to dispense pro-Israel propaganda and to discredit critical analysis of the Zionist state. The Israel lobby has evolved over time, yet its drives and single-minded dedication to pro-Israel advocacy have been remarkably stable and persistent since World War II.

The Israel lobby is the most powerful lobby acting in the interests of a foreign nation in all of American history. The little state of Israel—not the behemoths Russia or China, as many Americans might imagine or have been led to believe—intrudes more directly into American domestic politics than any other nation in the world.

The largest and most well-funded Israel lobby organization--the American Israel Public Affairs Committee (AIPAC)--is far and away the most powerful foreign policy lobby in Washington, D.C. A colossus in the world of Washington politics, AIPAC is often mentioned in the same breath as the gun, pharmaceutical and retired persons' lobbies.

AIPAC has long worked closely with prominent American Jewish representatives who comprise the Conference of Presidents of Major American Jewish Organizations. In addition to AIPAC and the Conference of Presidents, the lobby encompasses wealthy individual donors, political action committees, and myriad other Jewish and Christian organizations, Zionist pressure groups, media watchdogs, college campus organizations, and think tanks. Many are chronicled here but there are literally hundreds of such entities in existence.

The Israel lobby is not simply a front group for the State of Israel. AIPAC and other organizations are staffed by *Americans* who support Israel. That said, from its inception the lobby has worked in close collaboration with the Israeli state and usually in lock step with Israel's goals and actions in Palestine and the greater Middle East. AIPAC operates an office in Jerusalem (which it rarely acknowledges) and engages in planning and regular exchanges of information with Israeli government officials.

In the pages that follow I concentrate mainly but not exclusively on AIPAC, the most powerful, well-funded and best-known lobby entity. In the 2019-20 fiscal year, AIPAC was responsible for 86 percent of the $3.4 million expended on direct pro-Israel lobbying of the US Congress. Although $3.4 million may not seem like much, Israel lobby organizations must collectively raise nearly $200 million annually to sustain that level of direct pro-Israel lobbying expenditure on the Congress.[8]

"AIPAC uses the resources of wealthy people in the American Jewish community to enforce a kind of political orthodoxy in Congress, on the White House and on the media," declares M.J. Rosenberg, a man who should know, having worked as an AIPAC propagandist himself for many years in the past. "Its purpose is to make sure no one in a position of power deviates from the Israel line."[9]

As this book will show, AIPAC and its allies have influenced and sometimes dominated public discourse as well as executive authority, but the lobby has been most dominant in the Congress of the United States. Under AIPAC oversight, the Congress, as political scientist Kirk Beattie has pointed out, has become a "consistent, unrelenting agent in making Israel a regional behemoth impervious to worldwide criticism of its long-lasting violations of international law."[10]

In addition to myriad other sources, this book is the first to draw on comprehensive research into the *Near East Report* (NER), the influential lobby newsletter which for decades has been sent to every member of Congress, among other recipients. Serving as a crucial conduit linking Israel, AIPAC and the nation's elected representatives, the NER has proven to be a valuable source in illuminating the initiatives, discourse and methodologies of Israel and the lobby.

AIPAC and its cohorts have played a pivotal role in shaping and policing American policy throughout the history of the Palestine conflict. The lobby has helped to enable the Israelis to carry out aggressive policies with the assurance that the United States, the most powerful country in the world, would offer its full support. Over the years the lobby grew in size and expanded the scope of its propaganda campaigns in an effort to manage the political fallout stemming from Israel's aggressive actions in and beyond Palestine. The lobby has thus played an essential role in helping to insulate Israel from facing consequences for violations of human rights and of international law.

The lobby's skillful disinformation campaign has succeeded in convincing generations of Americans that Israel is a besieged innocent, but the history of the Middle East conflict reveals a much more complex story and a pattern of Israeli aggression. Americans appear especially naïve about realities on the ground in West Asia. When asked in a representative poll, the citizens of Mexico, the UK and Canada say they believe Israel occupies Palestinian territory. The majority of Americans believe the opposite is true.[11]

The Israel lobby is not comprised exclusively of people of the Jewish faith, nor does it speak for all Jews, nor all Protestant evangelicals, nor even all Zionists. The term "Jewish lobby," which has been applied in the past, is an incorrect and inappropriate term, as some American Jews—in fact more with each passing day—do not support Israel's aggressive course in the Middle East. While the lobby does depend heavily on a relatively small number of mostly right-wing and Orthodox Jewish donors, a growing number of Jews and Jewish organizations actively oppose Israeli repression of Palestinians and advocate a just peace in the Middle East. Moreover, linking the lobby with Jews alone obscures the growing number of Christians, notably evangelical Christians, who embrace Israel and the lobby. While they do relatively little direct lobbying as compared with AIPAC and other Jewish groups such as Anti-Defamation League and the American Jewish Committee,[12] Christian Zionists nonetheless mobilize significant and typically uncritical public support for Israel.

This book does not purport to represent the last word on the history of the Israel lobby. While *Architects of Repression* offers the most comprehensive assessment to date, much more research remains to be done on the structure, strategies, goals, tactics, and individual participants (Including notably studies of individual members of Congress) and covert activities of the most powerful lobby representing the interests of a foreign country in American history.

Settler State Symmetry

The framework of settler colonialism helps explain the Palestine conflict and the role of the Israel lobby in the United States. Settler colonialism is a relatively recent concept but one that has increasingly been applied to studies of Israel and Palestine.[13] Israel's settler colonial identity, its aggressive course in Palestine, and US support for these policies are all inextricably linked.

Settler colonization helps explain the core identity of *both* the United States and Israel. Indeed, the shared identity as settler colonial states goes a long way toward explaining the "special relationship" between the two nations, as proclaimed by President John F. Kennedy in 1962. The reciprocal relationship, in turn, profoundly influences the character and evolution of the Middle East conflict.

Surveying changes that were remapping the world as a result of the First World War, President Woodrow Wilson declared that "Jewish Palestine" should "never go back to the Mohammedan apache."[14] Through his pejorative linking of Arab Muslims and the southwestern American Indian tribe, which had relatively recently been violently subdued by the United States, Wilson invoked the shared history of settler colonization.

Just as American settlers had "tamed" their own frontier—"Winning the West," as Theodore Roosevelt put it in his multi-volume pop history--many Americans would assume that the Zionists were on a similar mission of settling and bringing civilization to the backward Islamic world. As the British politician Richard Crossman explained, owing to the "frontier mentality . . . the American will give the Jewish settler in Palestine the benefit of the doubt, and regard the Arab as the aboriginal who must go down before the march of progress."[15]

The United States and Israel--like Australia, New Zealand, Canada, South Africa, and many others—evolved as imperial settler societies. Animated by powerful nationalist, racial and religious drives, settler states cultivate their identities as chosen peoples destined to inherit a new land. Settler colonialism is a zero-sum game: through mass migration and violent removal policies settlers mean to drive indigenous residents from the land in order to take it for themselves.

Settler colonialism is worth emphasizing because it helps explain *the drives, aggression, and continuity* that have characterized the history of Zionism, as well as the history of the United States and other settler societies. Unlike conventional European colonialism, which focused on economic exploitation of colonies, *settlers* come to stay rather than merely to exploit labor and natural resources for profit. Settler societies create structures of permanence and work relentlessly to establish enduring facts on the ground. As the goal is elimination of the indigenous people, settler colonialism rarely gives way to a peaceful resolution of land conflict.

From the outset leading Zionists sought to *displace* rather than coexist with the indigenous Palestinian population. Success depended on following a simple formula: the migration of masses of Jews and their takeover of as much land in Palestine as possible with as few indigenous people as possible remaining on that land. "The Zionists look forward to a practically complete dispossession of the present non-Jewish inhabitants of Palestine," an international study group advised Wilson in 1919. The King-Crane Commission warned that an effort to displace the indigenous population of Palestine would generate a major conflict, but its report on the Palestine question was ignored.[16]

7

From 1931 to 1936, as the Nazi regime consolidated power in Germany, Jewish migration to Palestine more than doubled from 175,000 to 370,000 and land purchases accelerated as well. In the wake of the massive influx, episodic ethnic conflict gave way to a major armed clash between the European settlers and the Palestinians. In 1937 Great Britain, which had received colonial dominion over the former Ottoman province following World War I, proposed to partition Palestine between the Arabs and Jews in an effort to quell the violence.[17]

David Ben-Gurion, head of the executive committee of the Jewish Agency, whose mission was the promotion of Zionist settlements in Palestine, made it abundantly clear that partition of Palestine would be merely the first step in the quest to secure control over *all* of Palestine. A Polish migrant formerly known as David Grün, Ben-Gurion explained in a personal letter to his 17-year-old son in October 1937 that under "this proposed partition we will get more than what we already have, though of course much less than we merit and desire . . . What we want is that the whole and unified land be *Jewish* [emphasis in original]. A unified *Eretz Israel* [biblical or greater Israel] would be no source of satisfaction for me— if it were Arab."

Ben-Gurion went on to explain that the indigenous Palestinians as well as Arabs from the surrounding nations could be expected to resist an expanding Zionist state. It was therefore urgently necessary to bring in "all the Jews we can. We firmly believe that we can admit more than two million." Under the direction of the Jewish Agency, the migrants would "build a multi-faceted Jewish economy—agricultural, industrial, and maritime. We will organize an advanced defense force—a superior army which I have no doubt will be one of the best armies in the world. At that point I am confident that we would not fail in settling in the remaining parts of the country, through agreement and understanding with our Arab neighbors, or through some other means.

"If we are compelled to use force," he continued, the Zionists would in the end prevail, "not only because we will be better organized and equipped, but also because behind us stands a force still greater in quantity and quality. This is the reservoir of the millions in the Diaspora." The bottom line was clear to the Zionist patriarch, who now shared it with his son: "We must expel Arabs and take their place."[18]

As Ben-Gurion made clear, settler states anticipate the resort to violent solutions. In Palestine, cleansing operations, war, massacre, collective punishment, regimentation and incarceration have been used continuously to establish and maintain the settler state.

While vigorously resisting external constraints that might impede their project, the Zionist movement at the same time depended on powerful nations, first Great Britain then the United States, to support the new settler colony. The United States--itself an aggressive settler society and long the home of the majority of Jews in the world—became the crucial special ally enabling and funding Israel's expansionism.

Distinctiveness of Zionist Settler Colonization

While Israel had much in common with other settler colonial societies, in certain crucial respects Zionist settlement was and remained *sui generis*. The uniqueness stemmed mainly from two factors: one, the horrific intensity of historic anti-Semitism; and two, the belatedness of the Zionist settler project.

Zionist migrants carried with them to Palestine the devastating burden of historic anti-Semitism, culminating in the Nazi genocide that took the lives of some six million Jews. Anti-Semitism and pogroms against Jews (discussed in greater depth in the Appendix) had been deeply rooted for centuries. By the nineteenth century European and especially Russian anti-Semitism had driven Jews into the east-European "pale of settlement." By the 1930s Jews were trapped in the "bloodlands" of Europe, the site of terror, death, and destruction at the hands of the competing Soviet and Nazi empires. Europe's Jews were among the millions of victims of famine, disease, deportation, forced labor, rape, torture, and murder even before the Nazis implemented the "final solution."[19] They suffered the wrenching impact of loss of family members and destruction of their communities in Poland, Ukraine, Lithuania, and other areas.

The leaders of the Zionist movement, including several future Israeli heads of state, migrated from these very bloodlands. In the wake of World War II, Zionists determined to replace the stunning images of emaciation and of Jews appearing to go meekly into the gas chambers with a new, masculinized Jew, the *sabra*, who like the eponymous desert plant, thorny and tenacious, was determined to thrive in a hostile environment.

The Zionist leaders thus inherited, internalized, and perpetuated a Hobbesian worldview rooted in the traumas of Jewish history. This time, they vowed, the Jews would be the aggressors, not the victims. In one of the most dreadful ironies of modern history, European Jews--themselves horribly victimized by a genocide of unprecedented scope and intensity--became the aggressors in a new land.

From the outset Zionists were quick to resort to violence against their Arab foes as well as British colonial administrators. They constructed powerful militias notably the *Haganah* and went on to become—with massive assistance from the United States--by far the most heavily militarized state in the modern Middle East.[20]

Scarred by the traumas of war and genocide, the early Zionist leaders projected onto the indigenous Arabs the violence that had been inflicted onto the Jews. In 1947 Ben-Gurion accepted partition and citizenship for Palestinians within Israel, overcoming the right-wing opposition of "revisionist" Zionists in the process, but he and other Israeli leaders remained distrustful of Arabs and contemptuous of Palestinian refugees. Perennially invoking memory of the Nazi genocide, Israeli leaders proved quick in subsequent years to compare Arab leaders such as Gamal Abdel Nasser and Yasser Arafat with Adolf Hitler. From Ben-Gurion to Netanyahu, Israeli leaders frequently disdained negotiations with Palestinians and Arab leaders, comparing such talks to appeasement of the Nazis at the infamous 1938 Munich Conference.

Temporality and the Role of the Lobby

In addition to the legacies of anti-Semitism, the other major distinction between Israel and other settler societies pertains to timing. This distinction brings into sharp relief the role of the Israel lobby.

Zionist settler colonialism came to fruition well into the twentieth century—much later than the establishment of the Anglophone settler societies of the United States, Australia, New Zealand and Canada. Of crucial importance, Zionist settler colonialism thus coincided and clashed directly with the post-World War II rise of human rights consciousness and growing awareness of the historic exploitation and unjust treatment of indigenous and colonized peoples. In December 1948--the same year that Israel gained international recognition--the United Nations ratified the historic Universal Declaration of Human Rights of all peoples.

The confluence of Israeli settler colonialism and the postwar discourse of international human rights consciousness is fundamentally important. While established as a democracy and recognized by the UN, Israel was at the same time a *reactionary* settler colonial state. The Israeli policies of borderland aggression, militarism and the establishment of illegal settlements were more characteristic of an eighteenth- or nineteenth-century style of settler colonialism. Israel's settler aggression thus represented a stark contrast with the postwar norms of decolonization, national self-determination, international justice, human rights and the rights of indigenous people.[21]

The Zionist state uprooted some 750,000 indigenous Palestinians and expanded its borders during the first Arab-Israeli War of 1948. Thereafter Israel remained highly aggressive along its borders, as it mounted frequent punitive raids before invading Egypt in 1956. The June 1967 War, the subsequent decision to occupy and settle Arab territory, and the myriad attacks on neighboring states that followed all underscore *Israel's core identity as a congenitally aggressive and expansive settler state.*

Throughout this history Palestinians and the surrounding Arab states did not always act wisely, to be sure, but they did not cause the Palestine conflict. Palestinians sought self-determination just as myriad other peoples had done all over the world especially since the First World War. Just as we do not blame "Indians" for American settler colonialism, or African and Asian peoples for European colonialism in those lands, it is ahistorical to ascribe causation to anyone but the external invaders and their benefactors. This fundamental knowledge of causation has long been elided by Israel and lobby propagandists and their apologists.

While the Arab world, the UN, and to varying extents the nations of Western Europe all condemned Israel's violations of international norms, the country that mattered most was the United States of America. Far and away the most powerful and influential nation in the postwar world, the United States was also the home to the greatest number of Jews outside Israel and was the heartland of Christian Zionism as well. Parallel histories of settler colonialism combined with deep-seated religious attachment to the "holy land" enabled the special relationship to take hold and to thrive. Ultimately, the special relationship with Israel evolved from the deeply rooted affinities of race, religion and culture.

The American cultural affinity for Zionism did not pre-determine American diplomacy in the Middle East, but it made certain inclinations and choices more amenable to large numbers of Americans while foreclosing other options. American culture thus provided fertile ground for the cultivation of pro-Zionist sympathies and the emergence of a full-blown Israel lobby.

Israeli leaders and American Zionists fully understood that the United States was the one nation that could enable Israel to thrive in defiance of the Arab world, European and Third World critics, and the UN. Louis Lipsky, one of the founders of the Israel lobby, grasped this reality early on. In 1951 he declared that pro-Israeli propaganda in the United States supplied "the armor Israel cannot get along without."[22]

In their efforts to take charge of congressional and public perceptions of Middle East politics, Israel and the nascent lobby confronted persistent opposition from the US Department of State. The professional diplomats assiduously chronicled and regularly criticized the aggressive policies of borderland expansion, disdain for the plight of Palestinian refugees, and efforts to establish Jerusalem as Israel's capital in defiance of the UN agreement for an international trusteeship over the holy city. State Department diplomats regularly reported that Israel posed the primary obstacle to the quest for peace in the region. The diplomats and other national security officials advised the executive branch and therefore posed a threat to impede crucial financial assistance or otherwise deter the Zionist state from pursuing its goals. The State Department criticism was evidence-based and rooted in political realism rather than reflecting, as Zionists often charged, a "pro-Arab" or even worse anti-Semitic disposition.

Fully aware of the threats posed by the State Department criticism, the Israel lobby strove to undermine, discredit and overcome opposition within the US national security establishment. The lobby would go over the heads of the national security elite and appeal directly to the public and its elected representatives.

The lobby succeeded in these efforts by dispensing propaganda, mobilizing its supporters and most especially by exerting a growing influence over the Congress. Asked in 1973 to define AIPAC's mission, Isaiah Leo Kenen, the key figure in the first generation of the Israel lobby, responded, "I put it very succinctly. We appeal to local leadership to write or telegraph or telephone their Congressmen and urge them to call upon the President to overrule the Department of State."[23] Abraham Feinberg, a lobbyist and Democratic campaign fundraiser from the 1940s to the 1960s, was equally blunt, explaining, "My path to power was cooperation in terms of what they [members of Congress] needed—campaign money."[24]

Taking advantage of its influence over the Congress, the lobby regularly thwarted efforts by the American executive branch to rein in Israeli aggression in pursuit of a more balanced and realistic diplomacy that might bring peace to the region. A well-ensconced canard of Israeli propaganda holds that--to quote the Israeli diplomat Abba Eban in 1973--"The Arabs never miss an opportunity to miss an opportunity [for peace]."[25] That quotation actually much more accurately describes *Israeli* policy, often in defiance of the United States, or at least in defiance of the State Department and the executive branch.

Israel's persistent opposition to pursuing a Middle East peace flowed from the logic of Zionist colonization in which the settlers sought to gain control of as much land as possible with as few Arabs as possible living on it. Israeli leaders—Ben-Gurion, Moshe Dayan, Menachem Begin, Yitzhak Shamir, Ariel Sharon, and Netanyahu, among them--often explicitly advanced this very policy in these very terms. Israel belatedly did make peace with Egypt and Jordan but efforts to forge a peace with the Palestinians confronted an iron wall of right-wing resistance.

With respect to Palestine and the Golan Heights, the "peace process" thus became a sham, providing cover for the establishment of ever-increasing numbers of Jewish-only settlements. Moreover, the combined forces of settler colonialism, religious affinity, and the Israel lobby have rendered problematic efforts to highlight these facts, to criticize Israel, or hold it responsible for an illegal and unjust occupation. Knowing that the lobby had its back on the American home front, Israel ignored the State Department and frequently defied American presidents when they did seek to rein in its aggressive instincts.

Israel and the lobby thus warded off diplomatic pressure while at the same time ensconcing the United States as Israel's primary sponsor and protector. The lobby also tapped into American financial largesse, which dramatically aided Jewish migration to the Zionist homeland. The US funding--unmatched by that which it supplied to any other foreign government--also enabled Israel to become the military powerhouse of the Middle East. The Israeli militarist Moshe Dayan's famous quip thus had a ring of truth: "Our American friends offer us money, arms, and advice. We take the money, we take the arms, and we decline the advice."[26]

Management of public opinion within the United States through campaign contributions, propaganda and disinformation spearheaded by the lobby, played a crucial role in mobilizing support for Israel. Policing the Congress ensured the continuous flows of massive American financial assistance as well as the domination of pro-Israeli discourse in Washington and indeed across much of the nation. In sum, as this book will conclusively demonstrate, the Israel lobby has long played a powerful role in shaping and policing American Middle East diplomacy.

Lobby Discourse

For decades Israel and the US lobby have successfully promoted an image of Israel as the beleaguered and vulnerable "sole democracy" of the Middle East. This framing depicts Israel as a tiny nation that sought only the right to exist within the "tough neighborhood" to which, citing biblical justification, it claimed divine sanction to "return" (see Appendix). In 1970, a survey found that "three-quarters of Americans agreed that 'Israel is a small, courageous democratic nation which is trying to preserve its independence.'"[27] This propaganda framework obscured Israel's congenital aggression, illegal settlements, marginalization of minorities, and its rejection of opportunities to negotiate a viable peace settlement.

The discourse promoted by Israel and the lobby was not utterly without foundation. Israel is a bona fide parliamentary democracy within its own borders. The Palestinians who live inside Israeli borders, about 20 percent of the total population, have voting rights. They, however, along with other minorities such as the Druze and Ethiopian Jewish migrants, have been marginalized and subjected to racist discourse. A wealth of studies "have proved definitively," as Israeli scholar Arnon Degani points out, "that, contrary to its self-image, Israel never had a fundamental commitment to upholding basic democratic values and has treated the Palestinian Arab minority, at best, as second-class citizens."[28]

Israel, to be sure, is not unique in marginalizing minorities or seeking to obscure a history of settler aggression behind a cloud of discursive mythology. Throughout history settler societies have policed their pasts and distorted their actual histories of removing and colonizing indigenous people. Nineteenth century Americans famously claimed it was their "manifest destiny" to seize vast tracts of land from Indians and Mexicans, who were depicted as backward and racially inferior. In subsequent generations Americans internalized a mythical past, obscuring an actual history of white supremacy and imperialism by essentializing the nation as a land of "liberty and justice for all" and a champion of global democracy.

Unlike nineteenth century America, however, Israel and the American lobby encountered serious global challenges to settler colonial expansion in the late twentieth and early twenty-first centuries. Revolutionary transformations in mass media, beginning with television and expanding to satellite technology and the Internet, offered a world-wide web to present alternative views to counter Israeli and lobby propaganda depicting Israel as a peace-seeking democracy. Global public opinion thus presented a growing challenge to unilateral Israeli settler colonization in Palestine.

While we can only imagine the horrific visual imagery generated by the "trail of tears" of the 1830s, in which the United States cleansed the American southeast of five indigenous bands, the Palestine Intifada of the late 1980s and the repeated pummeling of the Gaza Strip in the 2000s, to cite two examples, produced immediate and visceral worldwide coverage replete with disturbing video. By the twenty-first century millions of people not only had immediate video access but could also discuss developments in world politics through Internet sites and on social media platforms.

As this book will show, the Israel lobby exerted significant influence over US Middle East policy throughout Israel's history, but beginning with the 1982 Israeli invasion of Lebanon the challenges of managing worldwide and especially US public opinion began to mount. AIPAC and other lobby organizations responded to the increasingly interconnected world with an expansion of fund-raising and intensification of propaganda efforts.

Over the ensuing decades AIPAC and the broader lobby continued to exert considerable influence over the Congress and much of American public opinion. Today, however, the Israel lobby faces unprecedented challenges. In addition to the advances in communications technology and the Internet that have made more and more people aware of the growth of illegal Israeli settlements and the ongoing violent repression of

Palestinians, the lobby confronts a growing divide in perceptions of Israel on the part of a core constituency—American Jews.

Until relatively recently, support for Israel was virtually inseparable from American Jewish identity. However, in recent years it has become clear that while the majority of American Jews continue to embrace, as they have long done, a liberal worldview, a minority of wealthy, older, and mostly Orthodox Jews are more-right wing. Their wealth anchors unconditional US support for Israel even as the Zionist state carries out aggressive and illegal policies. The gulf between majority liberal American Jewish opinion on one side, and Israeli aggression backed by a right-wing minority of American Jews on the other, constitutes an escalating "crisis of Zionism."[29]

A broad spectrum of Americans has grown frustrated with the nation's deeply flawed Middle East policy, which has failed to deliver peace and justice in Palestine while at the same time embroiling the United States in a series of inconclusive "forever wars." Injustice in Palestine has been a primary and persistent source of political instability and warfare in the Middle East since World War II. American postwar policy, which centered on anti-communism, controlling access to oil, and unstinting support for Israel, has done little to contain and much to exacerbate the instability that has wracked the region for decades. In sum, as is increasingly being recognized, US diplomacy in the Middle East has been an abject failure.[30] It is well past time for a new American approach to Middle East policy, a project that requires greater understanding and a meaningful reckoning with Israel and its American lobby.

Chapter 1
The Rise of American Zionism

Tall and distinguished, a skillful orator with a resonant baritone, Rabbi Abba Hillel Silver commanded the stage at the luxury Biltmore Hotel in the heart of New York City on May 2, 1942. He had prepared his whole life for this moment. Silver had given his first speech on Zionism in 1907 at the age of 14, only five years after his Orthodox Jewish parents had moved the family from Lithuania to the United States. Like his father, grandfather and great-grandfather, he had become a rabbi and by the time of the Biltmore gathering he presided over the largest Reform Jewish congregation in the United States in Cleveland, Ohio.

Silver's speech at the Biltmore marked a decisive moment in advancing the movement calling for the immediate establishment of a Jewish state encompassing as much of Palestine as possible. The time had come, Silver declaimed in a stirring address, to lend support to "those who have given their tears and their blood and their sweat to build for them and for us and the future generations, at long last, after the weary centuries, a home, a national Home, a Jewish Commonwealth, where the spirit of our entire people can finally be at rest."[1]

The audience roared its approval and subsequently passed a resolution known as the Biltmore Program demanding, "that Palestine be constituted as a Jewish Commonwealth integrated into the structure of the new democratic world."[2] Silver and like-minded Zionists went on to energize a powerful lobby dedicated to advancing first a movement, Zionism, and then a nation, Israel. Within two years of Silver's speech—and four years before Israel was created—the Zionist lobby was already well on its way to commanding the United States Congress and much of American public opinion.

Silver's speech marked the culmination of more than a generation of efforts by the Zionist lobby in the United States. In 1918 the Zionist Organization of America (ZOA) had convinced President Woodrow Wilson to throw his full support behind the historic British Balfour Declaration (1917), which called for "a national home for the Jewish people" in Palestine. Former President Theodore Roosevelt also endorsed the creation of a Jewish national homeland in Palestine, a reflection of growing bipartisan consensus. Lobbied by Zionists in the World War I era, the US Congress passed a series of resolutions in support of the Zionist project.[3]

Supreme Court Justice Louis Brandeis, a non-religious Jew but nonetheless an ardent Zionist, urged his friend Wilson to support converting *all* of Palestine into a Jewish state.[4] Thus from the outset many leading American Zionists sympathized with the drive to *displace* rather than coexist with the indigenous Palestinian population.

While Zionism gained increasing support, anti-Jewish prejudices remained a strong force in American life. From 1880 to 1914, as nearly three million European Jews, more than two-thirds of them Russian, poured into the United States, anti-Jewish sentiments flourished.[5] Jewish immigrants encountered hostility and grappled with poverty in the ghettos of New York and other East Coast cities.[6] The National Origins Act (1924) defined Jews as a separate "Hebrew race" and barred them from immigrating into the country. During the interwar period millions of Americans imbibed the anti-Jewish conspiracy theories propagated by the evangelist Gerald L.K. Smith, automobile manufacturer Henry Ford, and the Detroit Catholic "radio Priest" Father Charles Coughlin, among others.[7]

Popular perceptions began to change by the late 1930s, as Nazi extremism made it increasingly problematic for Americans openly to embrace prejudice against Jews. The United States still refused to open its borders to Jewish refugees from Europe, as nativists made it clear that they did not want the "scum of Southern and Eastern Europe" let into the country. At the same time, however, New Deal liberals enthused about Zionism, as Jews flocked to Palestine, establishing *kibbutzim* and seeming to bring progress to a primitive land. The settler agricultural communities "evoked idealized images of America's pioneer past," Amy Kaplan notes, adding that "liberals imagined New Deal-style public projects bringing social equality to the Middle East."[8]

As Nazi pogroms and aggression accelerated, Americans empathized with the plight of European Jewry and expressed mounting support for the Zionist movement. By the time of Silver's speech in 1942, "the Americanization of Zionism" was on a trajectory to "contribute significantly in preparing American public opinion for the establishment of a Jewish state."[9] Preoccupied with the Nazi threat to dominate Europe, Americans had little knowledge or interest in the plight of indigenous people on the ground in Britain's Palestine mandate.

At just under five million in 1940, the United States had the largest Jewish population in the world, yet many American Jews remained opposed or disengaged from Zionism. Since its creation in 1906 the American Jewish Committee (AJC) had promoted civil rights, economic, educational and social equality for Jews worldwide, but it was not a Zionist organization. The AJC advocated liberalization of immigration laws allowing more Jewish refugees in the United States while opposing formal affiliation between American Jews and the growing demand for a Jewish commonwealth.[10]

Even more sharply opposed to Zionism was the American Council for Judaism (ACJ), founded in 1942. The ACJ emphasized that Judaism was a religion and not a national movement hence the group was "unalterably opposed to the establishment of an independent national Jewish State in Palestine or elsewhere." In addition to embracing Judaism as a religion and not a theocratic state, ACJ members expressed concern about perceptions and potential charges of "dual loyalty" that would undermine the standing of Jews as patriotic Americans.[11]

American Christian Zionism

With Jews constituting a small minority of the US population, and not all of them Zionists in any case, American Christians from the outset played a critical role in the growing support for a Jewish homeland in Palestine. Millions of religious modernists as well as biblical fundamentalists embraced Zionism.

While Silver and others strove to unite American Jews, American Protestants provided decisive support rooted in the biblical tradition. Long before Zionism became a movement in world affairs Americans formed an enduring bond with the biblical Israel. In 1630 John Winthrop declared in his famous "City on a Hill" sermon at Massachusetts Bay, "The God of Israel is among us."[12] The Puritan covenant helped to ensconce in national identity the concept of American exceptionalism, a deeply held belief that Americans--like the biblical Israelites--were a chosen people. Americans "defined their place in prophecy" in Israel's image. As "God's favored nation," the United States would achieve greatness, "just as the Israelites had flourished when they walked in God's ways."[13]

While Christian Americans nurtured bonds with ancient Israel, they displayed disdain for Islamic cultures. In the early years of the nineteenth century, Americans expressed racial and religious contempt for the Islamic "Barbary pirates," who plagued American shipping off the coast of North Africa. The next generation of Americans came to the aid of Greek Christians against their "Muhammedan" oppressors in the Ottoman Empire. At the turn of the twentieth century, as the United States drove Spain from the Philippines, US forces massacred Islamic "Moro tribesmen" in the southern part of the Southeast Asian archipelago.[14]

The "uniquely American phenomenon of Christian Zionists" emerged as "more consistent supporters of Israel than any group in the United

States, including American Jewry." Many Christian Americans embraced Zionism out of conviction that the Jews belonged in the Promised Land. A Gallup Poll taken in 1945 found that 76 percent of Americans favored and only seven percent opposed allowing the Jews to settle in Palestine.[15]

Since the late nineteenth century, fundamentalists reacting to the theory of evolution had insisted that the Bible was the literal word of God. Millions of Americans, "the most religious people in the developed world," learned the same lesson as a result of the Sunday school movement. Dispensational pre-millennial theology, which views the return of the Jews to the Promised Land as a prelude to the return of Christ and the beginning of New Times, was "deeply imbedded in American conservative religious circles."[16]

Christian Zionists and influential modernists—notably the Protestant theologian Reinhold Niebuhr—lobbied in support of Zionism. Niebuhr did not invoke a biblical rationale but he endorsed a Jewish home in Palestine. He cavalierly opined that the resident Arabs could simply be relocated within the "vast hinterland of the Middle East."[17]

The Protestant-dominated American Palestine Committee (APC), created in 1931, advocated "reunion of the Jewish people with the land of its ancient inheritance." Sen. William King (D-UT) asserted that it was the duty of the United States in its "pre-destined role of arbiter of world affairs" to embrace the Zionist cause. The APC enlisted a bi-partisan array of eminent politicians, including future President Harry Truman (D-MO), future Vice President Alben Barkley (D-KY) as well as the 1940 Republican presidential nominee Wendell Willkie of Indiana. An "essential part of APC propaganda efforts" was to emphasize that a Jewish state would uplift the backward Arabs, thus eliding the actual Zionist quest to drive the Palestinians from the land. At its 1944 national convention, the APC) declared, "The Christian world must rededicate itself to the heritage it has received from Judaism, the mother faith of Christianity."[18]

While pro-Arab and anti-Zionist groups had virtually no members of Congress in their ranks, the APC counted scores of senators and representatives as members. In December 1942 the signatures of 63 senators and 182 representatives on a proclamation marking the twenty-fifth anniversary of the Balfour Declaration underscored the growing clout of the Zionist movement in the US Congress.[19] In 1946 the APC reorganized as the American Christian Palestine Committee (ACPC) and embarked on "a massive public relations campaign on behalf of the Zionist cause."[20]

Birth of the Israel Lobby

Ben-Gurion and other leaders of the *Yishuv*--the Hebrew term for the Zionist settlement movement—recognized the significance of the growing American support, especially as their relations with the British deteriorated. The United States possessed the largest Jewish population in the world and New York City was at the global center of Zionism. By the early 1940s it was becoming clear that the United States would emerge from the Second World War as the dominant global power—the one nation that could make or break the Zionist movement.

During World War II American Zionists in collaboration with the *Yishuv* formalized the modern Israel lobby. In 1939 the Jewish Agency legally registered as a foreign lobbying agent with the US Department of Justice, as required under the Foreign Agents Registration Act (FARA), which had become law the previous year.[21]

In May 1942 *Yishuv* leaders Ben-Gurion and Chaim Weizmann attended the historic Biltmore meeting along with 586 American Zionists and 67 from other countries. While moderate Zionists led by Rabbi Stephen Wise had pursued a patient approach working through the administration of President Franklin D. Roosevelt, a longtime Zionist, mounting evidence of the Nazi genocide added urgency to the movement. Denouncing as "cruel and indefensible" British efforts to limit Jewish migration to Palestine, the Biltmore resolution insisted on unrestricted Jewish immigration as well as the creation of the new Jewish commonwealth.[22]

During World War II, the growing Zionist lobby strove to marginalize the American Council for Judaism and other anti-Zionist Jewish organizations. Zionist leaders claimed that the "ideological disputes" that had previously "divided the Jewish community" were "no longer in existence."[23] They claimed to represent "the overwhelming majority of US Jews."[24]

Having vaulted into the leadership of American Zionism as a result of his electrifying Biltmore address, Silver spurred the creation in 1943 of the American Zionist Emergency Council (AZEC). The organization "heralded a new and forceful public relations campaign aimed at winning the American government's support for Jewish statehood in Palestine."[25] Raising money to lobby for the creation of a Zionist state, AZEC secured declarations of support from thousands of non-Jewish as well as Jewish organizations, state and local governments, and ever-growing numbers of Congressmen.[26]

To anchor an AZEC campaign of publicity and persuasion, Silver turned to a little-known fellow Clevelander, Isaiah Leo Kenen. Born in

Canada to Jewish immigrant parents from east-central Europe, Kenen migrated to Cleveland where he became a journalist, completed law school, and became president of a Zionist organization in the city. A tireless workhorse for the nascent Israel lobby, Kenen spearheaded "a political and public relations offensive to capture the support of congressmen, clergy, editors, professors, business, and labor."[27]

Kenen's tireless publicity and organizational efforts quickly established the lobby as a major force in national politics. The signature strategy of the lobby—lining up support for the Zionist state in the US Congress—made an immediate impact on the 1944 electoral campaign. In February Kenen reported that lobbying for the creation of the Jewish Commonwealth had "profoundly impressed the Capitol, evoking many assurances of support from Congressmen." He called for a "similar and immediate approach to President Roosevelt."[28]

In 1944 AZEC secured the endorsement of both major political parties in the presidential campaign. The Democratic platform endorsed "unrestricted Jewish immigration and colonization" and establishment of a "democratic Jewish commonwealth." On the Republican side, Silver collaborated with Benzion Netanyahu, a professor at Cornell University, supporter of the rightwing Revisionist Zionists and father of the future long-running Israeli prime minister, in crafting a platform that also called for unfettered immigration while condemning Roosevelt for failing to do more to back the Balfour Declaration.[29]

While the Zionists mobilized, Arabs and Muslims lacked unity and organizational clout. The Arab League, founded near the end of World War II partly in an effort to contain the burgeoning Zionist movement, failed to unite the "Arab world" as a coherent political entity. Divided into factions, Palestinians lacked leadership, as the Mufti, the Islamic religious leader, Mohammed Amin al-Husseini, and others had been forced into exile after the British and the Zionists repressed the Arab revolt of the late 1930s. Transjordan's King Abdullah opposed creation of a Palestinian state as he sought control of the West Bank of the Jordan River.[30]

King Saud of oil-rich Saudi Arabia, a wartime US ally, sharply opposed creation of a Zionist state in Palestine. He warned Roosevelt that a Zionist settler state would provoke Arab resistance and war. Roosevelt reassured Saud that no decision would be taken "with respect to the basic situation . . . without full consultation with both Arabs and Jews." On April 12, 1945, Roosevelt wrote the same message from Warm Springs, Georgia, to the Syrian president. Roosevelt died at his desk later that same day.[31]

Truman Embraces Zionism

A devout Baptist and member of the ACPC, Harry Truman sympathized with the well-publicized plight of Jewish refugees. As he assumed the presidency the Zionist lobby was demanding an end to British restrictions on Jewish immigration into Palestine and the creation of a Jewish commonwealth. The Department of State, however, opposed the immediate creation of a Zionist state that would alienate the Arab world. The State Department urged Truman to "refrain from supporting a policy of large-scale immigration into Palestine" until a political solution could be arranged.[32]

Bowing to the growing American Zionist movement, Truman rejected the advice of the professional diplomats as well as his British ally by deciding to "let as many Jews into Palestine as is possible."[33] Confronted with a livid response from the Arabs, Truman like Roosevelt scrambled to reassure King Saud that his humanitarian support for Jewish refugees did not signal a full-scale tilt toward Zionism.[34] The Arabs tried to explain that a massive influx of Jews and creation of a Zionist settler state would entail the forced relocation of Palestinians, but Truman failed to grasp the point.[35]

AZEC succeeded in its "all-out effort . . . to impress the President with the fact that Americans generally" favored admission of Jewish refugees into Palestine.[36] Wise praised Truman's decision "to overcome the obduracy" of the British while the Jewish Agency expressed "profoundest satisfaction" with the president's decision.[37]

The British emphasized that the influx of refugees would strengthen the irregular Jewish militias Lehi and *Irgun*, which strove to drive the indigenous population from as much of Palestine as possible. US support for increased Jewish immigration would undermine "patient efforts to achieve a settlement," and ultimately result in "the loss of still more lives in Palestine," the British warned, but Truman had made his decision to side with the Zionists.[38]

As a provincial politician well attuned to public opinion, Truman grasped the growing domestic political clout of the Zionist lobby. He utterly failed, however, to grasp the situation on the ground in Palestine. Oblivious to the intensity of the drives that inhered in the Zionist settler movement, Truman declared in January 1947 that the Jewish leaders had "no intention of expelling now or at a later date the indigenous inhabitants of that country." In view of how much Jews suffered in the war, it seemed to him "inconceivable that responsible Jewish groups or leaders could be contemplating acts of intolerance and aggression against Arabs in Palestine."[39]

In 1947, as the British in frustration handed off the matter of Palestine to the new United Nations, the Zionist lobby mounted an intensive campaign behind partition of the mandate. Kenen mobilized AZEC "to get members of Congress alerted" and urge Jews all over the country to "call on their respective Congressmen or Senators."[40] Truman later wrote in his memoirs that he never had "as much pressure and propaganda aimed at the White House as I had in this instance."[41] The administration was "inundated with thousands of letters urging it to adopt a patently pro-partition stance."[42]

On November 29 the UN General Assembly voted 33-13 with 10 abstentions (including Great Britain) to partition Palestine into separate Arab and Jewish states. The Zionists immediately embraced Resolution 181 while all 11 of the Arab states voted against the non-binding resolution.[43]

To the Arab world it was clear that "Zionist pressure" had helped sway the Truman administration in support of the "mutilation" of Palestine.[44] The Zionists, in contrast, praised Truman for his "unflagging efforts." The president of B'nai B'rith declared Truman "would go down in history" as a hero to Jews worldwide. Weizmann expressed his "profound sense of gratitude" directly to Truman.[45]

State Department career diplomats argued that the pro-Zionist policies, culminating in partition, betrayed the British ally, alienated the oil-producing Arab states, would empower Arab extremists, and create opportunities for the Soviet Union to exploit in fomenting communist expansion in the region. Siding unequivocally with Zionism would thus undermine the Cold War containment policy, damage national interests, and promote global instability.[46]

In late 1947 the start of the first Arab-Israeli war prompted Truman to reverse himself and reluctantly endorse a trusteeship in an effort to check the "bloodshed descending upon the holy land." Arab leaders reiterated support for the creation of "one independent state for the whole of Palestine whose constitution would be based on democratic principles and which would include adequate safeguards for minorities and the safety to holy places."[47]

Zionists resolutely opposed this basis for a solution to the growing conflict and condemned the "reversal of the American position regarding the partition of Palestine." The Zionist lobby demanded that Truman abandon the trusteeship and furthermore "lift the arms embargo" that had been instituted in an effort to contain violence in the region. Weizmann claimed that the Zionists were at "risk of extermination" yet the United States would "not even grant them the arms to provide for their own defense."[48] Eleanor Roosevelt publicly backed partition and called for the

Jews to be "equipped with modern armaments" to defeat the Arab opposition in Palestine.[49]

Truman blamed all sides for the impasse, including the Zionists. He resented the political pressure on the administration and declared privately that a combination of terror groups in Palestine backed by domestic Zionist militants, notably Silver, had impeded a diplomatic solution. While Truman disliked Silver, he considered Weizmann "one of the wisest people I ever met."[50]

Working through Truman's Jewish friend and former business partner from Kansas City, Edward Jacobson, Weizmann secured a pivotal private meeting with Truman in the White House. Lamenting that the Palestine conflict "has been a headache to me for two and a half years," Truman agreed by the end of the extended discussion on March 18 to abandon trusteeship, revert to partition, and ultimately to recognize the new Jewish state. "You two Jews have put it over on me," he jocularly told Weizmann and Jacobson as they left the Oval Office.[51]

On May 14, having been assured that Truman would proffer immediate de facto recognition, Israel declared independence in the midst of a campaign of dispossession waged against the indigenous residents of Palestine.[52] Within minutes of the Israeli declaration, Truman announced de facto US recognition of the new state of Israel. Domestic adviser Clark Clifford noted that Truman had been "under unbearable pressure to recognize the Jewish state promptly."[53]

Truman's decision to reject the advice of his foreign policy advisers and make the United States the first nation in the world to offer de facto recognition of Israel stemmed at least in part from biblical motivations. Truman was a devout Baptist who claimed to have read the Bible "at least a dozen times" before age 15.[54] In going against Israel, Truman seems to have decided, he would be going against God. "Truman's biblical background at least predisposed him to favor prompt recognition," historian Irvine Anderson notes.[55]

The "reversal of US policy from truce plus trusteeship" to recognition of the new Israel marked the beginning of decades of siding with Zionism over the objections of the UN--the organization the United States had spawned to promote international peace and security. The tilt to the Zionists "deeply undermined confidence of other delegations in our integrity," UN Ambassador Warren Austin reported. British Foreign Minister Ernest Bevin denounced US policy as, "Let there be an Israel and to hell with the consequences!"[56]

Domestic advisers, including a Zionist lobby insider in the White House, David K. Niles, urged Truman to continue to accommodate Israel, especially amid the 1948 presidential campaign. Having achieved a breakthrough in the 1944 presidential canvass, Kenen spearheaded lobby efforts that secured the support of both major political parties in 1948.[57]

Israel and the lobby opposed a UN effort to secure a peace treaty entailing recognition of Israel, resolution of disputes over Israel's borders--which had expanded as a result of the Zionist victory in the war--and some accommodation for the hundreds of thousands of Palestinians driven from their homes in the *Nakba* ("The Catastrophe," in Arabic). Count Folke Bernadotte of Sweden championed the effort to bring peace to the holy land

On September 17, 1948 Lehi terrorists responded to the threat of an equitable peace by gunning down the UN mediator at a Jerusalem roadblock. Following the assassination of Bernadotte, American Zionists took out full-page advertisements, launched a letter-writing campaign, and lobbied through Niles, Jacobson and other "friends in Government circles" to preclude Truman's support for the martyred mediator's UN peace plan, which Republican presidential candidate Thomas Dewey also condemned.[58]

By the time of the ceasefire in January 1949, Israel had increased in size from the 55 percent under the UN partition to possession of 77 percent of the former British mandate of Palestine. With some 750,000 Palestinians driven out, a census conducted in November 1948 counted 782,000 Jews to 69,000 remaining Palestinians in the new Israel. The Zionists had orchestrated a population shift of dramatic proportions through a campaign of ethnic violence. By the end of 1949 the Jewish population soared to one million, a third of those having entered the country in the past eighteen months, now coming mostly from the Near and Middle East rather than as refugees from Europe.[59]

After winning decisive US political support on partition and recognition, the Zionists set their sights on establishing Jerusalem as Israel's "eternal capital." Under the UN partition agreement as well as Resolution 194, Israel had agreed to a "permanent international regime for the Jerusalem area," but Ben-Gurion and his colleagues had no intention of abiding by the UN resolutions. In September 1949 the State Department affirmed US backing of Resolution 194 preserving the international status of Jerusalem.

The American Zionist Council (AZC), which replaced AZEC in 1949, mounted a lobbying campaign against the internationalization of Jerusalem. Ben-Gurion avowed, "It would take an army to get the Jews out of Jerusalem." Israel's chief diplomat urged the lobby to "enlighten" the Truman administration on the Jerusalem issue.[60]

The UN General Assembly reaffirmed the call to designate Jerusalem as a *corpus separatum* in accordance with the 1947 partition, but the United States voted against it. Truman directed Secretary of State Dean Acheson to "take sides with the Israeli delegation against the Arabs" in the UN. Resolution 303 passed the UNGA 38-14 with seven abstentions. Catholic nations and all of the Arab states except Jordan--which received a trusteeship over East Jerusalem and the West Bank of the Jordan River in the former British mandate--voted in favor of an international trusteeship overseeing the holy city, as did the Soviet Union and its allies. Contemptuous of the UN, Ben-Gurion responded within days by moving his office into the city.[61]

Although still officially opposed to establishment of Jerusalem as the capital of the new state, the United States sided with Israel and the lobby as it cast one of the 14 negative votes against the majority of world opinion in the UN--a precedent that would play out repeatedly in the ensuing decades. Eban expressed his gratitude for "the harmony that had existed between the Israeli delegation and the US delegation in the assembly concerning the Jerusalem question."[62]

In January 1949 under intense pressure from Israel and its American supporters Truman granted Israel $100 million (more than $1 billion in 2020 dollars), thus inaugurating what would become a massive program of US financial assistance to the Zionist state. Israel and the lobby mobilized a successful propaganda campaign ensuring there would be no linkage between the financial assistance and efforts to compel Israel to compromise over borders, refugees, and the status of Jerusalem.[63]

Israel thus rejected an opportunity to negotiate with its Arab neighbors. "After the sobering experience of military defeat at the hands of the infant Jewish state," the Oxford scholar Avi Shlaim has pointed out, the leaders of the Arab states were, "prepared to recognize Israel, to negotiate directly with it and even to make peace with it. Each of these rulers had his territorial price for making peace with Israel but none of them refused to talk."[64]

Cementing the Power of the Lobby

A child of Lithuanian parents but educated from a young age in Great Britain, Abba Eban was an erudite scholar-diplomat and ideally suited to forge the special relationship between the new Israel and the American Jewish Diaspora.[65] Eban found a key ally in Louis Lipsky, a veteran American Zionist from Rochester who replaced Silver at the head of AZC. Together with Kenen, these three men laid the foundation for the powerful national lobby that arose in the wake of Israeli independence. Lipsky perceived that "American Zionist political support" would provide the "armor Israel cannot get along without."[66]

Convinced that the American Diaspora was the key to "strengthen ties" and thereby get the United States "to grant Israel preferential treatment," Eban persisted over several months in the effort to close ranks within the American Jewish community. Eban, who became ambassador to the United States in June 1950, created an advisory group that would convene on a regular basis for "utterly private and unofficial" consultations aimed at securing US support for Israel's security aims. The group included Lipsky, Niles, Democratic fundraiser Abraham Feinberg, and representatives of several prominent Jewish organizations. In subsequent years the advisory group evolved into the Conference of Presidents of Major American Jewish Organizations, a key decision-making body within the US lobby.[67]

Successful in warding off US and UN efforts to achieve a settlement on borders and refugees, Israel and the lobby launched a campaign to tap the "vast financial resources" of the US Government. Israel needed the funding primarily to finance resettlement of the massive influx of Jewish migrants.[68] In July 1950 the Knesset passed the Law of Return enabling any Jew in the world to relocate to Israel and gain citizenship. Three months later, Israel and its lobby collaborated in drafting a memorandum to Truman outlining the Zionist state's need for emergency financial assistance for resettlement of Jewish refugees.

In 1950 the Israel lobby initiated the campaign by mobilizing local Zionist committees to "contact at once all incumbent Congressmen and Senators, as well as all candidates for Congressional and Senatorial offices." Kenen lined up Sens. Robert Taft (R-OH) and Paul Douglas (D-IL) behind a $150 million grant-in-aid request for Israel.[69]

Alarmed by the growing strength of the lobby, which had clearly tilted US policy sharply in Israel's favor, the State Department opposed special funding for Israel "based upon an obvious claim for favoritism." In March 1951 the National Security Council went a step further, issuing NSC 47/5, a policy paper formally declaring American "impartiality" in the Palestine conflict.[70]

Israel and the lobby issued a flurry of condemnations of the State Department diplomats, falsely equating the impartial policy with a pro-Arab position. "Distraught" over once again being caught in the middle between his national security advisers and the aggressive lobbying of the "political Jews," Truman turned to Feinberg, the Democratic Party fundraiser and Zionist insider. Feinberg orchestrated a "compromise" in which Israel received $65 million for Jewish migrants with the same amount allocated to Palestinian refugees and the Arab states.[71]

Kenen celebrated a "decisive victory" for the lobby, as Israel received the same allocation as the *entire Arab world*--including the refugees that it had driven from their homes in the *Nakba*. The funding represented a "revolutionary change" in which the US Congress, "now aware of Israel's needs," as Kenen put it, would in the future ensure "the inclusion of Israel in our country's foreign aid program."[72] In 1952 Congress authorized another $73 million to assist Jews to resettle in Israel.[73]

Congressional funding paled in comparison with the windfall Israel received from the newly created Federal Republic of Germany. Seizing the momentum of broadened awareness of the full scope of the Nazi genocide and attendant calls for atonement, Israel secured a massive long-term financial package of $845 million in reparations to diaspora Jews. Eban thanked the Truman administration for its "sympathetic assistance" in brokering the negotiations between West Germany and Israel.[74]

By the end of the Truman administration the Israel lobby had become a powerful force in Washington. The lobby had proven instrumental in Israel's establishment, the expansion of its borders, resistance to international status for Jerusalem, and rejection of calls to cooperate in the resettlement of Palestinian refugees even as Israel received hundreds of millions of dollars to facilitate resettlement of Jews in the Zionist state.

By the time he left office Truman had come to believe he had fulfilled a divine mission to reunite the Jews with the holy land. In his farewell address Truman declared that as a result of US support, "Israel can be made into the country of milk and honey as it was in the time of Joshua." Truman embraced the mantle of the modern-day Cyrus, the Persian king who in the sixth century BCE ended the Babylonian captivity and authorized rebuilding of the Jewish temple in Jerusalem. Believing that he had been part of a divine plan to establish the New Israel, Truman at one point proclaimed, "I am Cyrus, I am Cyrus."[75]

While Truman may have felt he was doing the Lord's work, Kenen attributed Israel's success under Truman to the more-earthly activities of the increasingly potent Zionist lobby. It was the "effective coalition of Israel's friends—Jews and Christians, Zionists and non-Zionists—who united in unprecedented cooperation" that had enabled the growing support for Israel.[76]

In 1952 the Israel lobby essentially wrote the planks on Middle East policy for both major parties in the presidential campaign. Kenen and Feinberg wrote the Democratic plank, which pledged "continued assistance" to Israel. Working closely with Israel, Silver wrote the Republican plank. However, the eventual Republican nominee and soon to be president, the hero General Dwight D. Eisenhower, posed a major challenge for the powerful new lobby, as he had no track record of support for Israel.[77]

Chapter 2
Taming Two Presidents

Dwight Eisenhower's secretary of state, John Foster Dulles, the preeminent Republican internationalist of his era, intended to rein in the Israel lobby, resurrect the State Department's impartial policy, and pursue a Middle East peace plan. Dulles condemned the Truman administration for acquiescing to "the wishes of the Zionists in this country," which "had created a basic antagonism with the Arabs." The new administration meant to stare down the lobby and compel Israel to compromise on a range of issues including "the internationalization of Jerusalem as foreseen by the 1948 UN Resolution."[1]

Israel and its American lobby launched a propaganda campaign against the administration's effort to assert the impartial policy. Denouncing the "change in American foreign policy in the Middle East, favoring the Arab states," Kenen strove "to stimulate our people to greater activity." He mobilized local Jewish councils linked with AZC and dispatched hundreds of "Dear Friend" letters warning of a "reduction of support and aid for Israel."[2]

Following a visit to the Middle East, which included a meeting with Gamal Abdel Nasser, the new leader of Egypt, Dulles announced that the United States was withholding millions of dollars scheduled for allocation to Israel "in view of the problems that exist in that area between the United Nations and Israel."[3] AZC denounced the funding cutoff as "an unwarranted act of duress" that would compel Israel to "suspend economic development in surrender to its enemies." Working in concert with the Israeli embassy, Kenen sent out an "emergency bulletin" condemning the "misguided course of policy undertaken by the State Department towards Israel."[4]

As lobby propaganda condemned Dulles, Rep. and later Sen. Jacob Javits (R-NY), a lobby stalwart, arranged a meeting between the secretary of state and a group of executives of the major Jewish organizations. Admitting to being "disturbed" by the "various inaccuracies and distortions" of the lobby campaign, Dulles explained he was trying "to support the UN" and to "dispel the Arab notion that the United States backs Israel right or wrong." He advised that the "Jewish fraternity" should focus on "the Israeli government to try to change their policy of presenting the world with *faits accompli*. Cooperation seemed to be a one-way street as far as Israel is concerned."[5]

Dulles soon learned the futility of appealing to Israel and the lobby's sense of fair play and balanced diplomacy. Two days after the meeting the nation's top diplomat restored the funds earmarked for assistance in return for Israel's pledge to end the unilateral diversion of waters of the Jordan River, which had precipitated conflict with neighboring Syria. Israel, however, later resumed the pressures on Syria and eventually prevailed in the "water war."[6]

Israel's borderland aggression included repeatedly lashing out against Palestinian refugees and farmers attempting to return to their land along the elongated border with Jordan.[7] In October 1953 a massacre by the Israeli Defense Forces (IDF) of 69 people, about two-thirds women and children, in the West Bank village of Qibya, created a crisis for the lobby. The act of collective punishment came in the wake of the killing of a Jewish woman and her two children. Jordan was helping Israel track down the perpetrators, but the IDF launched a characteristic unilateral indiscriminate assault nonetheless.[8]

Kenen acknowledged privately that the massacre--perpetrated by Major Ariel Sharon at the head of the elite IDF commando Unit 101--had "undermined the moral position of the Jewish people . . . discredited the premises of our propaganda and has given the color of truth to Arab propaganda." A campaign of damage control was urgently necessary. Kenen thus mobilized the "friends of Israel, Christian and Jewish" to emphasize putative Arab threats to Israel and to condemn as "one-sided" the US-backed UN censure of the Zionist state.

In response to Qibya, the lobby's local councils showed that they could "spring back to life and action in a crisis," Kenen later reported, and "impress upon the Government that an anti-Israel program would be deeply resented by large sections of American opinion." The massacre of the innocent villagers thus ironically ultimately strengthened the lobby by alerting it to the need for "intensification of our work in the field of public relations." The stepped-up propaganda effort included greater emphasis in the future on mobilizing local councils, churches and college campuses to complement the already in-place congressional lobby.[9]

By the early Eisenhower years, the Israel lobby had thus established a strategy and structure for dispensing propaganda, one that would operate for decades to come and to the present day. Hundreds of Jewish Community Relations Councils in every major population center could now be quickly mobilized to carry out a propaganda campaign in the event of a crisis, such as the Qibya attack. More routinely, the local councils remained vigilant and at the ready to denounce or suppress any unfavorable news or comment on Israel that might arise. By the early

1950s the lobby's *modus operandi* to exercise a chilling effect on criticism of Israel was ensconced.

The Israel lobby managed the fallout from a massacre, thwarted a popular president, and fended off a wide range of government agencies, including not only the State Department but the IRS, the FBI and the CIA. In 1951 the CIA, headed by Dulles's brother Allen, covertly and illegally organized a domestic front group, the American Friends of the Middle East (AFME), to counter the influence of the Israel lobby. The group worked with the State Department, the anti-Zionist American Council for Judaism, and the popular journalist Dorothy Thompson, among others, in an effort to counterbalance the Israel lobby's growing clout in Congress and with the public.[10]

AFME also collaborated with Henry Byroade, assistant secretary for the Near East, who condemned Israel for its borderland aggression, its "demand for complete control of the Jordan River," and "arrogant and obstructive attitudes toward the United Nations." While acting "to preclude a reasonable settlement," he charged, "Israel has made considerable progress in the propaganda battle to convince the American public of the justice of her case."[11]

When the Israel lobby lashed back at Byroade, Dulles initially defended him, telling Lipsky that the area expert's argument was "basically sound, and I am not disposed to repudiate it."[12] However, as the clashes with the lobby intensified, Dulles reassigned Byroade as ambassador in Egypt and subsequently moved him out of the region altogether to a post in South Africa.[13]

Dulles tried in vain to generate support for his Project Alpha Middle East peace plan under which Israel would take in a small percentage of refugees--75,000 out of some 800,000 Palestinians now displaced by the *Nakba*--over a five-year period, with the rest being absorbed by the Arab states. Border adjustments would provide a corridor connecting Jordan and Egypt through the Negev Desert, which Israel would nonetheless retain. Finally, the United States would contribute generous financial inducements to accommodate Palestinian refugees as well as Jewish migrants; economic boycotts of Israel by the Arab states would end; and peace would come to the region.[14]

While Nasser and other Arab leaders did not reject Alpha, which was co-sponsored by the British, the peace plan was dead on arrival because Israel proved unwilling to compromise its settler drives. The Zionist state rejected any proposal to take in refugees, discuss borders, compromise on Jerusalem, or to conduct diplomacy with Arabs. Even the moderate Eban dismissed Dulles's plan with the standard trope that it was a reprisal of appeasement at Munich in 1938. Dulles implored Javits as well as White House advisers with links to the Jewish community to do some "missionary work" to promote a spirit of compromise "among friends of Israel in this country," but to no avail.[15]

As the 1954 Midterm elections loomed, the Israel lobby resumed the offensive, mounting a campaign against military aid to Arabs and in favor of economic and military assistance to the Zionist state. In April Eisenhower pledged to "continue our present policy of impartiality" and "not be deterred by political pressures . . . in connection with the forthcoming elections."[16] Dulles vowed he would "not allow himself to be stampeded" into arming the Israelis, explaining that it would "be interpreted throughout the Arab world that we have capitulated again. All we have tried to do will be lost."[17]

Continually frustrated by the successful efforts by Israel and its lobby to stymie a more balanced US Middle East diplomacy, Dulles summoned Eban for a private meeting to complain about "Israeli Embassy activities which seemed clearly to go beyond the bounds of what was proper for a foreign government in that they involved domestic political action." Dulles asked the Israeli diplomat to take "proper steps" to rein in activity that went "beyond the bounds of propriety." Eban promised to "look into the situation," which merely reflected a "natural desire on the part of his Government and his Embassy to develop friendships on the part of the American people."[18]

Four days later Kenen trumpeted growing Zionist domination of the US Congress. He announced that more than 300 candidates in House races from 36 states, as well as 25 Senate nominees, had pledged to support Israel and "declared their opposition to the sending of arms to the Arab states."[19]

Eisenhower Stands Firm after Suez

As the lobby fended off the Eisenhower administration's effort to conduct a balanced diplomacy in the Middle East, the Zionist state's borderland aggression escalated dramatically. In 1954 Israel launched a failed covert operation against Egypt that included wanton destruction of American property. The false-flag-operation entailed the bombing of US Information Service libraries and other Western targets in Cairo and Alexandria, blaming the attacks on Egyptian Islamists and radicals, all in an effort to undermine Nasser and "damage US-Egyptian relations." The plan failed spectacularly, as the bombs did little damage and eight Egyptian Jewish agents were arrested, tried publicly and two were executed (two others committed suicide).

Israel's aggression in Egypt increased tensions not only with the Eisenhower administration but with the American lobby as well. The lobby received no advance warning of either the covert assault targeting the US facilities or subsequent aggression against Egypt. In February 1955 Israel launched a military incursion into the Gaza Strip, killing 39 Egyptians and setting the stage for the Sinai War the following year. Kenen later complained that he had been stonewalled by the Israeli government in his efforts to gain information in order to spin Israeli militarism as favorably as possible.[20]

The 1956 Israeli invasion of Egypt created a crisis for the lobby, which received no advance warning from Ben-Gurion.[21] The Eisenhower administration's subsequent decision to force Israel, Britain, and France to withdraw from occupied Egyptian territory placed the lobby between a popular American president and the Zionist state, creating the prospect of American Jews being confronted with the dreaded charge of "dual loyalty." After the Conference of Presidents of Major American Jewish Organizations convened in emergency session, Eban offered the telling comment, "For the first time in our memory there was reluctance" of Jewish leaders "to justify Israel's actions without reserve."[22]

Although polls showed that most Americans including many Jews had responded negatively to the tripartite Suez invasion, the lobby's influence in Washington remained strong. The Israeli embassy orchestrated "comprehensive *hasbara*" (foreign propaganda) activities while Kenen sent letters urging "friends" to "form committees of your local Zionist councils—together with all Jewish organizations willing to cooperate—to visit leading officials, clergymen, editors, teachers, labor leaders, and others." Kenen carefully tracked the statements and positions of representatives and senators on proposed sanctioning of Israel and the US demand for withdrawal from the Gaza Strip and the Gulf of Aqaba.[23]

The lobby took credit for unleashing the "uproar on Capitol Hill that deterred the Administration from imposing sanctions" on Israel after its initial refusal to withdraw.[24] Once again, as in the aftermath of Qibya, Israel and its lobby had emerged from a crisis in a stronger position than ever. "American-Israel relations were never better than they are at this moment," Kenen declared in December 1957.[25]

The Eisenhower administration forced Israel out of Suez, but otherwise had failed to assert the impartial policy and been stymied in efforts to pursue the Alpha Middle East peace plan. Backed by the crucial propaganda support from the lobby, Israel had successfully parried the Palestinian refugee issue, laid claim to Jerusalem, held onto its expanded 1949 boundaries, carried out border aggression culminating in a full-scale war with Egypt, and had solidified continuing US financial assistance and guarantees of its security in the process. When disputes arose, the Israel lobby was quick to intervene and to mobilize its growing support in the Congress and in communities across the nation.

Eisenhower and Dulles, who entered office with every intention of reining in the Israel lobby, in the end were rendered virtually powerless to shape Middle East diplomacy. Dulles complained that the "pressure of the Jews" was causing a "very nasty situation on the [Capitol] Hill" and influencing media coverage.[26] "Except for Israel," Eisenhower declared privately in July 1958, "we could form a viable policy in the area."[27]

Religious and Cultural Support for Israel

Once the architect of an ambitious Middle East peace initiative, Dulles, worn down by the relentless opposition of Israel and the lobby, left the matter in God's hands. He explained he "had been reading the Old Testament and they had the same problems as we have today . . . It did not make sense to think that he could solve problems which Moses and Joshua with Divine guidance could not solve."[28]

The devout Presbyterian secretary of state was not the only one influenced by an upsurge of American religiosity in the 1950s. Following World War II, the Cold War became a global crusade, as "one nation, under God" took the lead in the battle against the "evil" of atheistic world communism. Church attendance soared, as a renewed "great awakening" of heightened religious devotion, a recurring phenomenon in American history, unfolded in the 1950s. In 1956 "The Ten Commandments," dramatizing the biblical story of Moses on the big screen, became a runaway box office hit and won seven Academy Award nominations.[29]

It was another film, however—"Exodus," released in 1960--that propelled millions of Americans into an embrace of Zionism. Based on the popular novel of the same title by Leon Uris, published in 1958, "Exodus" presented a "narrative of Israeli innocence and self-defense" that "effaced the violent dispossession of Palestinians," Amy Kaplan notes. "The impact of Uris's story was unparalleled," Michelle Mart points out, "solidifying the image of Israel and the American relationship to that country for years to come." No less an authority than Ben-Gurion declared, "As a piece of propaganda, it's the greatest thing ever written about Israel."[30]

In "Exodus" Paul Newman brilliantly evoked the persona of the *sabra* in his lead role as Ari Ben Canaan. "Leaving behind the stereotype of a weak victim, a 'new Jew' was discursively constructed who embodied the virtues and aspirations of the American past and present," Mart explains.[31]

"Exodus" paved the way for President Kennedy's pronouncement in 1962 of the special relationship. Uris's novel, peppered with "overtly racist stereotypes" of Arabs, together with the film "provided a ready-made template" for Americans to side a few years later with the righteously aggressive Jews over their putatively uncivilized Arab foes in the June 1967 war.[32]

Building on growing popular support for Israel, Kenen shored up the ability to mobilize state and local councils to lobby their congressional representatives and thwart the executive branch as well as the national security bureaucracy. Fully aware that Congress was the lobby's proverbial ace in the hole, Kenen amassed extensive files on the voting records of all members, categorizing elected representatives as "active champions," or merely "sympathetic," "leaning toward Israel," "indifferent," and "leaning away." He alerted local councils as to when their representatives "will be home" in order to provide an "an opportunity" to meet with them to urge funding and support of Israel.

Kenen urged supporters to compose "letters written by Christians as well as Jews," advising that they "should be original and personal. Please do not send mimeographed appeals—they provoke an adverse reaction."[33] The lobby also sponsored "a series of dinner parties," each attended by scores of House members and Senators, "private functions at which Ambassador Eban" and other featured guests could "present [their] country's views."[34]

Restructuring the Lobby

Israel and the American lobby were not without challenges. The lobby faced declining revenues as a result of IRS and FBI investigations into its funding. The probes forced the AZC to rely on taxable rather than tax-exempt contributions.

In 1957 Kenen responded brilliantly, as he launched the *Near East Report* (*NER*), which quickly became the signature publication of the Israel lobby. While Jewish and other organizations could not legally contribute to the lobby owing to their tax-exempt status, they could purchase as many subscriptions to the lobby newsletter as they wished. Within months the *NER* circulation topped 5,700 with a goal of 20,000 by 1959.

Trained as a journalist, Kenen produced a well-edited propaganda bulletin with the outward appearance of a news-style format. Within months he exulted, "The *Near East Report* has caught on" and "proved to be a godsend."[35] Circulating to all members of Congress, the *NER* featured speeches and resolutions by the lobby's stalwarts in Congress. The favorable publicity prompted other representatives and senators to assert their pro-Zionist sympathies. As the newsletter evolved, Kenen began to publish 30-page special supplements, took in advertising, added book reviews, and other features.[36]

Along with introducing the *NER*, the lobby reinvented itself as the American Israel Public Affairs Committee (AIPAC) in August 1959. The reorganization was designed to spur fundraising and focus political influence squarely on the Congress. The AIPAC executive committee sought "to co-opt leading American Jews. It also established a National Council in order to stimulate fundraising." Kenen asserted, "We speak for the American Jewish community as a whole."[37]

From this point forward, the Israel lobby framework for dispensing propaganda in the United States was set: the Israeli government, working in collaboration with the Conference of Presidents of Major American Jewish Organizations, coordinated fundraising and communicated policy goals to AIPAC; the US lobby then took the desired policies before the Congress in order to secure their approval and funding. Meanwhile AIPAC closely monitored every member of Congress while ensuring that each received regular copies of the *NER*. Everyone in Congress quickly learned that AIPAC, backed by local councils and Zionist groups across the country, was monitoring their every move on Middle East policy.

As the 1960 presidential campaign neared, AIPAC bolstered its visibility in Washington by staging the first in a series of what were to become its signature annual policy conferences. The conference attracted politicians from both parties and "served to inform American Jewish leadership, as well as the public at large." AIPAC followed up by making its presence felt as both major political parties drafted "strong pro-Israel declarations" in their 1960 platforms.[38]

While most American politicians sought to stay on the good side of Israel and the lobby, a notable exception was Sen. J. William Fulbright (D-AR). Famous for sponsoring the acclaimed overseas educational exchange program that bore his name, Fulbright had since the Sinai War used his influence on the Senate Foreign Relations Committee (SFRC), which he chaired, to challenge the lobby's growing domination of Middle East policy.

Fulbright condemned unstinting US support for Israel despite the "intransigent" Zionist state's refusal to "receive and discuss in a forthcoming spirit" issues that might lead to a just and peaceful settlement of the Palestine issue.[39] Carefully tracking the actions of all members of Congress, Kenen warned in 1961, "Fulbright cannot be appeased. He is simply anti-Israel and will show it."[40]

Fulbright was not the only government official interested in AIPAC. In November 1962 the Department of Justice ordered AIPAC's parent organization, the AZC, to register as a foreign agent of Israel.[41] The following year Fulbright stunned AIPAC by conducting two days of closed SFRC hearings, which revealed evidence that Israel working through the Jewish Agency had funneled millions of dollars into domestic lobbying operations. By means of indirect funding--or, less charitably, money laundering--the Jewish Agency had funded Kenen and his activities; underwritten the *Near East Report* as well as the Jewish Telegraphic news agency; sponsored speakers; and promoted myriad other pro-Israeli "public information" initiatives including efforts to influence Congress and divert attention from Israel's budding nuclear reactor research program. Drawing on FBI wiretaps and subpoenaed documents, the investigation revealed abundant evidence of the lobby's fundraising, which included contributions from mobsters Aaron Weisberg and John Factor, known as "Jake the Barber."[42]

Delving into the financial dealings of the lobby, the FBI had become aware that the Jewish Agency--headquartered in Jerusalem but with an "American section" office in New York--was purchasing subscriptions of the *NER* and diverting revenues to the lobby. The JA was also making $5,000 direct quarterly payments to Kenen. From January 1, 1955 through the end of 1962 the JA made more than five million dollars in payments in support of lobbying, without proper itemization in its filings as required under federal law.[43]

In separate one-day hearings in May and August 1963 Fulbright grilled representatives of the JA as well as an AIPAC attorney. Fulbright homed in on Kenen's activities, demanding to know "why he shouldn't register" as a foreign agent. In 1951 Kenen had been registered as a foreign agent for lobbying purposes but in subsequent years declined to do so on the grounds that the lobby was a domestic enterprise and did not represent the Israeli state. However, the SFRC investigation showed, as Fulbright pointed out in the hearings, "In order to insulate him, you took the indirect way of paying him."[44]

The revelations emerged in the midst of a broader SFRC probe into foreign agent violations by several other countries, but Fulbright did not shy away from including Israel and AIPAC despite pressure from President Kennedy, Vice President Lyndon Johnson, and several senators and representatives. Jewish affairs adviser Myer Feldman informed Kennedy of the "detailed investigation of the interconnection between the various Jewish organizations in the United States and the use of the funds they raise," adding, "The Jewish community is very uneasy about this investigation."[45]

Under pressure from domestic supporters of Israel, Fulbright agreed to hold the hearings in closed session but he planned to have them read into the Senate record. He desisted only after Johnson focused his notorious powers of persuasion on the Arkansas senator. Transcripts of the hearings remained classified for decades. The hearings produced substantive modifications of federal law, including new provisions requiring registration by agents of foreign interests and full disclosure of financial arrangements.[46]

Fulbright's investigation exposed and shut down the indirect funding "conduits" to AIPAC, but by that time the lobby had registered with Congress in accordance with laws governing domestic lobbies, and had recovered from the financial challenges of the late 1950s.[47] The hearings ultimately had greater consequences for Fulbright than for the lobby. AIPAC kept the Arkansas senator in its crosshairs and eventually helped defeat his reelection bid in 1974.[48]

Cultivating Kennedy

Israel and AIPAC welcomed the return of the Democrats to the White House in the closely contested 1960 election in which Kennedy dominated the Jewish vote in his narrow victory over Vice President Richard M. Nixon. Kenen had "preferred Kennedy to Nixon," as the Massachusetts senator had developed into a strong supporter of Zionism, whereas Nixon was tarred with the Eisenhower-Dulles legacy.[49]

Kennedy had shored up his Zionist credentials in a series of speeches before Jewish groups leading up to the 1960 presidential campaign. Throughout the campaign as well as his 1,000-day presidency, Kennedy received advice on Jewish affairs from Feldman, a Philadelphia businessman and attorney. During the campaign, Feldman organized a large gathering of "the leaders of the Jewish community" for a meeting in fundraiser and lobbyist Abe Feinberg's New York apartment.[50]

Named deputy special counsel to the president, Feldman essentially functioned as a member of the Israel lobby inside the White House. He perceived his identity as "a Jew, as an American, as a Government official" in "harmonious relationship." Acting as the liaison between Israel and the lobby, Feldman "felt perfectly free to go to [Kennedy] at any time."[51]

Secretary of State Dean Rusk expressed frequent frustration over Feldman's access to the president and his ties with the lobby, which included regular communication with Kenen and a close friendship with Avraham Harman, a veteran of Israeli *hasbara* efforts who had replaced Eban as ambassador in 1959. Rusk objected that it was "improper for an Israel diplomat to call on [Feldman]." Other US diplomats complained that Feldman had become "the primary White House staff influence" on the Middle East conflict. "Actions dealing with Israel and Arab-Israeli matters and which could have a domestic political impact must now be cleared with the White House," they complained.[52]

Feldman played a central role in Israel's successful quest to achieve a breakthrough in securing advanced US military hardware beginning with

Hawk surface-to-air defensive missiles. Rusk, the State and Defense departments all opposed the sale, particularly as Israel was proving characteristically aggressive and contemptuous of diplomacy in relation to disputes over the Jordan River water diversion and resettlement of Arab refugees, as well as the status of Jerusalem. In an effort "to regain some degree of Arab confidence in us," Rusk wanted to push for "significant unilateral concession by Israel," a position that was sure to inflame Israel and the lobby.[53]

Kennedy hoped the sale of the Hawks would convince the Israelis to consider the administration's modest refugee resettlement plan, which had been carefully crafted by the president of the Carnegie Endowment for International Peace, Joseph Johnson. The plan envisioned only a limited number of refugees returning, as it included financial incentives designed to encourage them to choose not to return to Israel. Johnson's proposals thus took into full consideration Israel's sensitivity on the issue of Palestinian refugees.[54]

Kennedy and his advisers acquiesced to Feldman's advice that making the Hawk sale directly conditional on a refugee resettlement plan would alienate Israel and the lobby.[55] Rusk, however, warned against providing the Israelis with the Hawks before the Johnson Plan "could even be given a good try."[56]

Just as Rusk feared, Israel took possession of the Hawks while summarily rejecting the Johnson Plan. On August 20 Ben-Gurion wrote Kennedy of his "profound appreciation" for the missiles, but settlement of the refugee problem was "feasible only if the Arab refugees are integrated in the Arab countries."[57] Consistent with its position since 1948, Israel refused to accept the return of any Palestinian refugees who had been driven from their homes in the *Nakba*.

Originally charged with selling the Israelis on the Johnson Plan, Feldman in actuality acted as a lobbyist against the resettlement proposals. He argued inaccurately that the plan would "flood Israel with refugees" and, accurately, that it had caused "considerable furor in the [US] Jewish community." Feldman told Kennedy he could not "stress too strongly his firm conviction that the faster you disengage from this plan the better." Years later a US diplomat averred that Feldman "was being used as a pipeline not just by American Jewry but by the Israeli embassy" and that "his contacts with the Israeli ambassador were considerably closer than either of them talked about in public."[58]

Deception over Dimona

The decision in 1962 to sell the Hawk missiles stemmed in part from hopes that if Israel received advanced conventional weapons it would refrain from pursuing nuclear weapons. However, on his secret trip to Israel to hand over the Hawks Feldman had not raised the subject of nuclear research despite a State Department request that he do so.[59]

Beginning in December 1960, when US intelligence sources revealed that the Israeli nuclear complex at Dimona in the Negev Desert could develop a reactor capable of producing weapons-grade plutonium, the United States had pressed Israel for inspections and renunciation of any plans to introduce nuclear weapons into the Middle East. The Israelis repeatedly dissembled, fended off or manipulated the inspections, and carried on a determined effort to do precisely what they promised not to do--introduce nuclear weapons into the Middle East.[60]

As Kennedy took office the State Department informed Congress that the United States had been "assured categorically at the highest level of the Israeli Government that Israel has no plans for the production of atomic weapons."[61] Responding to the administration's request for inspections, Harman declared he "could not conceive why there should be continuing interest in Dimona in the United States or anywhere else," as Israel had "no intention of manufacturing the bomb."[62]

Despite such seemingly categorical reassurance, Kennedy remained skeptical about Israel's true intentions on the nuclear issue. He resolved to take up the matter directly with Israeli Foreign Minister Golda Meir during a summit meeting in Florida.

On December 27, 1962, the 64-year-old Meir met with Kennedy, nineteen years her junior, at the "Winter White House," a sprawling white beachfront mansion with an orange-tiled roof in sunny Palm Beach, Florida. Meir understood the United States well, having grown up as an American in Milwaukee after her parents emigrated there from Kiev, Ukraine, in 1906. At age 21 Meir had moved with her husband to Palestine to join a *kibbutz*. She began to work her way up the ranks of the Zionist labor movement and into the higher reaches of Israeli politics, eventually achieving the summit as prime minister (1969-73).

Adorned in a simple white dress and matching hat, the matronly Meir and the trim, handsome, besuited Kennedy exchanged views, as the president gently rocked in a chair specially designed to accommodate his arthritic back. The tough-minded Meir, an acolyte of Ben Gurion, began by dismissing the efforts to curb Israel's aggressive borderland policies, saying she was "not really surprised when people do not see Israel's security problems as the Israelis do."

Kennedy had already bowed to Israel and the lobby on refugees and the dispute over diversion of the Jordan River waters, but the president wanted clear assurance from Meir that the Israeli reactor at Dimona would not be used to produce nuclear weapons. He began, however, by making the historic acknowledgment that with Israel the United States shared a "special relationship . . . comparable only to that which it has with Britain."

Kennedy hoped that by pronouncing the existence of the special relationship--offering reassurance that the United States as a close ally would always safeguard the essential security of the Zionist state--that Israel would back off on the nuclear program. Turning to "our problems on this atomic reactor," Kennedy explained, "We are opposed to nuclear proliferation. Our interest here is not prying into Israel's affairs but we have to be concerned because of the overall situation in the Middle East." In response, a US diplomat present at the talks reported, "Mrs. Meir reassured the president that there would not be any difficulty between us on the Israeli nuclear reactor."[63]

Golda Meir returned from the meeting at the Palm Beach White House with a historic acknowledgment from a popular president that the Americans were committed to a "special relationship"—including substantial long-term economic assistance--with her country. In return, she had offered only a vague and disingenuous pledge pertaining to Dimona.

Less than three months after Kennedy received Meir's reassurances on the Israeli nuclear program, US intelligence sources revealed that Israel remained in active pursuit of a nuclear weapon. Committed to nuclear non-proliferation in the wake of the Cuban Missile Crisis (1962) and the signing of the Limited Test Ban Treaty with the Soviet Union (1963), Kennedy declared, "We should attempt to get every country that is not yet agreed to inspection to accept some form of international inspection."[64]

The Arab states posed no threat of nuclear proliferation. Nasser, who reacted "in a restrained manner" to revelations of the Israeli nuclear program as well as to the Hawk sales, reassured the Americans he "had no intention whatsoever" of seeking nuclear weapons and also "no intention of attacking Israel." On July 22, 1963, Nasser pledged in a public speech that Egypt was not planning to attack, nor seeking to destroy the Zionist state.[65]

Kennedy stepped up demands for a new round of inspections and warned Ben-Gurion, "This Government's commitment to and support of Israel could be seriously jeopardized if it should be thought that we were unable to obtain reliable information" on Israel nuclear activities.[66]

In response to the pressure from the Kennedy administration over its nuclear weapons program, Israel and the lobby initiated an asymmetrical propaganda counter-attack by charging Kennedy with appeasing the

Arabs. The administration had sought dialogue with Nasser and even considered inviting him to the United States on a state visit. Despite his sale of the Hawks and abandonment of the Johnson Plan, Kennedy had been "a disappointment to AIPAC," Kenen declared, because he had considered a rapprochement with Nasser and failed to support uncritically ongoing Israeli aggression against Syria.[67]

At its annual meeting in May 1963, AIPAC emphasized the threat posed by Nasser, offering the standard depictions of a Hitler-like Arab world seamlessly dedicated to the destruction of Israel. In response US diplomats pointed out, citing a proxy war in Yemen and tensions between Nasser and Jordan's King Hussein, among other fissures, "The Arab unity movement is confronted by strong divisive forces that will not be overcome for years, if then."[68]

Israel and the lobby regularly countered realistic assessments of Arab capabilities and intentions and refused to acknowledge the "cold war" raging within and among the Arab states.[69] Such assessments threatened to undermine the propaganda framework that depicted Israel as a small and vulnerable nation besieged by a united and relentless Arab world that would settle for nothing less than its destruction, thus leaving the Zionist state in desperate need of American money and support. "With Israel and the Zionists no logical arguments will be effective," advised the diplomat Robert Strong. "The Zionists will keep the maximum pressure on senators and congressmen until they achieve their principal objective."[70]

Angered by the Kennedy administration's efforts to engage with Nasser, the Israel lobby went on the offensive. On May 1, 1963, the *New York Times* reported that Javits and Sen. Hubert Humphrey (D-MN) "have begun attacking the administration's allegedly pro Nasser and pro-Arab policy in the Middle East." Charging the State Department with "appeasing Nasser ever since he came into power," Sen. Ernest Gruening (D-AK) offered an amendment to the Foreign Assistance Act of 1963 complementing a House version introduced by Javits targeting US foreign aid to Egypt. The amendment passed overwhelmingly making aid to Egypt including food supplies vulnerable to cut off.[71]

Asserting that the United States had been guilty of appeasing Nasser, lobby stalwart Rep. Leonard Farbstein (D-NY) introduced an AIPAC-generated resolution calling on the United States, Britain, France, and other nations to form a collective defense treaty with Israel. The proposal was anathema to American diplomats who were committed to preserving the "delicate balance" in the Arab-Israeli conflict.[72]

Kennedy fought off Israel's quest to propel the United States into a "defensive alliance with close joint planning" along the lines of NATO. The Americans rejected repeated Israeli claims of vulnerability to a "growing Arab threat," especially with the Arab world disunited and

Nasser's army bogged down in Yemen. On August 7, 1963, the Joint Chiefs of Staff declared, "The Israeli forces have the capability of defeating aggression by any combination of Arab states which might oppose them."[73]

To many diplomats it was becoming "increasingly clear that the White House is under steadily mounting domestic political pressure to adopt a foreign policy in the Near East more consonant with Israeli desires." Diplomats charged, "Contrary to proper diplomatic procedure, the Israel Embassy here has actively sought in dealing with American newspapermen, members of the Congress and others to undermine our policy."[74]

Noting that Israel had received the Hawks while the Americans and the Arabs had "gotten nothing for our efforts," Kennedy adviser Robert W. Komer advocated adopting a "tougher line toward Israel." Komer, who was Jewish, confronted Israeli diplomat Shlomo Gazit, a regular lunch partner, about the stepped-up lobby pressure on the administration. Gazit told Komer that the pressures exerted by the lobby "were a fact of life with which we would have to live." Komer appealed to Gazit for a "moratorium on propaganda maneuvers," but concluded that Israel was determined "to press us for all the traffic would bear. Its consistent policy seems to be to force us into an openly pro-Israeli stand despite our protest that this would undermine us with the Arabs and give the Soviets a field day." Komer was left wondering: "What kind of a relationship was this?"[75]

The lobby's powerful influence over American domestic politics left the Kennedy administration hamstrung in the pursuit of a balanced Middle East diplomacy. By the time of Kennedy's assassination on November 22, 1963, Israel and AIPAC were in command of the now officially proclaimed special relationship with the United States.

Chapter 3
Enabling Israeli Aggression

"You can be sure I have always been pro-Israel and will continue to be so," Lyndon Baines Johnson assured a group of constituents in San Antonio in 1953.[1]

Four years later, Johnson, as majority leader of the Senate, underscored his dedicated support of the Zionist state by effectively defending it against the Eisenhower administration's threat of censure and sanctions in the wake of the Sinai War. Israel and lobby cultivated and rewarded Johnson for his support. Indeed, Fulbright's Senate investigation revealed that the Jewish Agency "paid the expenses of Johnson and his entourage at the 1960 Democratic National Convention."[2]

Johnson's embrace of Israel was rooted in his religious faith, his close friendship with Jewish Americans such as Abe Fortas and Arthur and Mathilde Krim, and his naïve belief that Israel was a small and vulnerable state that merely sought to "live and let live." He also cultivated the support of liberal American Jews for his ambitious Great Society reform program.

Much like Truman, Johnson came from "very religious stock" and "liked to have the Bible read to him," as his good friend the Rev. Billy Graham later recalled. Johnson took seriously an admonition from his favorite aunt, who had advised, "Lyndon, always remember this, don't ever go against Israel . . . The Jews are God's people, and they are always going to be . . . that's their land . . . and nobody is going to take it away from them."[3]

Despite his reverence for Israel and Jewish tradition, Johnson like all American presidents episodically clashed with Israel and the lobby, yet he acquiesced to the Zionists on myriad crucial occasions. He became in fact the most significant enabler of Israeli aggression in the entire history of the special relationship.[4]

Following the Kennedy assassination, Johnson retained Myer Feldman, whom he dubbed in a telling phrase, "prime minister on the question of Israel." Feldman offered Johnson a spate of pro-Israel advice, including to avoid using the terms "Palestine," which "went out of existence in 1948," as well as "resettlement" of the "so-called refugees."[5]

On June 1, 1964, Johnson received Prime Minister Levi Eshkol in the first formal summit with an Israeli leader hosted by the United States since Chaim Weizmann had visited Truman in 1949. Johnson officially recognized Israel's expanded 1949 borders but like his predecessors got nowhere on the issue of refugee resettlement. Eshkol deployed the standard dehumanizing *hasbara* line dismissing the displaced Palestinians as "not people within the classic meaning of refugees. They are used by the Arab nations to develop enemies against Israel."[6] Johnson sided with Israel in ongoing disputes over the Jordan River, adding that the United States stood "foursquare behind Israel on all matters that affected their vital security interests." Unlike his predecessors, the appreciative *Near East Report* noted, Johnson had not succumbed to the fear that "overt display of friendship" with an Israeli leader "would antagonize the Arabs."[7]

Kenen helped draft the Democratic Party platform on Middle East policy in 1964, as the lobby enthusiastically supported Johnson in his landslide victory over Republican Barry Goldwater.[8] Retained as secretary of state, Rusk warned Johnson that his pro-Israeli policies were putting relations with Arab nations "in increasing jeopardy." Support for Israel on the Jordan water dispute and disdain for the refugees were bound to strengthen the Palestine Liberation Organization (PLO), formed in 1964, among other resistance groups.[9] This appeared to be news to Johnson, who scrambled to "assure all the Arabs that Johnson is just a much their friend as Kennedy was."[10]

Working through Feldman, Israel and the lobby followed up on the sale of the Hawks by pressing Johnson to supply American tanks and strategic aircraft. Noting, "I have rarely been exposed to as much pressure as I have had recently on the question of tanks for Israel," Feldman took credit for convincing several members of Congress and "the Anglo-Jewish press" to remain patient with Johnson on the contentious issue of Middle East arms sales.[11]

While seeking American weapons, Israel and AIPAC condemned a modest arms package proposed for Jordan and designed to deter King Hussein from doing business with the Soviet bloc. Although the proposed sale had the full support of the national security bureaucracy, Johnson hesitated to approve it. To Komer it was "crystal clear" that Johnson's inaction stemmed from "his concern over the US domestic reaction," a euphemism for lobby propaganda and political pressure.[12]

In a stunning private acknowledgement of the lobby's influence, Johnson declared, "I'm not prepared to take on the *New York Times* and Mike Feldman and everybody else." The president actually left the ultimate decision on a US arms sale to a third country for Israel and the lobby to decide. "I'm gonna let them make the decision," he told lobby go-between Abe Feinberg by telephone. Showing his fear of the political clout of the lobby, Johnson declared, "We don't want it laid on to a man from Johnson City. I'm not gonna get in the middle of these clashes and have one of them leak it on me that I want to join up with the Arabs."[13]

American diplomats insisted that the Israeli "campaign to stop all aid" to Arab countries impeded US efforts to promote stability, arms control, and to deter Soviet influence. The professional diplomats resented being bypassed by "backdoor negotiating with the White House through unofficial emissaries" notably Feldman and Feinberg.[14] In February 1966 Johnson, as Dulles had done, appealed to Eban to urge "well-meaning friends of Israel . . . to stop coming in the back door, or writing, or sending telegrams, or talking to the newspapers" and instead allow the two governments to "handle these matters" diplomatically.[15]

In the end Israel and the lobby parlayed the threat of waging a propaganda campaign over the arms package to Jordan to secure additional offensive weapons for the Zionist state. After Feinberg questioned whether "he could reassure various groups of US Jewry who were hearing about arms to Jordan and wondered how Israel could be protected," Israel received 210 M-48 Patton tanks as well as 48 A4E Skyhawk fighter jets in return for acquiescing to the sale of 36 secondhand F-104 jet aircraft to Jordan.[16] In 1966 Johnson approved "a military aid package for Israel, far more ambitious than Kennedy's" already elevated levels of assistance.[17]

Feinberg arranged for Johnson to meet "off the record" with "a select group of Jewish leaders" to smooth over any remaining tensions.[18] "US support for Israel has never been as clear or as certain as under the Johnson Administration," the *NER* merrily proclaimed.[19]

Johnson forwarded to Feinberg a report entitled "US Help for Israel, 1964-1966," which opened with the statement, "Perhaps the best way to characterize US-Israeli relations in this period is to say that they are closer today than ever." Eban concurred, characterizing the Johnson years as "a high point in the evolution of American-Israel friendship." Eban added that Johnson personally had "contributed in abundant measure to the reinforcement of Israel's strength and spirit."[20]

The Johnson administration, like his predecessor, held out hope that the US conventional military assistance could deter the Israeli nuclear program. Israel, however, continued undeterred on the path to developing nuclear weapons--and continued to deceive its special ally in the process. In March 1965 Israel declared that it "will not be the first to introduce nuclear weapons into the Arab-Israel area." Fully aware that Israel had "deliberately misled us initially about the nature of the nuclear facility at Dimona," Rusk warned Eban that cultivation of the bomb could have "a disastrous effect" on US-Israeli relations. Responding with blatant mendacity, Eban insisted, "We haven't got and hope we will never have" nuclear weapons.[21]

The Israelis kept the veil over their nuclear weapons program, which reached the threshold in 1966. Throughout 1967 Israel continued to deny any intention of developing a nuclear weapon, which it had already done in all but testing. The Johnson administration ultimately gave up the effort to head off the Israeli nuclear program.

Israel's Road to War

Israel went on the offensive in the months leading up to its initiation of the pivotal June 1967 War. In November 1966 Israel attacked the West Bank town of Samu in "the worst single incident since Suez," according to the CIA.[22] In an act of collective punishment, the IDF targeted the village in response to a land mine that had killed three Israeli soldiers. Once again Jordan's King Hussein had been working with the Israelis to combat isolated rebel forces, but the West Bank village was subjected to an indiscriminate assault, nonetheless. The IDF admitted to destroying 41 houses; a subsequent UN assessment put the number at 125 homes destroyed.[23]

The Johnson administration sponsored a resolution of censure in the Security Council over the disproportionate Samu attack, but the *NER* reassured its readers that the only reason the United States took the action was to preclude the Soviet Union from posing as the sole defender of the Arab world. The lobby praised UN Ambassador Arthur Goldberg--a dedicated Zionist--who condemned the Samu assault, but in what the *NER* called an "even-handed American reaction," Goldberg added, "We also deplore the terrorist incidents" that provoked it.[24]

The lobby erupted when the United States announced another modest arms supplement to Jordan meant to reassure Hussein as he grappled with the political fallout from the Samu assault. Even as Israel launched surprise assaults and deceived its special ally about nuclear weapons, Eban had the *chutzpah* to complain that Israel should have been "taken into confidence" by the administration before it decided on an arms supplement for Jordan.[25]

For a second time Israel exploited a US arms shipment to Jordan to demand more advance weaponry of its own. "The entire US Jewish community felt it was isolated after Israel's censure by the US," Feinberg explained, thus it was "extremely important" to resupply the Israelis "in order to give a sense of security."[26] The United States had threatened to "reexamine" arms sales to Israel, especially after US supplied tanks were deployed in the Samu attack. However, "continuing pressure in New

York"—a euphemism for the lobby--prompted Johnson to direct Goldberg, assisted by Feinberg, to facilitate the arms request.[27]

Well on the way to replacing France as Israel's main arms supplier, Washington at the same time delighted the lobby by withholding food aid to Egypt, precipitating a bitter rupture in US relations with the Nasser regime.[28] AIPAC, which had long urged termination of the aid program to Egypt, was getting everything that it wanted from the Johnson administration. "American policy has become more independent of Arab pressure in recent years," as the *NER* delicately put it.[29]

The Samu assault was a watershed event for Hussein and thus "proved to be a decisive moment in the march to war" in the Middle East. The attack spurred Hussein's fears that Israel coveted the West Bank—the territory east of Israel's legal borders and west of the Jordan River--which Palestinians had earmarked for a future state of their own. Hussein concluded that Israel could not be trusted nor would it be compelled by the Americans to respect the independence of Arab territory or Jordanian security. Driven to "seek alternative solutions to secure the volatile West Bank," Hussein "sought an alliance with Nasser."[30]

Serious tensions prevailed with Syria as well as with Jordan. Having won the water war, Israel coveted the Syrian Golan Heights, overlooking the Galilee (Lake Tiberius). Control of the heights would dramatically improve the Israelis' strategic position vis-à-vis Syria as well as neighboring Lebanon. The Israelis thus continued to make aggressive thrusts in an effort to provoke the Syrian regime. "Israel's strategy of escalation on the Syrian front," historian Avi Shlaim points out, "was the single most important factor in dragging the Middle East to war in June 1967."[31]

On April 7, 1967, Israel initiated a major conflict by precipitating a border clash and then escalating it into a full-scale military onslaught. The battle raged "most of the day and involved mortar, artillery and tank fire and several aerial dogfights." In a harbinger of the full-scale war to come, Israel commanded the air, shooting down six Soviet-made MIG fighter aircraft including two on the outskirts of Damascus, humiliating the Syrian regime. After flaunting their dominance of the air over the Syrian capital, all the Israeli jets returned safely to their base.[32]

Under pressure as the titular leader of the Arab world, Nasser responded to Israeli aggression in Syria by closing off to Israeli shipping the Straits of Tiran, which linked the Red Sea to the Gulf of Aqaba. Nasser's response increased the possibility of war, as Israel had demanded and received access to the Gulf of Aqaba as a condition of withdrawal at the end of the Sinai War.

Siding with Israel in the dispute over the Tiran Straits, Johnson referenced an Egyptian "blockade" of an "international waterway" even though a full-blown blockade never materialized. Moreover, the status of the Tiran Straits, actually a closed gulf, was disputed rather than unambiguously "international." In his May 23 speech, Johnson did not allude to Israel having been the first to change the status quo in the Gulf of Aqaba during the Sinai War. At that time the Eisenhower administration had acquiesced to Israel's demand of free navigation on the Gulf of Aqaba, prompting the Arabs to complain with good reason that Israel had used aggression, namely the attack on Egypt, to gain previously nonexistent navigation rights.[33]

While buttressing the Israeli interpretation of the status of the waterway, Johnson at the same time declared that the United States "strongly opposes aggression by anyone in this area, in any form, overt or clandestine."[34] Thus the Johnson administration, while blaming Nasser for the growing crisis, did not believe Egyptian actions constituted a casus-belli.

Nasser condemned the United States for its "hypocrisy," pointing out that it had responded far less resolutely to Israeli aggression at Samu and in Syria. In a May 26 pubic speech Nasser declaimed, "Nobody spoke about peace or threats to peace" when the Israelis carried out aggression against Syria, but when Egypt acted in pursuit of its "legitimate rights" the Western powers "turn the world upside down and speak about threats to peace and about a crisis in the Middle East."[35]

Johnson received a mixed response from the Israelis following his May 23 address on the crisis in the Straits. Eppie Evron, the Israeli minister in the Washington embassy who since his arrival in 1965 had nurtured a close friendship with Johnson, conveyed his "deep personal gratitude" for the administration's support, adding that the Israeli Embassy "was flooded with telephone calls from people we both respect that were deeply gratified by your statement."[36]

Although Johnson had backed Israel in the dispute, Eban conveyed concerns about the president's statement that Egypt's actions did not justify a war. While insisting that Israel "had no intention of taking initiatives," Eban declared that Israel was "disturbed because it had not sensed the kind of identification, the kind of special support that it had hoped to receive" from the administration.[37] While Israel sought a guarantee of US backing if it went to war, Johnson and his top national security advisers rejected fictive Israeli claims that they faced an imminent pan-Arab attack and annihilation. "Our best judgment is that no attack on Israel is imminent," Johnson told Eban on May 26. Moreover, "if Israel was attacked our judgment is that the Israelis would lick them."[38]

Concerned by the threat of a backlash from the lobby and irritated by Israeli suggestions that the United States was "retreating" in the face of Arab aggression, Johnson emphasized that he would work with the UN, Congress, and US allies to reopen the Straits of Tiran, obviating the need for aggression. There was no need for Israel to launch a war. "We will pursue vigorously any and all possible measures to keep the Strait open," Johnson pledged. "At the same time Israel must not make itself responsible for initiating hostilities."[39]

Israel and the lobby stepped up a campaign of alarmist rhetoric misrepresenting the crisis and sounding the drumbeat of war. The *NER* declared that Nasser had "won a major skirmish" and this was "the fruit of appeasement." Deploying the familiar trope of "another Munich," the newsletter opined, "The cost of US surrender would be incalculable." Hyperbole proliferated, as Harman insisted that Israel was "threatened not with aggression but with genocide." The United States must not "let the valiant people of Israel be driven into the sea," Sen. Javits ominously declaimed.

While Israel campaigned for war, a group of Arab ambassadors in Washington sought a special meeting with Johnson's advisers at which they emphasized that none of the Arab states "wanted to start a war." It was clear, however, that Israel was determined to have one.[40] Flying to Washington to lay the groundwork for war, Meir Amit, the head of Mossad, the Israeli intelligence service, met with Defense Secretary Robert McNamara on June 1. Amit returned home with assurances that Washington would not obstruct Israeli aggression and moreover would, if necessary, deter the Soviet Union from intervening on behalf of the Arab states.[41]

Most important of all, Amit left Washington with assurance that Johnson--increasingly overwhelmed by the war in Vietnam and thus lacking enthusiasm for a conflict in the Middle East--nonetheless could be counted on to step in if the war went badly for Israel. Israel's key American "assets"—Feinberg (*Andre*, to the Israelis), Goldberg (code-named *Menashe*) and Fortas (Ilan)—all affirmed that Johnson would back Israel. The Israelis understood that Johnson "intended to see this through even if, in the end, the United States was the only nation standing behind Israel." But the United States did not anticipate that it would be necessary to intervene, as the CIA accurately predicted Israel would win the war handily.[42]

Israel was determined to strike while it enjoyed military superiority. Backed by the lobby and its "assets" within the accommodating Johnson administration, Israel was confident the United States could be managed. Only a few doves in Congress notably Fulbright called for the matter to be resolved in the UN and not on the battlefield, but Israel rejected diplomacy and chose war. When the IDF forced Eshkol to name the militant Moshe Dayan as defense minister, Rusk realized it would "be impossible to hold the Israelis."[43]

Rusk's aide, the Middle East expert Harold Saunders, spelled out the approach to the conflict that the Johnson administration ultimately adopted. Although he blamed the crisis on a failed US policy of siding almost exclusively with Israel over the years, Saunders concluded that war was now inevitable. He recommended that the United States stay out of it and *"let the Israelis do this job themselves."* [italics in original][44]

On June 5 Israel launched the war without informing its special ally prior to the attack. The Israelis followed up with false claims that Egypt had attacked first. Over the ensuing six days of war Israel ignored US and UN calls for a ceasefire until it had pummeled Egypt, Jordan, and Syria.[45]

The United States acquiesced to the Israeli aggression--including a timid response to the unprovoked Israeli air and naval assault on the intelligence ship the *USS Liberty*, killing 34 and wounding 171 American sailors. On the morning of June 8 Israeli fighter jets carried out strafing attacks, firing rockets and napalm at the lightly armed spy ship as it cruised in international waters off the Sinai coast. Twenty minutes later three Israeli torpedo boats followed up, one of them blasting a hole in the hull in a clear effort to sink the *Liberty*, which managed to stay afloat.

Israel insisted the attack was a case of mistaken identity amid the fog of war, but officials in the Johnson administration, the Navy, and the CIA believed it should have been obvious on a clear day that the ship was an American rather than an Egyptian vessel. The *Liberty* flew the American flag and, with its array of antennae and communications equipment rather than weaponry, posed no military threat and should not have been confused with an Egyptian warship. US crewmen, many of them sunbathing on the deck of the *Liberty*, identified the Israeli jets and even waved to them prior to the attack.

Israel apologized and provided compensation for the American casualties while insisting that the two separate attacks, by air and by sea, were a case of mistaken identity. Decades later previously secret recordings surfaced, showing that the Israelis had identified the ship as American. Some investigators have cited alleged Israeli desires to bring a swift halt to the spy ship's monitoring of Israel's actions on the battlefield--which included indiscriminate killing of Egyptian prisoners as well as an eminent attack on Syria--as the rationale for launching a deliberate assault on the *Liberty*.

At the time, the Johnson administration joined the Israelis in containing the fallout from the attack, which threatened to undermine support for Israel in the midst of the war and even to call into question the special relationship. The *Liberty's* injured captain and surviving sailors were sworn to secrecy and calls for a full-blown investigation were shut down. Since the incident the surviving *Liberty* crewmen, among others, have repeatedly called for a serious investigation, but both Israel and the US Congress have ignored these demands for decades.[46]

From War to Occupation

From the outset Israel sent the message through the lobby that the war of June 1967 would not be a reprise of the war a decade earlier in which Eisenhower had acted as honest broker and compelled Israel to withdraw from occupied territory. On June 5, when a State Department spokesman declared the United States was "neutral in thought, word, and deed," the Israel lobby erupted with a propaganda onslaught. An official alerted Johnson that the neutrality statement was "killing us with the Jews in this country." As letters and telegrams poured into the White House in support of Israel, Rusk put out a statement in an effort to divert media focus away from the statement on neutrality.[47]

While the lobby and Israel's assets policed the discourse in Washington, the Zionist state embarked on a quest for the Greater Israel. On the second day of the war, Goldberg informed Rusk, "The Israelis have a frigid attitude toward any declaration supporting withdrawal."[48]

AIPAC and other American Zionist organizations also rejected calls for a ceasefire and withdrawal from newly conquered territory. AIPAC's Kenen upbraided Javits, who had made the mistake of drafting a resolution invoking "territorial integrity." Kenen "complained bitterly" and forced the New York senator to desist. "This is not what we wanted at this stage," he explained. "What we really want is fluidity" hence a resolution upholding the 1949 armistice lines would have been "disastrous."

Javits quickly got the message that the June war was to be a war for Israeli expansion and not for a return to the territorial status quo. The New York senator also quickly learned that Israel and AIPAC, and not a member of the US Congress, would frame the public discussion on Middle East policy.[49]

Determined to fend off a reprise of Eisenhower's insistence on an Israeli withdrawal after the Sinai War, the lobby worked overtime to mobilize Congress and the public against an anticipated State Department diplomatic offensive. Fearing that the attack on the *Liberty*, "alleged mistreatment of Egyptian prisoners," ongoing expulsion of Palestinian refugees, and efforts to absorb Jerusalem could undermine support for Israel, AIPAC strove to gauge the attitudes of "as many senators as possible." On June 14, after speaking with some 35 senators, "The report we get is that just about everybody is voting in support of Israel's position, that it cannot withdraw prior to a peace settlement," Kenen advised. An Associated Press poll found that 365 out of 438 responses from members of Congress "were opposed to withdrawal without peace." After conducting a "roundup of American editorial, columnist and magazine opinion," the Anti-Defamation League reported "considerable comment favoring Israel retaining strategic territory."[50]

Kenen was thrilled with the response. "The US position is all that can be desired," the lobby propagandist declared. "The US is working like never before." In addition to support from the public and on Capitol Hill, donations were flowing into AIPAC at an unprecedented level in the wake of the six-day war.[51]

Johnson's closest advisers emphasized that Israel and the lobby were demanding "assurances" that he would not "sell Israel down the river" by forcing it to withdraw from the seized Arab territory, as Eisenhower had done a decade earlier in the wake of the Sinai War. They advised that Johnson "ought not to mention 'territorial integrity'" as the basis of a settlement of the war.[52]

Abe Fortas (*Ilan*)--the Supreme Court Justice, dedicated Zionist, and close friend of Johnson--advised the president against trying to force Israel to return to the prewar boundaries. "The post-ceasefire situation is going to be the trickiest from the viewpoint of domestic politics," he advised in a reference to the clout of the lobby.[53]

Johnson also heard from his close friend Mathilde Krim, who was sleeping in a White House guest room when the war erupted. Johnson treasured his friendship with Mathilde—a scientist who had been married to a member of the *Irgun* terror group amid the 1948 war--and her second husband Arthur Krim, a United Artists film executive and Democratic fundraiser. For years the Krims had cultivated Johnson's Zionist sympathies over many hours of dinner parties and conversation in Texas, New York, and Washington. Johnson showed Krim top secret documents and found Mathilde, an intelligent and articulate "blonde beauty," to be "stimulating" company. Amid the war, the Krims lobbied Johnson for Israel's retention of new territories and for insisting upon regime change in Egypt.[54]

Johnson had a shallow grasp of Middle East territorial issues and had been well-schooled by the Krims and other friends of the lobby to view Israel as a besieged innocent. "They just want to live and let live," he told a senator on June 12, and could be counted on to "get out of there" except for "this little area there"—apparently a reference to the West Bank--that they wished to retain.[55]

Johnson thus dramatically underestimated Israel's settler state drives and ambitions, which ultimately entailed retention of not some "little area" but rather an area much larger than the existing Israel, encompassing East Jerusalem, the West Bank, the Gaza Strip, the Golan Heights, and the Sinai Peninsula.

On June 19 the President reversed US policy upholding the territorial integrity of the 1949 borders, announcing instead that new boundaries should be negotiated "on the basis of peace between the parties."[56] By sanctioning for an indefinite duration the occupation of Arab territory, the Johnson administration paved the way for an enduring Middle East crisis.

Johnson embraced the position of Israel and the lobby that the Arabs had to capitulate, recognize Israel, and hope for the best on borders. But the Israelis had no intention of returning land for peace. After "crushing" the Arabs in war, Israel had "changed the map of the Near East," the *NER* proudly proclaimed, and would "not return to the UN armistice lines . . . No American diplomat could justify pressure to roll back Israel." Buoyed by a massive "flow of contributions to AIPAC" and sweeping support in the Congress, Kenen exulted, "Everyone likes a winner, and Israel is a spectacular one."[57]

Rusk and the State Department vehemently opposed the unfolding occupation, but Johnson tapped McGeorge Bundy to steer a special committee on the Mideast crisis. Bundy rejected efforts to uphold "territorial integrity," endorsed the AIPAC discourse that the State Department operated under a "pro-Arab bias," and advised Johnson to sideline Rusk, who was "not right for you" on Middle East policy.[58]

Israel and the lobby retained the support of the Johnson administration, fending off efforts by the Soviet Union and the UN to forge a Middle East peace settlement. Meeting with the Soviets in New Jersey in late June, Johnson rejected calls for an Israeli pullback to the 1949 borders. Goldberg, who championed Greater Israel, sided with his fellow Zionists against the consensus in the UN calling for an Israeli pullback from occupied Arab territories.[59]

On the volatile issue of Jerusalem, the United States declined to join the overwhelming majority of nations in condemning Israel's takeover of the historic holy city. On July 4 the UN General Assembly voted 99-0 with 20 abstentions--the United States among the latter--in favor of a Pakistani-sponsored resolution that condemned Israel for actions designed to "alter the status of Jerusalem."[60] Goldberg linked the status of Jerusalem to an overall settlement, explaining to Johnson: "We said that the whole kit and caboodle has to be settled" in order for Israel to withdraw. The administration thus essentially acquiesced to the Israeli takeover of East Jerusalem.[61] When the UN adjourned on July 21 with no resolution of the conflict, Eban expressed his elation over the "favorable impasse."[62]

Believing that his compromise on territorial integrity would allow Israel to negotiate from a position of strength, Johnson only belatedly came to the realization that Israel meant to expand rather than to negotiate. Declaring on July 18 that "the clock is ticking" and "the Arabs have no confidence in us," Johnson now urged meaningful negotiations, but

AIPAC inundated the White House with protest. Johnson felt so hounded by the propaganda campaign that he directed aides to "channel future requests by Jewish leaders to Bundy and not to the President. The President said he was seeing too many." On July 26 Bundy reported that he met with lobbyists Feinberg and David Ginsburg, directing them to "not bother you for a while."[63]

Lobby insiders warned that efforts to "pressure the Israelis to be more amenable" on determining borders and on Jerusalem "had to be resisted."[64] Bundy realized that the Zionist position was "hardening" and that the Israelis were proceeding with "great confidence" in plans "to keep not only all of Jerusalem but the Gaza Strip and the West Bank." However, Bundy embraced a colonialist solution, as he advised against efforts to "make the Israeli view of Jerusalem or the West Bank into a federal case." He advised that Johnson should "not affront the Israelis" and acknowledged, "We may well be heading toward a de facto settlement on the present cease-fire lines."[65]

Bundy counseled aligning the United States with "the rights and hopes of Israel," not merely as a matter of expediency or to appease "the Abe Feinbergs or even the Arthur Krims," but rather because the special relationship was rooted in the "wider grounds of national sympathy and interest." As he saw it, State Department opposition to the "heavy-handed agents of the Jewish community like Mike Feldman" had caused the professional diplomats to "weight their advice . . . against any pro-Israel course."[66]

While Goldberg and Bundy, isolating the State Department, anchored the pro-Israeli policy inside the White House, AIPAC acted as watchdog against any moves toward a settlement with the Arabs. Using its favorite tropes, the *NER* urged Johnson to steer clear of "appeasement" and to "beware of any Munich-like compromises." The lobby propaganda organ assured Johnson that he had "Congressional support for a firm policy insisting on negotiations and a peace settlement."[67]

With the Israelis laying claim to Jerusalem and driving Palestinians from their homes, there was no chance that the Arab leaders meeting at a summit in Khartoum in August would acquiesce to the Israeli demand of direct negotiations and de jure recognition of Israel in the absence of agreement to withdraw from the Occupied Territories. The Khartoum summit thus concluded with the "three No's": "No peace with Israel, no recognition of Israel, and no negotiations with it" amid the Israeli occupation.[68]

The emphasis on the "three No's" played into Israeli propaganda emphasizing Arab intransigence driven by a desire to destroy the Jewish state, but in actuality the Khartoum summit had marked a breakthrough in Arab attitudes in the wake of the humiliating defeat. The summit marked "a turning point," as Hussein put it, in which the moderate forces had prevailed by warding off calls for military liberation of Palestine and committing the Arab states to pursue a settlement through indirect negotiations under international auspices. As usual the Arabs were far from united at the meeting, as Syria boycotted the Sudan summit and together with Algeria advocated a "large-scale and sustained guerrilla campaign" against the Israeli occupation. By contrast Nasser and Hussein had acknowledged their defeat in the war and showed a willingness to come to terms, as both the Americans and the Israelis recognized.[69]

As Shlaim points out, Israel "deliberately misrepresented the conclusions of the summit as the climax of Arab intransigence in order to justify the toughening of their own posture."[70] The three No's were "less categorical than they sounded," former Israeli foreign minister Shlomo Ben-Ami concurred, obscuring the most important result of the Khartoum summit that for "the first time in its history that the Arab League contemplated the principle of a political solution to the Arab-Israeli conflict."[71]

Even the *NER* acknowledged that the Arabs "made conciliatory gestures at the Khartoum summit conference" and have "toned down" their anti-Zionist rhetoric, but the newsletter dismissed the actions as merely "calculated to win votes" in the UN. Lobby propaganda emphasized the Arab states' rejection of immediate recognition of Israel in the aftermath of an aggressive war and the midst of the cementing occupation, rather than the Arab leaders' turn away from calls to wage a war of liberation in Palestine.[72]

UN Resolution 242, passed by the Security Council in November, declared "the inadmissibility of the acquisition of territory by war" and called for Israel to "withdraw from territories occupied in the recent conflict." However, the binding resolution did not mention Palestinians nor did the English version compel an Israeli withdrawal from all of "the" occupied territories.[73]

Israel and the lobby celebrated their semantic triumph of precluding the inclusion of "the" territories in the English version of 242. The UN resolution "intentionally does not say *all* the territories" meaning that the June war had "changed the map of the region's ever-shifting boundaries," the *NER* emphasized. Trumpeting its close monitoring of the American legislative branch, the newsletter declared, "Congress did not want Israel to lose the peace . . . Israelis have returned to their ancient capital" of Jerusalem, which would remain "under Israel rule."[74]

Goldberg, himself a proponent of *Eretz Israel*, collaborated with the Israelis in rendering the withdrawal resolution feckless and fending off UN efforts to make the Israelis responsible for launching the war. The avoidance of responsibility for initiating the June conflict was important, as it sanctioned "expanded versions of self-defense" based on the legitimation of "preemptive war." Similar justifications would be cited in an effort to legitimate future Israeli attacks against Iraq, Lebanon, and the Gaza Strip.[75]

By the spring of 1968 the UN effort to promote a diplomatic settlement of the Middle East conflict was clearly failing as a result of Israeli intransigence and Johnson's acquiescence to Israeli aggression and occupation. Overwhelmed by the escalating Indochina War, particularly in the wake of the Tet Offensive, Johnson abandoned plans to seek another term in office and became a lame duck president. Hussein continued to plead for a settlement, but Bundy bluntly told the king that the Americans were "heavily preoccupied with the war in Vietnam and with elections, and that there was little incentive to expend energy on a no-result exercise in the Arab-Israel contest."[76]

As in 1949, Israel's aggressive settler identity drove it to reject an opportunity to forge peace accords with its Arab neighbors in the wake of war. Some Palestinian factions and King Hussein proved willing to negotiate with Israel, which summarily rejected them in deference to a diplomacy of annexation. "Israel preferred land to peace," Avi Raz explains in a definitive account of Israeli policy in the wake of the Six-Day War, "and thus deliberately squandered a real opportunity for a settlement with its eastern neighbors."[77] Ben-Ami concurs, declaring that as a result of "hubris" and "triumphalism" an "opportunity was missed to turn the tactical victory in war into a major strategic victory for Zionism that could have made the Six-Day War into the last major war of the Arab-Israeli conflict and an avenue to a settlement with at least part of the Arab world."[78] Instead of peace, a prolonged a highly destabilizing expanded settler colonial occupation ensued.[79]

More Arms for Israel

After sidestepping UN Resolution 242, the Israelis backed by AIPAC threatened a public relations "confrontation" if the United States maintained an arms embargo, which had been placed on all belligerents with the outbreak of the June War. The outcome of the war, in which Israel had destroyed massive supplies of military equipment and installations, left the Zionist state militarily far superior to its neighbors, but the Soviet Union responded with stepped up arms shipments to Egypt and Syria. The *NER* demanded rearmament of the Zionist state in a special 30-page supplement, "The Arms Race in the Near East."[80]

The Soviet resupply threatened to put US-Israeli relations on a "collision course" if the Americans refused to lift the embargo or tried to link the renewal of arms sales to Israel with demands for withdrawal from the Occupied Territories.[81] At this point veteran diplomat W. Averell Harriman resigned in disgust as "ambassador at large," citing "the excess of Jewish chauvinism which existed on the Hill in some of the less responsible Congressmen who were clamoring for a stronger pro-Israel attitude on the part of the United States."[82]

Saunders, who had complained since October that the administration was "weaseling in the face of Israeli intransigence," proposed to link the resupply with forcing Israel to make "an honest effort to reach a settlement with its neighbors," but Bundy shot down the call for linkage. Rearming the Israelis was "not a great cosmic issue," he declared, adding that "the whole New York crowd" would come down on the administration if sale of Skyhawk aircraft were not resumed. Johnson subsequently lifted the embargo and arms sales to Israel resumed.[83]

Not content with the Skyhawks, Israel and the lobby set their sights on receiving a shipment of the qualitatively more advanced Phantom F-4 supersonic fighter-bomber aircraft. Spurred by the lobby, the 1968 presidential candidates weighed in with their support for sale of the jets, including Sen. Robert F. Kennedy (D-NY). Following Kennedy's endorsement of the Phantom sale in the midst of the California Democratic primary, Sirhan Sirhan--a 24-year-old Jordanian national whose family had been ousted by the Israelis from their West Bank village--shot Kennedy to death. "I did it for my country," Sirhan cried, as he was wrestled to the ground.[84]

A diplomat advised Rusk that sale of the F-4s would "end our long-standing policy" of avoiding becoming "the principal supplier of Israel's military needs." The State Department noted, "The Arabs are upset" about the prospect of sale of the Phantoms. Moreover, Gunnar Jarring, the UN mediator, "very much hopes that the negotiations on the subject will be used as leverage on Israel to move them toward a political settlement."[85]

When Israel flatly rejected tying sale of the Phantoms to the UN negotiations, diplomats advised that the administration should "link the F-4s to Israeli concessions on its nuclear and missile policy" in order to secure Israel's signature on the Nuclear Non-proliferation Treaty (NPT) of 1968.[86] While the vast majority of nations in the world—including all the Arab states—have embraced the landmark treaty, Israel from the outset rejected the international effort to contain the spread of nuclear weapons.[87]

Saunders pointed out that "no one is prepared to recommend that the President release the Phantoms to Israel" without getting some diplomatic cooperation in return, but Israel abetted by AIPAC launched an intensive propaganda campaign for the jets.[88] The lobby was "up in arms . . .

mounting this reaction deliberately to press us to separate the Phantoms and NPT," Walt Rostow observed.[89] Seemingly "every Jew in the country" was "hepped up" about the issue, Johnson told Rusk.[90]

Johnson caved in to lobby pressure, deciding to sell Israel the Phantom jets with no strings attached. On November 1 Rusk reported that Johnson was "strongly opposed to twisting arms on the nuclear thing in connection with the Phantoms. Doesn't want them linked."[91] Feinberg, Arthur Krim and others then complained about the financial terms, arguing that the Shah of Iran was receiving a more favorable price for his purchase of a shipment of Phantoms. "Everybody was mad . . . may blow the whole deal," Krim told Rostow. Johnson again backed the Israelis and on November 23 demanded, "Wrap it up . . . I'm getting a lot of heat."[92]

While the State Department, the Arabs, and the UN mediator had suffered another defeat, the Israelis and AIPAC were "overjoyed" by the sale of the Phantoms.[93] As Johnson left office in January 1969, the State Department noted that the United States "is presently Israel's principal arms supplier—Hawks, tanks, 100 Skyhawks, 50 Phantoms and many million dollars annually of miscellaneous supplies and equipment." Thanks to the American military assistance, "Israel today is militarily superior to any and all of its immediate neighbors."[94]

In January 1969 Johnson retired to his Texas ranch amid widespread condemnation of him as a failed president who had consigned the promise of a "great society" to a torturous death in the rainforests and rice paddies of Vietnam. While Johnson had deeply divided the American people by escalating the futile war in Indochina, Israel and the lobby could not have been more pleased with him. As the Israeli diplomat Eppie Evron put it, Lyndon Johnson had proven to be "the best friend that Israel could have."[95]

Chapter 4
Cementing the Occupation

As he entered the presidency, Richard M. Nixon knew that most American Jews had voted in 1968 for his opponent, the longtime Zionist Hubert Humphrey, whom he had narrowly defeated. Well acquainted with Zionist advocacy dating back to his two-terms as Eisenhower's vice president, Nixon privately avowed that he would not allow the "Jewish lobby" to bully his administration. Yet, preoccupied during his first months in office with the ongoing Indochina crisis, Nixon had no desire to stir the simmering Middle East pot.

Despite his vows to stand up to the lobby, Nixon secretly sabotaged his own secretary of state's peace plan in order to keep the Middle East on the back burner. While diplomats advocated holding back a supply of Phantom jets to put pressure on Israel to negotiate, Nixon and Henry A. Kissinger, his national security adviser, secretly ordered attorney Leonard Garment "to organize some Jewish Community protests against the State Department's attitude on the Middle East situation."[1]

With the White House working with Israel and the lobby against them, the State Department diplomats had no hope of getting Israel to consider a negotiated settlement based on UN Resolution 242. At the same time, Nixon also acquiesced to Israel's status a nuclear power, giving up on the demand for inspections and the pressure to sign the NPT.[2]

Nixon and Kissinger subscribed to a hardline realism over morality in foreign policy. Their top priorities were securing "peace with honor" in Vietnam and orchestrating détente with the USSR and China, but secrecy and executive authority characterized their approach to all matters of foreign policy, including the Arab-Israeli conflict.

The Eurocentric Kissinger had little knowledge of the Middle East but as a German Jewish emigre whose family had been victimized by the Nazi genocide he identified with Israel. He and Nixon also viewed Israel as a strategic asset and bulwark of anticommunism in the region. The "Nixon Doctrine" envisioned arming and equipping regional allies in order to avoid the type of direct US military intervention that had led to the Indochina debacle. Moreover, Kissinger opposed efforts to force an Israeli withdrawal from occupied Palestine and would ensure that none occurred on his long watch (1969-1977).[3]

Secretary of State William P. Rogers, by contrast, advocated "a balanced position" in which Israel would negotiate a land for peace agreement under Resolution 242. The propaganda campaign by Israel and the lobby, secretly abetted by Nixon and Kissinger, quickly stymied the Rogers Plan. At the annual AIPAC Conference in April 1969, lobby stalwart Rep. Emanuel Celler (D-NY) read a statement signed by 227 members of Congress demanding support of the Zionist policy under which the Arab states were to recognize Israel on its terms rather than negotiate through the UN peacemaking process.[4] "Israel has staked out its firm opposition to the positions we have taken," the hapless Rogers advised Nixon, including encouraging "criticism from the Jewish community in the US."[5]

Successful in opening the American arms spigot under Johnson, Israel and its lobby stepped up the pressure on the Nixon administration for unprecedented flows of military support, particularly as the Soviet Union increased aid to Egypt and Syria. Israel and AIPAC demanded regular delivery of Skyhawks, Phantoms, and other weapons and supplies with no strings attached—that is without giving up any of the Arab lands seized in the 1967 war or signing the NPT.

The Presidents of the Major American Jewish Organizations kept up the pressure by mobilizing a "national emergency conference" in Washington, which the group claimed demonstrated that "American Jews are virtually unanimous in their criticism" of the Rogers Plan. Max Fisher, a Midwest oil and real estate executive, acting as Nixon's liaison with the lobby, read a statement at the rally in which the president pledged support for direct negotiations and avowed there would be no American effort to "impose the terms of peace."[6]

The *NER*, which increased to weekly publication in 1970, stepped up the drumbeat of anti-Arab propaganda while championing unquestioned support for Israel in the Congress. In May 1970 the lobby newsletter published "Congress Speaks Out on US Policy," a 32-page "special survey" extensively quoting and then listing names of 280 representatives and 70 senators who endorsed the Israeli policy of "direct, unhampered negotiations" bypassing the UN and all intermediaries.[7]

The lobby campaign paid off—literally—as the Nixon administration and Congress rewarded Israeli diplomatic intransigence with a military assistance package of more than $500 million (more than $3.4 billion in 2020 dollars). Celebrating the "convergence of US-Israel interests," the *NER* called the deal "the major 1970 development in US-Israel relations."[8]

Remarkably underwhelmed with gratitude for the massive assistance package, Ambassador Yitzhak Rabin warned Nixon that failure to keep the pace on rearming Israel would result in increased political pressure on the administration. He instructed the administration that Israel required "a steady pipeline of material to be provided and with sufficient notification so that past turbulence"—a euphemism for lobby propaganda campaigns—"could be eliminated."[9]

By the spring of 1971, Nixon was becoming fed up with Israel's effrontery and its refusal to negotiate a Middle East settlement. He was equally irritated by Kissinger's acquiescence to Israel, telling his aides that because Kissinger was a Jewish emigre he was "irrational" on the subject of Israel. The president now decided that Rogers "could get a hell of a lot more done" if only Kissinger were not continually placating Israel and the lobby. Nixon decided he would encourage Rogers to "squeeze" the Israelis in contrast to Kissinger, who was "just taking the Jewish line."

Citing "the enormous influence of the Jewish lobby in the United States," Nixon told Rogers, "We have often subordinated US security interests to the interests of Israel." Sympathy for Israel was understandable, he went on, insofar as "Jews were horribly persecuted during World War II and it was the responsibility of all decent people to go an extra mile to rectify that blot on the conscience of mankind. But speaking in humanitarian terms we have almost totally closed our eyes to the terrible condition of Arab refugees."

In sum, the United States had "gone too far" enabling Israel against the Arabs and global public opinion, only to be confronted with unceasing Israeli demands for economic and military support. Frustrated by Israel's diplomatic stonewalling—they were "just sitting tight, not doing a damn thing," Nixon concluded, "We've got to pressure 'em and we're going to."[10]

Nixon decided to hold back on resupply of Phantoms, but this step spurred an immediate *hasbara* campaign by the Israelis in concert with extraordinary steps taken by Sen. Henry Jackson (D-WA), an intensely anti-Soviet and pro-Israeli hawk who aspired to the presidency. After being wined and dined in Israel, Jackson sponsored an amendment that would strip executive authority by *mandating* massive annual military assistance to Israel. Nixon beat back the Jackson amendment only by reopening the military supply spigot. Prime Minister Meir then demanded that Nixon take a "passive role in the negotiations" that were still officially under way but stalled at the UN. Israel instructed the United States "not put forward any compromise proposals."[11]

Meeting with Meir in Washington on March 1, 1973, Nixon again urged Israel to "get off dead center" and come to terms on disengagement with Egypt. He brought to the meeting only carrots and no sticks, however, as he informed Meir that he was releasing a new shipment of Phantoms and Skyhawks. "We never had it so good," the Israeli leader replied.[12]

Meeting with his Cabinet on March 18 Nixon made it clear that the lobby's ability to mobilize overwhelming bipartisan congressional support for Israel left the administration hamstrung. "In the Middle East the problem is Israel," he bluntly declared. "Israel's lobby is so strong that Congress is not reasonable . . . We have to have policies which don't allow an obsession with one state to destroy our status in the Middle East."[13]

Even more frustrated than Nixon was Egypt's Anwar Sadat, Nasser's successor, who had desperately pursued an interim agreement only to be stonewalled by Israel. In the summer of 1972 Sadat delighted the Americans by expelling Soviet advisers from Egypt, a move he hoped might spur the United States to put more pressure on Israel to compromise on eventual return of the Sinai Peninsula.[14] Washington offered little in response, however, leaving Sadat with no illusions about the ability of the United States to serve as an honest broker.[15]

Having failed to generate support for a peaceful return of the Sinai, Sadat in October 1973 launched another round of warfare with Israel. The surprise attack had the Israelis reeling until a massive US military resupply enabled Israel to mount an effective counteroffensive. When Israel, as it had done in the June 1967 War, blatantly violated a ceasefire agreement and advanced on the west bank of the Suez Canal, the Soviet Union threatened to intervene, at which point the Nixon administration went on heightened nuclear alert status (Defcon 3).[16]

Israel's disdain for diplomacy with the Arabs had brought the world to the brink of superpower confrontation. It also brought the oil-addicted Western world to its knees as the Arab oil producing states responded to all-out American support for Israel in the war with devastating price increases. Kissinger had previously scoffed at the possibility of the Arabs wielding oil as a diplomatic weapon.[17]

Imbalanced US support for Israel and its occupation, policed by the lobby, thus undermined American national interests by precipitating a major war followed by the economically devastating Arab oil embargo. The cutoff in oil supplies rocketed the price of oil skyward, spurring a broader "stagflation" of the US and Western European economies that prevailed through the 1970s.[18]

Now serving as secretary of state, Kissinger had enabled Israel's intransigence while ignoring Arab perspectives on the conflict. In 1975 he acknowledged, "I am sorry that I did not support the Rogers effort more than I did." He offered the devastating admission that an interim agreement with Egypt could have been negotiated and "would have prevented the 1973 war."[19]

The United States rewarded Israel for its intransigence with a mammoth $2.2 billion military resupply, which more than covered Israeli losses in the war. Kissinger told AIPAC and the Jewish Presidents group, with which he began to meet regularly, that Israel had "gotten seven times more equipment than in any comparable period in the history of Israel-

Arab relations. It was more than the Berlin airlift in terms of tonnages."[20] He added, "We are giving aid to Israel at a rate which would be unbelievable for any other country."[21]

Fully aware that the United States would back Israel militarily and politically, Egypt and Syria had no illusions about winning the October 1973 war, but they had succeeded in breaking the diplomatic logjam. Kissinger belatedly took an interest in the Arab side of the issues, as he began "shuttle diplomacy" to the Middle East as well as to Moscow. In January and May 1974, Kissinger secured disengagement agreements between a grudging Israel and Egypt and Syria, respectively, with the explicit understanding embodied in UN Security Council Resolution 338 (October 1973) that these were only the first steps toward a full and lasting peace based on UN Resolution 242.[22]

Rabin replaced Meir but neither he nor Kissinger pursued the possibility of a lasting peace with the PLO, which had stayed out of the war yet was relentlessly dismissed as nothing but a terrorist group. Contrary to the demonization campaign, the PLO had evolved considerably from an ebullient national liberation movement demanding the eradication of Israel to an organization that sought a seat at the diplomatic table in order to trade recognition of Israel in return for a Palestinian state.[23]

Recognizing that the PLO and Islamic radicals would gain growing international legitimacy, Kissinger urged the Israelis to come to terms with Jordan before it was too late. "For God's sake," he advised the Jewish Presidents, "do something with Hussein while he is still one of the players." Kissinger added, however, with cavalier and characteristic disdain for Resolution 242 and for the Palestinians, that the occupation of Palestine was "not an American interest, because we don't care if Israel keeps the West Bank if it can get away with it. So, we won't push it."[24]

Disdainful of Palestinians and disinterested in the quest for justice and human rights for non-Western peoples, Kissinger thus dismissed the pursuit of a comprehensive settlement of the Palestine conflict. Reveling in the fanfare of his much-publicized shuttle diplomacy, Kissinger celebrated style over substance. The Eurocentric diplomat thus sided with the Israelis in eschewing the opportunity to pursue a comprehensive settlement in the aftermath of the October 1973 war.

Despite Kissinger's palpable disdain for the Palestinians, the Arab League declared at an October 1974 summit meeting in Morocco that the PLO was "the sole legitimate representative of the Palestinian people." Under growing lobby influence, the United States failed to pressure the Israelis to negotiate with Hussein, much less the demonized PLO. These policies enabled Israel to perpetuate the destabilizing occupation.[25]

Ford Takes on the Lobby

As Nixon's presidency imploded in the Watergate scandal, Kissinger kept the focus on achieving an accord with Egypt and Syria, only to confront the iron wall of Israeli intransigence. Kissinger and President Gerald Ford—a longtime dedicated Zionist—found that Rabin like Meir still insisted on Egypt and Syria caving in with full declarations of non-belligerency in hopes that the expansive Zionist state might then benevolently return territory that it had seized and to which it had no legitimate claim.

"Mad as hell" because Israel was "stalling," Ford announced at the end of March 1975 an "immediate reassessment" of US policy toward Israel and Middle East, which meant the military supply spigot was to be turned off.[26] Previously laudatory, the *NER* turned against Kissinger, declaring that he "seems to have lost sight of the advantages to US diplomacy of a strong Israel."[27] Javits "came in very threatening," Kissinger told Ford. "If we went after Israel, he and [Sen. Abraham] Ribicoff [D-CT] would come after me. He said our interests were identical with Israel." "I know they will hit us," Ford responded, "but I kind of enjoy a fight when I know I am right."[28]

Ford would soon learn as other presidents had discovered that taking up the fight with Israel and the lobby was a losing proposition. Javits and Simcha Dinitz, Israel's ambassador to the United States, launched an intensive propaganda campaign. They condemned Kissinger and Ford for allegedly sacrificing the vulnerable Zionist state on the altar of détente with the Soviets, thus leaving Israel at the mercy of the terroristic Arabs. Sen. Jackson's neoconservative aide Richard Perle played a prominent role as a go-between in the lobby campaign.[29]

Stunned by a "bunch of lies" and "preposterous" misrepresentations of his shuttle diplomacy, Kissinger expressed "extreme outrage" over the turn of events.[30] "I showed you messages, telegrams, and wires from the Soviet Union and Egypt," Kissinger pleaded with Dinitz in an April meeting. He added in what Dinitz described as a "crying voice," that he "was a Jew before I was an American and now you are making me the scapegoat." Dinitz refused to back off, however, as the "maximum *hasbara* effort" was producing "practical results" in the form of an outpouring of congressional support for Israel.[31]

Indeed, on May 21 the propaganda campaign culminated when Ford received a letter signed by 76 of the 99 sitting American senators, demanding that the administration resume economic and military assistance to Israel, which in reality had never ended, as previous orders had continued to be shipped. The end game was that Israel moved in

Egypt's direction by relinquishing one-seventh of the territory it occupied, and Egypt made gestures toward non-belligerency without however recognizing Israel.[32]

American taxpayers paid off Egypt and especially Israel in order to achieve the "Sinai II" agreement, which by making no mention of the West Bank or the Golan Heights failed to advance the overall UN peace effort. Moreover, the United States secretly pledged not to recognize or negotiate with the PLO or make any diplomatic initiatives in the region without consulting Israel. In addition, Israel received a 200 percent increase in US economic and military aid, including pledges of F-16 fighter planes and Pershing missiles with conventional warheads. Washington had in effect entered into a military alliance with Israel, though it was not proclaimed as such, while enabling continuation of the broader occupation. The "good fight" Gerald Ford said he welcomed thus ended in a knockout punch for Israel and the lobby.[33]

Deepening Cultural Support for Israel

Growing public support for Israel smoothed the path for lobby propaganda campaigns, which in turn reinforced the staunchly pro-Zionist American Middle East policy. Hollywood film represented an important medium, reinforcing favorable popular perceptions of Israel.

Building on the success of the film "Exodus," an "extraordinarily close relationship" linked Hollywood studios, Israel, and the lobby. The relationship flourished in the wake of the famous real-life raid on Entebbe, Uganda, in 1976. The sensational mission, in which Israeli special forces flew 2,500 miles to free more than 100 hostages who had been taken to central Africa after an airline hijacking, coincided with the July 4 bicentennial celebration, contributing to an outpouring of pro-Israeli sentiment in the United States.

Immediately following the daring raid several Hollywood studios competed furiously for Israeli cooperation and film rights. By this time Israel and the lobby "not only considered Hollywood to be a powerful image-builder but an Israeli asset," as many of the studios seeking to produce the Entebbe films were owned or operated by Jewish supporters of Zionism. The three popular "Raid on Entebbe" films that ultimately were produced celebrated the heroic raid as righteous violence, were commercially successful, and had a "wide impact" in the United States. The Entebbe films thus "strengthened the Hollywood-Israel relationship and helped lay the foundations for the American film industry's depiction of Arabs as international terrorists in the decades ahead."[34]

Another powerful source of growing American cultural attachment to Israel was the emerging framework of the Holocaust. Since the latter stages of World War II, awareness of the full extent of the Nazi genocide had horrified the American public while fostering widespread sympathy for Jews as the victims of monstrous crimes. The Israeli capture of Nazi war criminal Adolf Eichmann in 1962, followed by his heavily publicized trial and execution, laid the groundwork for the evolution of the Holocaust as the hegemonic trope representing the Nazi genocide.

The term Holocaust, virtually unused in the first postwar generation, was widely recognized by the 1970s. In a seminal study, the historian Peter Novick analyzed the "sacralization of the Holocaust" as a distinctly *American* memory. This process of cultural adoption eventually culminated in the construction of the United States Holocaust Memorial Museum adjacent to the Washington Mall and opened in 1993.[35]

As political scientist Norman Finkelstein, whose parents were victimized by the Nazi genocide, points out, "unique suffering confers unique entitlement." The culturally driven "holocaust industry" spurred sympathy and garnered financial support for Israel while exercising a chilling effect on criticism of the "Jewish state."[36] The Holocaust framework in American culture emphasized Europe's anti-Semitism while "downplaying the discriminatory US immigration quotas before the war"; exaggerated "the US role in liberating the concentration camps"; and "silently passed over the massive US recruitment of Nazi war criminals at the war's end."[37]

Backed by unswerving US support, Finkelstein argued, the Zionist state had "total license" to carry out virtually any aggressive policies. Criticism of Israel increasingly became linked with anti-Semitism, exercising a chilling effect on critical thinking about the Israel-Palestine issue.[38]

Containing Carter

As in 1972 Israel and the lobby enjoyed broad support from both political parties in the 1976 presidential campaign. However, the victory of Jimmy Carter spurred anxiety, as the former Georgia governor emphasized human rights and became the first American president to lend rhetorical support to the idea of a Palestinian homeland as a part of a comprehensive peace. Israel of course sharply opposed any peace plan that entailed an end to the occupation or that would curb illegal settler colonization of the Occupied Territories.

"From the outset" the Carter administration believed "that the Arab-Israeli conflict should be given very high priority," but the election of

Menachem Begin as Israel's prime minister in May 1977 destroyed any hope of achieving a comprehensive peace. Begin, who had orchestrated terror attacks against the British mandate while a leader of the *Irgun* militia, was an uncompromising proponent of Greater Israel and the burgeoning settlement movement in the Occupied Territories. He had no intention of allowing Carter to "meet the fundamental Arab requirement of withdrawal to the 1967 borders with only minor modifications."[39]

In contrast to Kissinger, Secretary of State Cyrus Vance secured broad support from the Arab states to push for a settlement. Moreover, the PLO had informed the Carter administration through backchannel discussions that it could endorse Resolution 242, in which Palestinians had gone unmentioned, and recognize Israel in return for the establishment of a Palestinian state. "Palestinians accept Israel as a permanent fact in the Middle East," intermediary Landrum Bolling advised Carter. "They know Israel is here to stay, and they are prepared to live with it."[40]

Begin, by contrast, would not consider coexistence with the PLO, which he routinely equated with the Nazis. He adamantly opposed any relationship other than a colonial one with "the Arab inhabitants of Judea and Samaria," the biblical names Israelis had begun to apply routinely to lay claim to the occupied West Bank.[41]

While the election of Begin aroused some "private misgivings" among liberal American Jews, AIPAC and most other lobby groups lined up squarely behind the right-wing Likud government as it championed the continuing occupation and settlements. The Israel lobby thus continued to offer unconditional support for Israel, no matter what party was in charge, and rallied most American Jews as well as gentiles to the cause.[42]

It did not take long for Carter's top political adviser Hamilton Jordan to come to grips with the power of the Israel lobby. In June 1977 he urged Carter to "begin immediately with an extensive consultation program with the American Jewish community."[43] Concurring that "the Jewish community is getting restive about our policies," Vice President Walter Mondale, a longtime Zionist, followed up with a Middle East policy speech, but the *NER* dismissed it as a "disappointing . . . attempt to allay concerns over the disconcerting drift in US policy" toward a comprehensive land for peace agreement.[44]

In an effort to head off a major *hasbara* campaign, Carter met with American Jewish leaders and with Begin, who traveled to Washington. On July 7, 1977, after hearing one Jewish leader after another condemn the direction of his Middle East policy, Carter deemphasized the call for a Palestinian homeland. "On the Palestinian question," he explained, "we see it as tied in to Jordan, as an independent State would be a direct threat to Israel and could be captured by any of the Arab nations." He offered the added reassurance that he would "never repeat" the Ford-Kissinger cut off in aid "reassessment" gambit.[45]

Carter promised Begin he would also back off on discussion of the 1967 borders and abandon "the emphasis on a Palestinian homeland." Begin "committed himself to exercising restraint with respect to settlements and to consulting with us before undertaking any action in south Lebanon." Within days Begin violated the pledge on settlement activity and would later invade Lebanon.[46]

By the fall of 1977 the administration faced "a very intense domestic reaction" as Israel and the lobby mobilized their bipartisan support in the Congress against proposed resumption of settlement talks in Geneva.[47] The United States had issued a joint statement with the USSR in which the two powers sponsored resumption of the conference, which aimed to achieve "normal peaceful relations," including "the legitimate rights of the Palestinian people."[48]

Growing neo-conservative opponents of détente joined with the Israel lobby to squelch the proposed resumption of peace talks. The Likud government and the American lobby condemned Carter and sensationally equated the "legitimate rights" of Palestinians with the destruction of Israel. The *NER* condemned pursuit of peace "apparently at any price" as "the latest blunder by the Carter Administration."[49]

Meeting with Carter in New York amid a firestorm of domestic reaction, Moshe Dayan rejected "pressure or leverage on us to get us to accept a Palestinian state, even if it is tied to a Jordanian federation." Insisting on the maintenance of the colonial occupation, he explained, "We want to live together in the territories and we don't want to give them back. We need your understanding."

Carter responded that the Arab states "have been very cooperative and have given us some options," but Israel was being "adamant," had shown "no flexibility," and was "an absolute obstacle" to a negotiated settlement. Moreover, he went on, "It puts me in a difficult spot being attacked by the American Jewish community and by Congress publicly. If I respond, it seems like there is a cleavage between the United States and Israel . . . I hope you can be constructive."[50]

Israel and the lobby ultimately fended off a resumption of the Geneva talks and defeated Carter's effort to include Palestinian representatives in discussion of a Middle East settlement.[51] In November Sadat seized the initiative with a historic speech before the Knesset, which drove momentum further away from the comprehensive peace sought by Carter and the other Arab states and toward a separate peace between Egypt and Israel.

In September 1978 Carter sponsored the 13-day Camp David summit at which Begin again fended off a comprehensive settlement in deference to a separate agreement with Sadat. Sadat and Carter acquiesced, the former to achieve return of the Sinai and the American president bowing to pressure by the lobby. Ultimately an Egyptian nationalist rather than a leader of the Arab world, Sadat settled for a separate peace, prompting the resignation of his foreign minister, condemnation from the Arab world, and ultimately his assassination by Islamists in 1981.

In the months leading up to Camp David, Begin had skillfully shifted the frame of discussion away from land for peace by declaring his support of "home rule for the Palestinian Arabs," by which he meant only a limited cultural autonomy amid the continuing occupation. This colonialist framework stonewalled negotiations while Ariel Sharon boasted of plans to put "a million Jewish settlers on the West Bank," thereby establishing facts on the ground that would end all discussion as to who would be in control of Palestine.[52]

Carter continued to come under attack from Israel and the lobby as he attempted to get Begin to follow through with the "Framework for Peace in the Middle East," including the "legitimate rights of the Palestinian people," which had been agreed to at the Maryland summit. Begin continued to stonewall, reiterating the neo-colonial framework, dismissing the PLO as Nazis, authorizing Sharon to build more settlements, and stepping up *hasbara* attacks.

Amid the lobby propaganda campaign, incoming White House mail on Carter's Middle East peace proposals was "85% negative" and press coverage unfavorable as well. "Jewish opinion in the country is almost totally agreed that the Administration is insensitive to Israel's concerns about the peace treaty and its security requirements," Ed Sanders, Carter's liaison with the lobby, advised in January 1979.[53]

In August Carter bowed to pressure and fired his friend and UN Ambassador Andrew Young for breaking Kissinger's secret pledge that the United States would not negotiate with the PLO. Young had held a private meeting with a PLO representative in New York--which the Mossad had covertly wiretapped in violation of US law and then leaked to the press.[54]

During the one-term Carter presidency, Israel and the lobby thus fended off a major threat to the occupation. Returning the Sinai followed by peace with Egypt secured Israel's southwestern flank, which enabled the Zionist state to reinforce the occupation of Gaza, the West Bank, East Jerusalem, and the Golan Heights--and to lay siege to the PLO in Lebanon.

Mounting Christian Zionist Support

Israel and AIPAC again had no trouble lining up the political parties for the 1980 campaign, as both platforms offered "strong support for Israel."[55] The historic landslide election of Ronald Reagan in November included a "dramatic Republican shift in the Jewish vote," previously dominated by the Democrats but now about evenly split. While Jews constituted only 2.5 percent of the American population, they comprised nearly 5 percent of the participating voters as a result of their heavier than average turnout. The Republicans followed up by devising a "Jewish Strategy" to solidify and extend the support they had received in the 1980 election.[56]

Of greater numerical significance than the Jewish vote was, as the *NER* noted, the "broad Christian support" for Israel that permeated the country.[57] Israel and the lobby had long recognized the potential reward of tapping into American Christian Zionism. In pursuit of this cause, as Daniel Hummel notes, Zionists had engaged in "advocacy, organizing, and cooperation beginning after the founding of the state of Israel in 1948 and advancing significantly in the wake of the 1967 Arab-Israeli War."[58]

The most popular postwar American evangelist, Billy Graham, played a key role in "Judeo-Christian" reconciliation, a cultural project that had coalesced with the help of the Cold War struggle against communism and atheism. At the end of a pivotal 1960 trip to Israel, Graham told packed audiences that he had "committed his life to a Jew who was born in this country." Graham also stated that he rejected the popular canard that Jews had been responsible for the death of Jesus Christ. Golda Meir gifted Graham with a Bible inscribed to "a true friend of Israel."[59]

The American Jewish Committee cultivated Graham in a successful effort to generate greater support for Israel among American evangelicals in the wake of the June 1967 war. Israel's Ministry of Tourism followed up by establishing a "cooperative relationship" with Christian Zionists to spur rising levels of "Holy land tourism" in the late 1960s. Evangelical tour organizers, guides, marketers, and hospitality providers promoted "Israel as the homeland of Judaism and Christianity" and "the modern state of Israel as a sacred expression of biblical prophecy."[60]

The 1970s marked another periodic uptick of American religious "awakening." The decade began with Hal Lindsey's runaway bestseller *The Late Great Planet Earth* (1970), a tale rooted in dispensationalist theology featuring the apocalyptic consequences of Christ's return to the holy land.[61] Christian voters helped the self-professed "born again" Southern Baptist Carter win the presidency in 1976, which *Newsweek* magazine anointed, "the year of the evangelical."[62]

Not all evangelicals were necessarily theologically or politically conservative nor wedded to Zionism.[63] However, by the end of the 1970s evangelism had become more right-wing, more Republican, and more Zionist. The Falls Church, Virginia, ministry of the Rev. Jerry Falwell condemned communism, secular humanism, and emerged at the forefront of "the new guard of Christian Zionists."[64]

Under Begin, Christian Zionists became a key constituency in Israel's efforts to manage public opinion in the United States. Begin funded Falwell's visit to Israel, made him the first non-Jew to receive the Jabotinsky Award, which honored the right-wing founder of Revisionist Zionism. Begin also presented Falwell with a private Learjet and telephoned him personally to explain Israel's reasons for bombing the Iraqi nuclear site in 1981. Falwell responded by emphasizing the "Biblical view of the Promised land" and backing the ongoing occupation as well as the 1982 invasion of Lebanon. Falwell sent flocks of worshippers from his Moral Majority to visit the holy land.[65]

Growing numbers of American evangelicals thus identified with Israel and opposed any effort to compel it to compromise with the Muslim Arabs. "God would smite any nation that raises its hand against Israel," Falwell advised, "even the United States."[66]

Chapter 5
Beating Back Challenges

Elected by a landslide in 1980, Ronald Reagan had little knowledge of the Middle East, but he paid homage to the Bible, cultivated evangelicals, and had long expressed unshakeable support for Israel, including its "undivided sovereignty" over Jerusalem.[1] Both AIPAC and the number of illegal settlements in the Occupied Territories flourished in the favorable climate of the two-term Reagan presidency.

A perfervid anti-communist, Reagan condemned the Soviet Union as an "evil empire" and viewed all groups associated or allied with it— including the PLO—as forces of global unrest. Eager to exploit this theme, Israeli Prime Minister Begin told Secretary of State Alexander Haig that the PLO was a "satellite of the Soviet Union" and would ensconce communism in "Judea, Samaria, and the Gaza district" if Palestine were allowed to become an independent state.[2]

Seeking to bolster Israel as a Cold War ally in the Middle East, the United States stepped up joint strategic planning with the Zionist state. Quarrels erupted over Israel's bombing of the Iraqi nuclear site in 1981, the sale of sophisticated AWACS (Airborne Warning and Control System) air defense technology to Saudi Arabia, and Israel's abrupt annexation of the Golan Heights, but none of these acts posed a serious threat to the special relationship and growing US accommodation of Israeli aggression and illegal settlement of the Occupied Territories.

The Reagan administration condemned the unprovoked attack on the Iraqi nuclear facility in June 1981 and briefly suspended delivery of F-16's to Israel, but at the same time Reagan said Israel had "reason for concern." Asked about Israel bombing a neighboring state that was not on the verge of developing the bomb, while stockpiling its own nuclear weapons in disregard of the NPT, Reagan offered a response reminiscent of Truman and Johnson's naivete: "It is difficult for me to envision Israel as being a threat to its neighbors."[3]

Israel and the lobby vigorously opposed the US sale of the AWACS to the Saudi regime, but they confronted a president who just won the election by a landslide. In addition, the Israel lobby had to contend with another powerful lobby led by Boeing, the manufacturer of the E-3 Sentry, known as AWACS. Moreover, with the United States having already lost one repressive allied monarchy through the fall of the Shah in Iran in 1979, the Reagan administration was determined to shore up relations with the Saudi kingdom through the major arms sale.

The vigorous opposition campaign waged by Israel and the lobby nearly succeeded in achieving an almost un-heard of event: rejection of a US arms sale by the Congress. However, on October 28 the Senate voted 52-48 in favor of the AWACS deal. AIPAC attributed its defeat to a "last-minute blitz of Presidential blandishments."[4]

While skeptics invariably cite the political defeat suffered by AIPAC on the AWACS sale to argue that the power of the Israel lobby is overrated, such a conclusion is unwarranted. The AWACS sale had no effect on the overarching issue in Middle East politics, namely Israel's continuing occupation and construction of illegal settlements. Moreover, the narrow defeat actually served to strengthen the lobby. Vowing to use the defeat to turn future decisions in Israel's favor, AIPAC bolstered its propaganda apparatus enabling it to prevail the next time the issue of rearming the Saudis surfaced.

The AWACS sale angered Begin but did not impede pursuit of the Greater Israel to which he was dedicated. Just weeks after the Senate approved the AWACS sales Begin took a dramatic unilateral step by announcing the annexation of the Syrian Golan Heights. The United States joined the rest of the UN Security Council in declaring the annexation null and void by a vote of 15-0. In January 1982, however, the United States vetoed proposed sanctions against Israel over the Golan annexation, prompting the *NER* to laud Haig for his "excellent leadership" and "consummate diplomatic skill."[5]

Haig made the Israelis even happier when he explicitly green lighted the 1982 assault on Lebanon, which would be orchestrated by Defense Minister Ariel Sharon. "By any reasonable standard," as Avi Shlaim notes, Sharon, the perpetrator of the Qibya massacre, was "a man of war, the champion of violent solutions . . . a Jewish Rambo."[6] After Haig cynically informed Sharon that, as long as Israel could cite a "recognizable provocation," it was free to try to destroy the PLO in a neighboring state, indiscriminate killing of Arabs was sure to follow under Sharon's command. A week later Israel seized upon the attempted assassination of the Israeli ambassador in London—an attack in which the PLO had played no part—as a pretext to launch the assault on Lebanon.[7]

Deceiving the Israeli Cabinet and public as to the scope of his plans, Sharon initiated a full-scale military onslaught designed to root out the Palestinian refugees and the PLO from Israel's northern border while simultaneously igniting a de facto war with Syria. For weeks Israel carried out a punishing attack into the heart of Lebanon by air, land, and sea. Israel shelled and bombed the Palestinian refugee camps as well as Beirut, the historic coastal city known since the time of the French mandate as the "Paris of the Middle East."[8]

The Israelis intended to take out the PLO and install pro-Israeli Maronite Christian leadership in Lebanon--a vision first spawned by Ben-Gurion in the 1950s. The IDF cultivated a close relationship with the Phalange, the Maronite militia, which had a well-known track record of indiscriminate torture and murder of Palestinians. They were a "corrupt gang of murderers that reminded me of a pack of wild dogs," recalled Uzi Dayan, Moshe Dayan's nephew and the commander of an elite IDF unit in the Lebanon war.[9]

The plan to install the Christian right-wing in Lebanon imploded in the remote-control assassination of Bashir Gemayel, perpetrated by Syrian agents, in September 1982. Enraged by the assassination of his Christian ally, Sharon facilitated the Phalangist massacre of as many as 2,000 people at the Sabra and Shatila Palestinian refugee camps. The militia stormed in and slaughtered in their homes the population of mostly the elderly, women, and children. Rapes and dismemberment also occurred. Israeli forces provided illumination for the attackers, blocked escape routes, and then attempted unsuccessfully to cover up the massacre of the defenseless Palestinian civilians.[10]

Characteristically resisting international efforts to forge a ceasefire, Israel prolonged the violence, ultimately killing some 20,000 Lebanese and decimating the PLO, which relocated in Tunis. However, the bloody conflict precipitated mass protests and a growing peace movement inside Israel, which by 1985 had suffered more than 1,200 dead and thousands of soldiers injured. The investigating Kahan Commission revealed the sordid details of Sabra and Shatila as well as Sharon's brutality and mendacity throughout the conflict, revelations that resulted in his ouster. In October 1983 Begin resigned, replaced by another former terrorist from the mandate era, Yitzhak Shamir.[11]

The intensity of Israel's violent assault in Lebanon shocked Reagan, as it did many others, including Israeli citizens and American Jews. The brutal attack prompted a reassessment of Middle East policy and a revival of the diplomatic track under George Shultz, who replaced Haig. Reagan called for the resumption of Palestinian autonomy talks and an effort to forge a "realistic and fair solution" to the conflict. Begin promptly rejected the Reagan Plan.[12]

Reagan, who had originally declared that Israeli settlements in the occupied territories were "not illegal," now called for a freeze, as it had dawned on him "that Israel has a well thought out plan to take over" the West Bank. Begin, of course, rejected the call for a settlement freeze, responding, "What some call the West Bank, Mr. President, is Judea and

Samaria."[13] Reagan made no effort to back up his call for a freeze and the Israelis continued to establish facts on the ground.

From 1985-90 the number of settlers in the West Bank nearly doubled to a total of more than 80,000.[14]

Once again, in a pattern first established in the wake of the 1953 Qibya massacre, Israel and the lobby launched a propaganda offensive to mitigate the damage unleashed by an indiscriminate borderland assault. "Israel's lightning thrust into Lebanon has greatly enhanced American national interest in the Middle East," the *NER* cheerily proclaimed at the outset of the attack.[15] Lobby propaganda necessarily shifted as the debacle unfolded. The *NER* decried a "deliberate campaign of disinformation, falsely multiplying the numbers of casualties . . . for the express purpose of making Israel appear the ruthless aggressor." The head of the Jewish Presidents' Conference "categorically rejected" any Israeli responsibility for the Sabra and Shatila massacres, a position the Israeli Kahan Commission refuted with compelling evidence months later.[16]

In the wake of the massacres the United States redeployed a Marine contingent in order to keep its pledge to facilitate the safe withdrawal of the PLO under ceasefire, which Israel had sabotaged. Left "exposed without a clear mission in the midst of a civil war," the United States suffered two massive attacks in Beirut. In April 1983 a suicide bomber slammed a pickup truck into the US Embassy, killing 63 people including 17 Americans. On October 23, 241 US Marines along with 58 French soldiers died in another truck bomb attack.[17]

Not for the last time the United States suffered the violent consequences of blowback for its unconditional support of an aggressive Israeli regime--support that was demanded and policed by the Israel lobby. Reeling from the devastating assaults on the vulnerable American contingents, Reagan ignominiously withdrew the US forces that he had recklessly committed and left vulnerable to attack.

Israel and the lobby were unapologetic and undeterred. When the administration held back F-16s in an effort to force Israel out of Lebanon, the lobby promptly launched a propaganda campaign. The *NER* denounced the "disturbing" development "undermining America's interests" and rallied congressional opposition. Israel pulled back and the pipeline of offensive weapons resumed.[18]

Rather than placing Lebanon firmly in the hands of the right-wing Christians, Israel's war paved the way for the rise of the Shi'ite Muslims (the Palestinians were overwhelmingly Sunni Muslims) as the dominant force in the south of Lebanon. Long marginalized in Lebanese society, the southern Shi'ites received support and weapons from Iran and Syria as well growing popular support in Lebanon in the wake of Israel's punitive invasion.[19]

By 1985, as Israel pulled back to a security zone on the contested borderlands, the Hizbullah forces were digging in for a prolonged resistance. That same year Israel bombed Tunis—more than 2,000 miles from Israeli shores--killing 56 Palestinians, 15 Tunisians, and wounding about 100 more. The attack came in retaliation for the killing of three Israeli security agents in Cyprus.[20]

Despite the wrenching events of Israel's terror attacks, the Sabra and Shatila massacres, and the slaughter of the US Marines, the "pro-Israel Congress" remained steadfast, crowed the *NER*. Moreover, the Reagan administration rewarded Israel for its indiscriminate violence with generous military funding and an exalted new status as a "major non-NATO ally." The agreement on "enhanced cooperation" in military-security issues meant, the *NER* exulted, "After 35 years of US-Israeli friendship, an American president has unambiguously accepted the premise that Israel is a strategic asset to the United States." Noting that Reagan had "tilted" decisively toward Israel, the *NER* concluded that 1983 had been "a very good year" after all.[21]

As the 1984 presidential campaign unfolded, the American "consensus on Israel" once again manifested in the party platforms. "In essence, we have two pro-Israel documents," the *NER* proudly noted. "Republicans and Democrats—who have such fundamental differences on most of the key issues of the day—stand as one on this subject."[22]

An AIPAC poll found "by whopping margins" that congressional candidates "favor US economic and military aid to Israel, support strong military ties between the two countries, oppose dealing with the PLO, and oppose Israel's return to the pre-1967 armistice lines." The ensuing 98th Congress granted Israel $2.6 billion in economic and military assistance. In 1987 the 100th Congress upped the figures to $1.8 billion in military assistance and $1.2 billion in economic support.[23]

Israel and the lobby had their way throughout the second Reagan administration. Decrying a proposed arms sale to Jordan as "more dangerous than the Saudi sale of 1981," AIPAC gloated in February 1986 when the administration "backed down in the face of strong Congressional opposition." The next year Israel and the lobby got their revenge against the Saudis, as 67 senators and 170 House members signed a letter of opposition, forcing Reagan to withdraw an arms package for the regime in Riyadh.[24]

Israel and the lobby, like Reagan himself as a rival politician once complained, were Teflon-coated—the dirty deeds failed to stick to them as far as much as the American public was concerned. If Lebanon did not provide evidence enough, the infamous Iran-contra scandal might have done the trick, but Reagan remained popular and Israel suffered no diminished support for helping the Americans carry out an illegal covert operation to ship weapons to the hated terrorist regime in Tehran as part of a hare-brained scheme to generate funding for murderous militarists in Central America.[25] The fiasco was no match for the spin-doctors at the *NER*, who declared, "The apparent involvement of Israel as a conduit for US equipment does show, even in an ill-advised course, Israel's value to America as a dependable ally."[26]

Bulking Up the Lobby

During the 1980s the Israel lobby in the United States expanded dramatically and grew even more assertive in its propaganda campaigns. AIPAC's funding "massively increased following the 1967 war," enabling the lobby to achieve new levels of power and influence. The battles with Nixon, Ford, and Carter, followed by the rift over the AWACS sale, convinced lobby leaders of the need to assemble a more fully equipped tool chest to undermine critics of Israel and above all to maintain the grip on Congress.

After losing the AWACS fight in 1981, followed by criticism of the disastrous assault on Lebanon the next year, AIPAC and other lobby leaders hired consultants and publicists, conducted workshops and held strategy sessions, culminating in expansion and intensification of propaganda efforts. While AIPAC and the Conference of Presidents of Major American Jewish Organizations--closely linked through interlocking board members--remained the two most powerful pro-Israel groups, the lobby branched out and created new entities to carry out its propaganda and tactics.[27]

Under the pivotal leadership of Thomas Dine, executive director from 1980 to 1993, AIPAC accumulated money and power. A former adviser to Senators Edmund Muskie (D-ME) and Edward Kennedy (D-MA), Dine was a liberal who well understood national politics and the innerworkings of the Congress. He proved skilled at fundraising as well.

Tapping wealthy donors, AIPAC's annual budget soared from a little more than $1 million to $15 million (just under $45 million in 2020 dollars). As deregulation enabled large donations to enter ever more deeply into American politics in the 1980s, pro-Israel political action committees (PAC) funneled cash into the campaigns of reliable supporters of Israel—and into the campaigns of challengers to those opposed to the policies embraced by Israel and the lobby. AIPAC did not dispense money directly to candidates, rather it did so indirectly by targeting congressional candidates for support or defeat. Pro-Israel PAC and individual donors then responded by infusing money into the targeted campaigns.[28]

Pro-Israel PAC "quickly became a highly effective (and discreet) means of rewarding or punishing elected politicians for their track record on issues concerning Israel."[29] Practicing bipartisanship in its targeting as well as its support of officeholders, the lobby celebrated the ouster in the 1974 Democratic primary of Sen. Fulbright (D-AR), defeated after 30 years in the Senate by the lobby-backed candidate, Dale Bumpers. In 1982 AIPAC targeted Rep. Paul Findley (R-IL), who had championed the cause of a Palestinian state, by recruiting political novice Dick Durbin as the Democrat to run against him. Durbin ended Findley's run of 22 years in the House and years later won election to the US Senate where he became the reliably pro-Israel majority whip.

In 1984 AIPAC targeted Sen. Charles Percy (R-IL), who had voted for the AWACS sale, advocated "rights" for Palestinians, and used his position as chair of the influential SFRC to criticize Israel amid the onslaught in Lebanon. Percy explicitly challenged the power of Israel and the lobby, declaring it was wrong that "a foreign government gets this money without debate simply because it's organized to get it . . . Can Israel have more power than the entire Senate of the United States or the President of the United States?"[30]

AIPAC responded by recruiting and helping to finance the campaign of Paul Simon, the Democrat who narrowly defeated Percy.[31] After the 1984 elections Dine declared that "Jewish money" had played a decisive role in selecting "the most pro-Israel Congress in history."[32]

Openly trumpeting AIPAC's growing political clout, Dine boasted, "Jews in America, from coast to coast," had ousted Percy and "those who hold public positions now, and those who aspire—got the message." By the mid-1980s, as Dov Waxman notes, "The pro-Israel lobby, and AIPAC in particular, came to national attention and began to acquire the fearsome reputation it has today."[33]

In 1984 AIPAC insiders created the Washington Institute for Near East Policy as a putatively objective think tank on US foreign policy in the Middle East. In actuality WINEP functioned and continues to function as a front for lobby-endorsed positions on Middle East policy, one that journalists would often turn to in ensuing years while rarely if ever noting the linkage with AIPAC. At the same time, liberal Jewish donor Haim Saban funded the Saban Center for Middle East Policy at the Brookings Institution with a $13 million grant. The lobby thus had both conservative and liberal Middle East think tanks established to promote pro-Israeli discourse behind a veneer of scholarly objectivity.[34]

AIPAC and other lobby groups also became more active on college campuses and focused more on influencing and policing the media. The televised images of Israel bombing and shelling defenseless Lebanese civilians and the massacres at Sabra and Shatila had left a legacy of marginally more critical reporting on Israel, which prompted the lobby to go on the attack.

Marking its 25th anniversary in 1982 and claiming a circulation of 50,000, the *NER* lashed out at the media in a 30-page "special survey" alleging, as *Jerusalem Post* reporter Wolf Blitzer put it, that "coverage of Israel in recent years has become more-harsh." AIPAC accused the *Washington Post* of "waging a frontal war against the State of Israel" through critical coverage depicting the Zionist state as a "warlike, aggressive, colonial power."[35]

In 1982 lobbyists launched the Committee on Accuracy in Middle East Reporting and Analysis (CAMERA). Despite the lofty pretensions implied by the name, CAMERA was a watchdog attack group, notorious for launching vitriolic assaults on individuals and groups that criticized Israeli policies. CAMERA, based in Boston, spun off FLAME (Facts and Logic About the Middle East), based in San Francisco, to set up a coast-to-coast lobby organization to monitor and attack media accounts perceived as critical of Israel.

Containing the Intifada

By the late 1980s the Palestinian Intifada—a popular upheaval that strove to "shake off" the continuing occupation—revealed the depth of frustration on the part of the oppressed Palestinians. The uprising, including vivid imagery of rock-throwing youth facing off against Israeli tanks, circulated worldwide, prompting Israel and the lobby to counter with aggressive propaganda and attacks on media outlets.

By 1987 more than 40 percent of Palestinian land had been seized and tens of thousands of settlers were flooding into the West Bank.[36] From 1967 to 1982 Israel's military government had demolished more than 1,300 homes on the West Bank and detained more than 300,000 Palestinians without trial for various lengths of time. Economic dependency relegated Palestinians to menial labor jobs while a dilapidated infrastructure required many of them to live without electricity, running water, or sewage disposal.[37]

A generation of human and civil rights abuses had created simmering resentments primed for explosion. The spark came on December 7, 1987, at a refugee camp in the Gaza Strip when an Israeli transport truck driver plowed into a line of traffic killing four Palestinians and wounding 10 others.

The ensuing protests sparked an uprising as Palestinians took to the streets, chanting, throwing stones at Israeli security forces, and demanding an end to the occupation. Shocked by the outpouring of resistance, the

Israelis responded to the overwhelmingly non-violent civil disobedience with violent repression. Serving as defense minister, Rabin implemented an "iron fist" approach, tripling the number of troops and accelerating the use of deadly force, deportations, mass incarceration, torture, school and shop closures, curfews, and collective punishment. Israel further restricted access to Jerusalem and replaced Palestinians with foreign workers, causing a sharp rise in unemployment as well as homelessness.

The Intifada continued with varying levels of intensity for about six years. Israeli forces killed some 1,000 Palestinians and arrested about 120,000 others, many under the age of 16. As video and photographs circulated worldwide showing unarmed children confronting Israeli tanks with stones, Israel had been transformed into Goliath to the Palestinian David. As Neve Gordon points out, "The Intifada revealed Israel's occupation as a colonial project that was sustained through political violence."[38]

Amid the Intifada, the *NER* and other lobby organs routinely depicted Arabs and Palestinians as anti-Semitic terrorists determined to destroy Israel, as opposed to colonized people waging a grassroots struggle against entrenched oppression. The lobby closely monitored American media reports and sometimes sought to police them. CAMERA chose a vulnerable target--public radio and television. Many Republicans joined by some conservative Democrats had already pursued dramatic funding cuts if not outright dissolution of the public media outlets. CAMERA claimed that National Public Radio (NPR) reports reflected a "pro-Arab bias" with coverage "skewed toward the perspectives of Israel's enemies." In June 1992 CAMERA representatives met with NPR officials to demand curbs on critical reports on Israel, citing individual reporters by name as well as specific programs such as "Fresh Air" and "Talk of the Nation." NPR did not cancel the shows or remove the named reporters, but the publicly funded network had been put on notice.[39]

CAMERA and FLAME targeted the Corporation of Public Broadcasting over public television reports including the award-winning "Frontline," which had aired a film entitled "Journey to the Occupied Lands." The lobby media groups vigorously protested it as well as "Days of Rage," which presented the viewpoints of young Palestinians in the first months of the Intifada. The lobby groups succeeded in pressuring most stations that carried "Days of Rage" to enclose it with a "wrap-around" program in which critics condemned and countered the film. When the identical wrap-around was proposed for "Israel: A Nation is Born," a celebratory portrait hosted by Abba Eban, pressure from CAMERA, among others, fended off the effort.[40]

The media watchdogs monitored newspaper and magazine reports, encyclopedia entries and television and film, issuing Media Alerts as well as articles in the American Jewish Committee publication *Commentary* alleging anti-Israel media bias. CAMERA and FLAME urged followers to scan the shelves of bookstores and complain to the manager if they found books by critics such as Edward Said or Noam Chomsky while urging them to feature works by Joan Peters, Bernard Lewis and other friends of Israel. Lewis's son Michael at the time served as AIPAC's chief of "opposition research."[41]

While the lobby watchdogs exercised a chilling effect on critical reports of Israel's aggression and repression, Congress in 1990 provided more than $3 billion in financial assistance to Israel following passage by record margins of the "most expansive and comprehensive aid bill to date." As an added sweetener the 101st Congress endorsed Jerusalem as the "undivided capital" as well.[42]

The 1991 Persian Gulf War, in which the United States besieged Iraq following Saddam Hussein's invasion of Kuwait, further solidified the US-Israeli de facto military alliance. In September 1990 Rep. Stephen Solarz (D-NY), an AIPAC stalwart from Brooklyn, formed a committee heavily supported by "Jewish congressional leaders," which advocated the use of force to oust Iraq from Kuwait. By the time Congress began its formal debate of the decision to go to war in January 1991, "All the major Jewish organizations had come out for the use of force" against Saddam Hussein.[43] As Desert Storm got underway, Washington paid Israel an additional $650 million in "emergency aid" to deter it from retaliating when Iraq began lobbing Scud missiles onto Israeli territory, where they did minimal damage.[44]

In addition to military assistance, Israel also requested and received massive additional funding from the United States to facilitate resettlement of an influx of refugees from the Soviet Union, which had disintegrated. The lobby had long taken up the cause of Soviet Jews, who were often denied exit visas from the USSR. Persecution of Soviet Jewish dissidents had been well publicized in the United States. In December 1987, on the eve of Soviet leader Mikhail Gorbachev's arrival for a summit with Reagan, lobby organizations sponsored a march on Capitol Hill by some 200,000 Jews and their supporters to demand free emigration for Soviet Jews.[45]

Since its creation in 1948, Israel had taken in more than half a million Soviet Jews, the most from any country, followed by migrants from Romania, Morocco and Poland. By the time of the dissolution of the USSR in August 1991, about 8,000 Soviet emigres a month were pouring into Israel. Jewish and lobby organizations, facilitated by Congress, financed their resettlement—including thousands who settled illegally in the occupied territories.[46]

The "Lonely Guy" President

Entering office in 1989, President George H.W. Bush and Secretary of State James Baker challenged Israel and the lobby to an extent unseen since the Carter presidency (both were one-term presidents). While stopping short of calling for an independent Palestinian state, the Bush administration did call for a halt in new Jewish settlements and demanded a serious Israeli approach to negotiating with the Palestinians.

In what may well be the boldest speech an American politician has ever made before the annual AIPAC conference—normally the site of obsequious parroting of Israel lobby positions--Baker declared on May 22, 1989, "Now is the time, once and for all, to lay aside the unrealistic vision of a greater Israel."[47]

Shamir refused to call a halt to the new settlements, which had proliferated in the Reagan years and were undermining prospects of a future settlement by establishing ever more facts on the ground. The US lobby fully backed the right-wing Israeli leader. When Baker flatly declared, "I don't think that there is any bigger obstacle to peace than the settlement activity," AIPAC condemned him for "leaning toward the Arab position."[48]

The Israel lobby's propaganda line on settlements was that they were not really an important matter. The *NER* decried media reports "portraying Israel's settlement activities in the territories as a major object to peace." The lobby insisted that the construction of permanent new Jewish communities in the illegally occupied Arab territories--in actuality a war crime under international law--was merely "a side issue" that was being raised solely for the purpose of attacking the Zionist state.[49]

When Bush announced plans to withhold resettlement funds until Israel called a halt to settlements and engaged in diplomacy, Israel responded with *hasbara*. The lobby held to the position advocated by Israel since the June 1967 War, the demand for direct negotiations (the Arabs coming to them, hat in hand) rather than seeking peace on neutral ground through the UN or third parties. Through its support for convening Middle East peace negotiations in Madrid, Spain, AIPAC charged, the administration was "placing the onus on Israel to make all the concessions." When Shamir flatly refused to engage in diplomacy, Bush decided to hold back $10 billion in loan guarantees earmarked for resettlement of emigres in order to compel Israel to take part in Madrid.[50]

On Sept. 12, 1991, AIPAC, the Conference of Presidents, and other lobby organizations mobilized more than 1,000 Jewish leaders for a "national advocacy day" in which they descended on the Capitol to demand US funding for resettlement of Jews in Israel with no linkage to the construction of settlements or participation at Madrid. Bush, however, fought back effectively by depicting himself as David confronted by a lobby Goliath.

Amid the lobby campaign Bush appealed to the public, declaring, "There are 1,000 lobbyists up on the Hill today lobbying Congress for loan guarantees for Israel and I'm one lonely little guy down here asking Congress to delay its consideration of loan guarantees for 120 days."[51] Bush thus exposed the raw power of the lobby and its attempt to run roughshod over executive management of American foreign policy. Popular in the immediate aftermath of the decisive victory in the Persian Gulf, Bush argued that the war had created "exciting possibilities for peace in the Middle East" that he and Baker were determined to exploit by means of convening the international conference.[52]

The "one lonely guy" trope proved effective, as many Americans rallied behind the president. Calculating that they had more to lose than to gain, Israel and the lobby abandoned the propaganda campaign. Israel reluctantly agreed to take part in the Madrid conference in order to receive the resettlement funds.[53]

Bush won the skirmish with Israel and the lobby, but they prevailed in the ensuing "war" in which Israel continued to establish facts on the ground, stonewall negotiations, and receive American military assistance on uniquely favorable terms. Israel and lobby support for illegitimate settlement expansion in the Occupied Territories once again impeded the quest for peace. As nearly always seemed to be the case, the setbacks absorbed by Israel and the lobby were thus ephemeral and led ultimately to a renewed strengthening of AIPAC and its affiliates.

Republicans soon became keenly aware that Bush paid a heavy political price for pressuring Israel. AIPAC polls in the wake of the clash with the Bush administration found American Jews "growing more 'hawkish,'" reported the *NER*, whose circulation climbed to a new high of 55,000. Christian Zionists continued to back Israel and AIPAC was firmly in command of the Congress. In 1992 the thirty-third annual AIPAC policy conference brought a record at the time of more than 2,000 attendees including 46 senators and 78 House members wined and dined at the annual banquet.[54]

As always, both political party platforms adopted the lobby-backed positions on the Palestine issue in the runup to the 1992 presidential election. The platforms endorsed funding for Jewish emigres and stepped up support for Jerusalem as the "eternal capital." Bush and the Republicans did their best to recover from the previous clash, as the GOP forwarded an "excellent Middle East plank" showing that "support for Israel runs deep within the party," the *NER* reported. Citing the "increasing involvement of the Jewish community in the Democratic Party," the newsletter also praised that party's platform as "outstanding."[55]

During the campaign Democrat Bill Clinton of Arkansas, positioning himself as the pro-Israeli candidate, stooped to tarring Bush with a baseless charge of anti-Semitism. Campaigning in New York in April 1992, Clinton told a Jewish group that Bush's "strident rhetoric, public and private, against Israel, against the Jewish community" showed that the administration "has broken down the taboo against overt antisemitism." The Bush administration promptly rejected the "abhorrent" charge but the damage had been done.[56]

The Bush administration's clash with the lobby clearly factored into the 1992 election in which Clinton defeated Bush. The incumbent's support among American Jews plunged from the 35 percent that he had won in 1988 to 11 percent 1992--the lowest level of support for a Republican since Barry Goldwater had received 10 percent backing in 1964.[57]

Like Jimmy Carter, Bush reportedly blamed his defeat on Israel and the lobby, but in both cases the Arab-Israeli conflict was not clearly the decisive factor, as other economic, political and diplomatic issues played a role in the election in which both candidates were swamped in the electoral college.

The clash with Bush nonetheless dramatically underscored the political price for taking on Israel and the lobby. Clinton had capitalized by offering no criticism of Israel's expansion of illegal settlements while smearing Bush with the unfounded suggestion of anti-Semitism. In January 1993 the *NER* put out a special supplement to the newsletter entitled "Clinton and Gore: A Pro-Israel Team," praising the new administration for its unquestioned support, including Clinton's endorsement of Jerusalem as Israel's undivided capital.[58]

In 1992 the Republicans learned a lesson they would not forget. They "took a strategic decision," journalist Thomas Friedman explained, that "they will never be out pro-Israel'd again." The GOP thus became increasingly uncritically pro-Israel. For the next 30 years the Republican Party would make every effort to side with Israel and the lobby in an effort to cut into the traditional Democratic hold on the Jewish vote.[59]

Chapter 6
Fending Off Peace

In 1993 AIPAC's longtime and highly effective director Thomas Dine was forced out of his position. More than any other single individual Dine had been responsible for developing AIPAC into one of the most powerful lobbies in the country. Under Dine AIPAC membership had soared from 10,000 to 55,000; its staff from a few dozen to 150.

It was Dine who had arranged for the ever-increasing US financial assistance to Israel to come in the form of lump-sum grants rather than loans that would be repaid. Moreover, the grants were given out as quarterly payments so that Israel could collect the interest on the money right away, a perquisite enjoyed by no other nation. Dine had also pioneered a US-Israel free trade agreement, heavily one-sided in favor of Israel, before such accords had become fashionable.[1]

Dine's resignation followed leaked comments in which he declared that many "mainstream Jews" perceived Orthodox Jews as "smelly," "low class," and comprised of "*Hasids* and New York diamond dealers." (*Hasid* is a Yiddish term for a segment of ultra-Orthodox Jews.) The pejorative comments forced Dine's resignation on June 29, 1993, but they may not have been the sole cause. Orthodox Jews tended to be right-wing and more hostile to negotiations with the Palestinians, hence the ouster of the more moderate Dine reflected their efforts to move AIPAC further to the right.[2]

Amid the controversy over Dine's comments, questions thus arose about whether AIPAC and other lobby groups were in fact moving too far to the right—and further to the right than Israel's new Labor government under Rabin, who had replaced Shamir and sought to pursue the Oslo peace process that arose in the wake of the Madrid Conference. After years of stonewalling meaningful negotiations, AIPAC and other lobby groups were taken aback by the sudden momentum for peace talks. Under the new leadership of Morton Klein, the Zionist Organization of America (ZOA) "veered sharply to the right" and condemned the entire Oslo process.[3]

Labor Party official Yossi Beilin ignited controversy when he declared that "rightist forces in AIPAC and other Jewish organizations" were undermining a potential breakthrough in negotiations.[4] A meeting was arranged between Rabin, the new AIPAC executive Howard Kohr--a conservative who replaced the liberal Democrat Dine--and other Zionist insiders. They agreed that the lobby would not mount a campaign against the negotiations.

AIPAC and most American pro-Israel advocacy groups--though not the ZOA and other far-right groups—thus formally endorsed the Oslo process, but their support was, as Dov Waxman has noted, "half-hearted at best." Rabin tried to present a united front by declaring, "I consider AIPAC to be an important friend of Israel." Although he asserted that the "American Jewish community" remained "united in their support for Israel," Rabin knew he faced opposition from the American lobby as well as the right-wing Likudniks and Zionist settlers.[5]

While right-wing Jews in the United States as well as in Israel opposed the Oslo process, liberal American Jews had also become a concern for the lobby. Since the 1940s, when the initial challenges from the non-Zionist American Jewish Committee and the openly anti-Zionist American Council for Judaism were beaten back, the Israel lobby had built on a solid foundation of overwhelming American Jewish political support. However, the rise of the right-wing Begin government, the disastrous intervention in Lebanon, and violent repression of the Intifada had created a growing liberal American Jewish push for the Oslo process.

The vast majority of American Jews strongly supported Israel but the liberals in groups such as Americans for Peace Now and Israel Policy Forum increasingly advocated Palestinian rights and a two-state solution. Some acknowledged the illegality of the occupation and settlements, whereas the ZOA and other right-wing groups were reactionaries who condemned efforts to negotiate with the Palestinian "terrorists" or to compromise on the vision of the Greater Israel. American Jews were thus increasingly divided over Israel and Middle Eastern policy, divisions that complicated the work of the lobby.[6]

Polls showed that the Rabin government and the "peace process" were popular with the American public as a whole, hence AIPAC offered its public endorsement. Both Israel and the lobby remained committed, however, to "opposing the establishment of a Palestinian state," rejecting restrictions on settlements, or doing anything that might threaten exclusive claims to Jerusalem. The right of return of Palestinian refugees was not even open to discussion.[7]

While offering grudging public support for the Israeli government and the Oslo accords, AIPAC secretly launched efforts to undermine the agreements. "AIPAC couldn't act like they were rejecting what the government of Israel did," lobby insider Keith Weissman later acknowledged, "but the outcry in the organization about Oslo was so great that they found ways to sabotage it." Thus, AIPAC encouraged legislation, duly proposed in Congress, against providing the funding for Arafat and the Palestinian Authority (PA), provisions that were pivotal to securing their support for the peace process.[8]

In September 1993 the parties overcame the right-wing Zionist opposition and, with Clinton presiding, carried out the Oslo signing ceremony in the White House Rose Garden. Like the Camp David Accords in 1978, the Oslo agreements proved to be another diplomatic disaster for the Palestinians. In decline since Israel drove it out of Lebanon in 1982, the PLO had also lost the support of Arab monarchies in the wake of the Gulf War in which Arafat foolishly had sided with Saddam Hussein. Under challenge from the Islamist group Hamas as well as the wider Arab world, Arafat negotiated from weakness. He therefore consented to deferring to future discussions the critical issues of final borders, return of refugees, and status of Jerusalem. The PLO failed even to secure a freeze on Israeli construction of new settlements in the Occupied Territories.[9]

Not only had Oslo failed to secure Israeli concessions, it created a "double occupation" as the PA evolved into "a repressive police-state apparatus that sought to suppress and disarm any resistance to Israeli occupation and to crush any internal Palestinian dissent and criticism with increasing ferocity." It also embraced neo-liberal economic policies constructing a façade of economic growth to mask colonial dependency.[10]

For these reasons, many Palestinians and their supporters opposed the Oslo framework. The PA became increasingly discredited. The Palestinian intellectual Edward Said famously condemned Oslo as an "instrument of Palestinian surrender," declaring that the PLO had transformed itself from a liberation movement into an occupation-abetting "small-town government."[11]

In signing the Oslo Accords the PLO accepted the autonomy framework--originally proposed by Begin 15 years earlier--in hopes that the United States would play the role of honest broker and eventually pressure Israel into relinquishing the West Bank and the Gaza Strip. In sum, at Oslo the PLO made a bad deal in a desperate effort to preserve its own relevance.[12]

Two years later, under the Oslo 2 or Taba Agreements, Israel released substantial areas of the West Bank and Gaza to PA interim authority as part of the continuing peace process that was supposed to lead to final status negotiations. Right-wing Israelis railed against the prospect of sacrificing the dream of the total control over the biblical Israel even though Rabin made it clear any eventual Palestinian state would be demilitarized and Israel would retain control over Jerusalem. The Knesset ratified Oslo 2 by a razor thin margin of 61-59.[13]

Grants and resettlement assistance funds continued to flood into Israel, as did US rhetorical support for Jerusalem as the "undivided capital" of the "Jewish state." With encouragement from AIPAC, 279 House members dispatched a letter demanding assurance that Clinton would not "in any way support a Palestinian claim to the city."[14]

In concert with the right-wing Israeli and American opposition parties--Likud and the Republicans--as well Christian Zionists, the lobby wielded the emotional issue of the status of Jerusalem as a weapon to derail the Oslo process. In 1995 AIPAC encouraged the new Speaker of the House, Rep. Newt Gingrich (R-GA), to sponsor a bi-partisan effort to relocate the US Embassy from Tel Aviv to Jerusalem, which would be recognized as Israel's capital.[15]

Having learned their lesson from Bush's clash, the Republicans were only too happy to outdo the Democrats in embracing pro-Israel polices. The chief sponsor of the Jerusalem embassy bill was Sen. Robert Dole (R-KS), who hoped to win lobby support in his 1996 bid to unseat Clinton.

The proposed embassy relocation embittered the Arab and Muslim world while putting Rabin in an impossible situation. The move would infuriate the Palestinians and destroy the peace process in its cradle. In order to preserve the Oslo framework, a Labor Party official later explained, the prime minister of Israel was forced into the position of "telling American Jews, 'Don't ask for recognition of Jerusalem as our capital.'" Rabin quietly told AIPAC he opposed the bill, but it went forward anyway.[16]

In October 1995 the Republican-dominated Congress passed the Jerusalem Embassy Act by overwhelming margins of 93-5 in the Senate and 374-37 in the House. The *NER* celebrated the law, for which AIPAC had long campaigned, by declaring it "culminated a 30-year effort to correct an indefensible policy of our government."[17]

The law endorsed relocating the US Embassy in Jerusalem, which would be recognized as the capital of Israel. Under the Constitution, however, the executive branch alone had the power to recognize jurisdiction over foreign territory, hence the new law provided that the president could authorize a waiver of the law every six months for "national security" reasons. Every president--until Trump--did just that in deference to the understanding that East Jerusalem was supposed to become the capital of a Palestinian state at the end of the "peace process."[18]

Religious zealots in Israel and the United States celebrated the proposed embassy relocation to the "eternal capital" and bitterly opposed the Oslo peace process. The growing and increasingly vocal constituency of American Christian Zionists strengthened the lobby and bolstered resistance to the accords.[19]

Even though the Oslo accords had been lopsided in Israel's favor, and thus further weakened and marginalized the PLO, Likud politicians, notably Benjamin Netanyahu, vehemently opposed any compromise over the "land of Israel." The Israeli right wing and the militant settlers viewed the accords as treason and somehow a threat to Israel's existence, despite Arafat's emphasis on recognition and his explicit renunciation of terror attacks.[20] On February 25, 1994, a fanatic Israeli settler from Brooklyn, Baruch Goldstein, launched a devastating one-man terror attack, as he slaughtered 29 worshippers amid the Muslim commemoration of Ramadan in Hebron's historic mosque.

Brutally assailed over the handshake with Arafat, Rabin was depicted on opposition rally placards adorned in a Nazi SS uniform. "You are even worse than Chamberlain," Netanyahu told Rabin in a reference to British efforts to placate Hitler at the 1938 Munich Conference. "He imperiled the safety of another people, but you are doing it to your own people."[21]

Amid this toxic climate an Israeli religious extremist assassinated Rabin in November 1995. Prominent American evangelist Pat Robertson declared God had removed Rabin because he was seeking to give away the Promised Land. Texas fundamentalist minister John Hagee attributed Rabin's death to his "fanatical pursuit for peace."[22]

Mounting frustration empowered extremists in both Israel and occupied Palestine. After more than 30 years of brutal occupation, many Palestinians had become radicalized. Support for moderation and the "peace process" had brought new settlements, corruption, indiscriminate violence, and humiliation.[23]

Despite Israel's resort to violent repression during the first Intifada, "it is remarkable that the Palestinians preserved the tactics of nonviolent resistance," Eugene Rogan notes.[24]

By the mid-1990s, however, the Israel-Palestine conflict became increasingly violent. Hamas, the radical offshoot of Egypt's Muslim Brotherhood, flourished after its founding in Gaza amid the Intifada.[25] Ironically, Israel had initially covertly encouraged Hamas in an effort to undermine Arafat and the PLO through a divide and conquer stratagem. The Islamist movement, which offered an alternative and a sense of self-esteem to a colonized people, flourished far beyond expectations. Israel responded with repression, including arrests, mass expulsions, and ultimately assassination of Hamas leaders.[26]

Dedicated to the liberation of Palestine, the military wing of Hamas responded to Israel's violent repression with suicide bombings, the first of which it launched at an Israeli checkpoint in 1993. With few viable military options against the edifice of Israeli power, Hamas and other groups engaged in asymmetrical terror attacks--just as Begin, Shamir, and the Zionist terrorists had done in an ultimately successful effort to drive the British out of Palestine in the 1940s. In 1994 Hamas responded to Goldstein's homicidal rampage in Hebron with a suicide attack, killing 13 and injuring 70. Two years later, in response to Israel's assassination of one its top militants, Hamas retaliated with four attacks killing 57 Israelis and injuring 130.[27]

American diplomats, Jordan's King Hussein, and other Arab leaders had warned since 1967 that Israel's failure to compromise on land for peace would only serve to empower Arab extremists and Islamic fundamentalists.[28] The blowback onto the Israeli homeland duly arrived in the persons of suicide bombers.

Suicide bombings backfired, however, as the trauma they inflicted on Israeli society succeeded only in empowering the right wing embodied by Sharon and Netanyahu and backed by the American lobby. Whereas Israelis seemingly quickly forgot—although some celebrated—the Goldstein massacre, suicide bombings led to the widespread conviction that the Palestinians were nothing more than murderous fanatics against whom any level of violent repression would be justified and with whom no peace was possible. In sum, the assassination of Rabin, repression of Hamas, and the spate of suicide bombings destroyed the Israeli peace camp.

In the 1996 presidential campaign in which Clinton won reelection, both the Republicans and Democrats were in lockstep with Israel and lobby discourse vilifying the Palestinians as terrorists. As always, AIPAC maintained vigilance over the congressional elections. As 15 new Senators and 72 new House members won election in November 1996, AIPAC boasted that it was "the only grassroots organization that met with every new member of Congress." Kohr declared that "over 90 percent of the freshman class—a record high—issued supportive statements on US-Israel relations."[29]

At the end of 1997 *Fortune* magazine ranked AIPAC the second most powerful lobby in the United States, behind only the American Association of Retired Persons. Kohr publicly welcomed "this important recognition" of the lobby's growing clout."[30]

While Democrats and Republicans alike shored up their pro-Israeli credentials, the Likud returned to power under Netanyahu, who had condemned the peace process and vilified Rabin.

Even before his brother Jonathan had been killed in the famous counter-terrorist raid at Entebbe, Uganda, in 1976, Netanyahu had nurtured little but contempt for Palestinians. "A proponent of the revisionist Zionist program of the undivided Land of Israel, not of peaceful coexistence with the Palestinians," Netanyahu authorized explosive growth of new illegal settlements, especially in Greater Jerusalem.[31]

Netanyahu had spent much of childhood in the United States, where he graduated high school and university and attained graduate degrees from MIT in Boston. During the 1980s Netanyahu had worked in the Israeli Embassy in Washington, developing close ties with AIPAC's leadership. No Israeli leader had a better grasp of American culture and politics than Netanyahu, who once boasted, "America is a thing you can move very easily."[32]

The Likud leader showed little respect for the peace process or for Clinton, who declared in exasperation after their initial White House meeting in 1996, "Who the f--- does he think he is? Who's the f------ superpower here?" The following day Netanyahu received--and not for the last time--a "rapturous reception at the Republican-dominated Congress."[33] Defying the Clinton administration, Netanyahu authorized construction of 1,800 new homes in a West Bank settlement near Jerusalem.[34]

The *NER* assured newsletter recipients—including of course all members of Congress--that Palestinian and other criticism of the new settlements was merely a lot of "hype." The lobby line remained that because settlements had been constructed in the Occupied Territories since the June 1967 War, they were somehow therefore legitimate. "The units represent nothing more than a continuation of policies followed by every Israeli government since 1967," the propaganda sheet explained.[35]

Despite his irritation with Netanyahu, Clinton did not challenge Israel on its illegal settlement expansion. On February 22, 1998, the UN General Assembly voted 115-2—with the United States and Israel standing alone against the rest of the world—to condemn the new settlements in the "occupied Palestinian territory."[36]

Slow Death of the "Peace Process"

Clinton urged Netanyahu to honor the Oslo process by negotiating interim agreements with Arafat, including partition of the historic West Bank city of Hebron, a holy site to both Jews and Muslims. Jewish settlers had insinuated their way into wildcat settlements in and around the old city and wanted recognition and protection from the Israel government.[37] The Hebron accord pleased neither the settlers nor the Palestinians, but it kept the "peace process" on life support as Clinton appealed to Netanyahu and Arafat to make further concessions.

Netanyahu worked with his primary American constituency, the Republican right, including the Christian Zionists, to "blunt pressure from the Clinton White House." Upon his arrival in Washington in January 1998 Netanyahu proceeded directly to a fundamentalist rally, where the Rev. Jerry Falwell was busy demonizing Clinton. Falwell interrupted his speech to welcome the Israeli leader, who received a thunderous ovation.[38]

AIPAC, Christian Zionists, and the Republican right worked in tandem to contain the threat of peace. Gingrich accused Clinton of putting "pressure on Israel," alleging that he had issued an "ultimatum" to Israel to pursue the Oslo process or face consequences. Gingrich's hyperbole extended to Secretary of State Madeleine Albright, whom he accused of being "an agent of the Palestinians."[39] AIPAC heaped praise on Gingrich, citing his "powerful pro-Israel legacy" through 20 years of service in the House and being the first speaker to lead a congressional delegation to Israel.[40]

In an effort to keep the Oslo process afloat in October 1998, Clinton oversaw nine days of "tense negotiations" at the Wye Plantation in Maryland. The Palestinians denounced terror attacks and agreed to remove a clause in their charter denying the legitimacy of Israel's existence. After threatening to walk out on the negotiations, Netanyahu signed the Wye River Memorandum, in which he pledged to follow through on redeployments from the West Bank as envisioned under the Oslo and Hebron accords, but he subsequently refused to implement the agreements.

As the Oslo process broke down, a "passionate debate" emerged "among policy-makers and within the American Jewish community." Critics pointed to Israel's unfulfilled agreements coupled with ongoing illegal settlement construction, but AIPAC expressed outrage that anyone might blame Israel or the United States for the stalemate. It was "obvious," the lobby averred, that "Palestinian terrorism" was solely responsible for undermining "the peace process."[41]

In reality Israeli obduracy on the occupation and especially on settlements lay at the root of the collapse of the Oslo process. By the time the Camp David summit convened in July 2000, Israeli Prime Minister Ehud Barak headed a "crumbling" coalition and "was leading a minority government." The weakened political position made Barak "adamant about protecting the interests of the settlers," Ami Pedahzur points out, hence "the peace talks failed."[42]

Pro-Israeli sympathies and lobby influence loomed over Clinton's belated efforts at Camp David. Clinton's chief negotiator, Dennis Ross, was a Zionist long affiliated with AIPAC.[43] His colleague, Aaron David Miller, also a dedicated Zionist (both men were Jewish), later acknowledged, "Those of us advising the secretary of state and the president were very sensitive to what the Jewish community was thinking and, when it came to considering ideas Israel didn't like, too often engaged in a kind of preemptive censorship."[44]

The US delegation sided with Israel, which while willing to negotiate over the status of the West Bank, would only do so under the framework of the continuing Israeli occupation. The eventual Palestinian "state" was thus to remain disconnected, dotted with another country's expanding settlements, and divided into three cantons cut off by Jewish-only enclaves, bypass roads, and check points. Moreover, Israel insisted on ultimate authority over Jerusalem and made no "tangible offer" on the issue of refugees.[45]

Clinton and Barak responded to the collapse of the Oslo process by adopting the propaganda line that AIPAC had been pursuing for years, asserting that Arafat's obstructionism and support for terror attacks caused the breakdown of talks. Arafat--who had accepted handing over part of the Occupied Territories to Israeli settlements, including neighborhoods in Jerusalem, and had acquiesced to a demilitarized Palestinian state--was charged with rejecting a "generous offer" out of a bloodthirsty desire to ignite a campaign of terror. "Arafat chose violence rather than compromise at Camp David," as the *NER* put it.[46]

Blaming Arafat and the Palestinians for the ensuing violent unrest of the Second Intifada--which Ariel Sharon ignited by staging a deliberately provocative demonstration at a holy site in the heart of Jerusalem's Old City—finished off the "peace process." Talks had resumed and were marking progress, as both sides offered new compromises, but it was too late. Barak suffered a humiliating electoral defeat enabling Sharon--a confirmed enemy of peace and of Arabs and essentially a state terrorist-- to come to power.[47]

Second Intifada

What began as another largely peaceful protest movement became brutally violent as a result of the provocation by Sharon. On September 28, 2000, Sharon, flanked by hundreds of riot police, marched onto al-Haram al-Harif, the Dome of the Rock, the third holiest site in Islam after Mecca and Medina in Saudi Arabia. Jews also claimed the area, which they called the Temple Mount, a 35-acre esplanade in the Israeli-occupied Old City. Reviled by Arabs as the perpetrator of a series of massacres stretching over decades, but still revered by many Israelis as a military hero, Sharon provocatively declared, "The Temple Mount is in our hands and will remain in our hands."[48]

The action by Sharon ignited the Second Intifada, which proved far more violent and devastating to Palestinians than the first uprising. The deeper cause of the uprising was Israel's refusal to follow through on Palestinian statehood, combined with its growing reliance on violent repression. As Arnon Degani notes, the Second Intifada was "primarily born from the conditions of Israel's expansion of settlements and lack of commitment to end colonial control over Palestinians."[49]

Angry but initially overwhelmingly non-violent, Palestinians took to the streets where they met with a disproportionate brutal response featuring the full range of well-honed Israeli police state tactics including killings, detention, torture, home demolition and other forms of collective punishment. Within the Occupied Territories, Jewish settlers lashed out in "blatant disregard for Palestinian lives and property" and could act with virtual impunity. It remained "extremely likely," reported the Israeli human rights group B'Tselem, "that an Israeli who kills a Palestinian will not be punished or will receive only a light sentence." By this point settler violence was "not only tolerated by the state but is actually sanctioned."[50]

Israeli repression and Sharon's provocation at the Dome of the Rock provoked not only Palestinians but Muslims all over the world. Since the June 1967 war, the Islamist movement built popular support partly by pledging to rectify the widespread sense of loss, "a stain on the name of Islam," of the Israeli occupation of Jerusalem. As Beverley Milton-Edwards notes, "Islamists cannot accept occupation of their holy places by Israel, particularly the area of the Noble Sanctuary in Jerusalem."[51]

From the outbreak of the Second Intifada to 2006 more than 4,000 Palestinians were killed in the violence. By contrast, from 1987 to 2000 fewer than 1,500 had died in the original Intifada. For Israelis the number of those killed grew from 422 in the period 1987-2000 to 1,019 from 2000 to 2006.[52]

Sharon's provocations and the indiscriminate violence on the part of the IDF fueled the rise of Islamic militancy. As fanaticism and religious fundamentalism flourished, Israel tightened its control over the West Bank. Little remained of the original plans to colonize and integrate Palestinian territory and workers into the Israeli economy. Separation and iron fist repression now prevailed.

The extreme violence of the Second Intifada swept the Oslo process aside. The suicide bombings undermined the Israeli peace constituency as well as pressure on Israel and the lobby from liberal American Jews. AIPAC and the Conference of Presidents of Major American Jewish Organizations were back in command of a largely right-wing, uncritically pro-Israel lobby.

During the Second Intifada Israel began construction of a massive "security wall." Ostensibly an emergency measure, the edifice became a permanent divide between Israel and the West Bank. Israel seized Palestinian land, driving out the inhabitants and in some places cutting off farmers from fields, children from school, and communities from their sources of water. The UN, the EU and the International Court of Justice declared the more than 700-kilometer-long wall a violation of international law because it appropriated some 10 percent of Palestinian territory.[53]

Backed by the United States and the lobby, AIPAC dismissed the international criticism and derided the International Court of Justice as a "kangaroo" court.[54]

Bush and the Neoconservatives

Campaigning for the presidency in 2000, George W. Bush differentiated himself from his father, who had pressured Israel to compromise in an effort to forge a Middle East settlement. "My support for Israel is not conditional on the outcome of the peace process," he told a cheering crowd at the annual AIPAC conference in May 2000.[55] Proclaimed the winner of the tightly contested race, Bush won 19 percent of the Jewish vote, a strong performance for the Republicans considering that his Democratic opponent, Vice President Al Gore, had tabbed as his running mate Joe Lieberman (D-CT), a dedicated Zionist who became the first Jew selected for a major party presidential ticket.[56]

True to his word Bush endorsed Israel's rejection of further talks with the Palestinians and forged a close personal relationship with Sharon, whom he admired and even referenced in Orwellian fashion as "a man of peace" amid the repression of the Second Intifada. Inexperienced in foreign affairs or even in foreign travel, Bush assembled an administration divided between right-wing neoconservatives and moderates. The former included Vice President Dick Cheney, Defense Secretary Donald Rumsfeld, and adviser Elliott Abrams while the more moderate advisers included Secretary of State Colin Powell and National Security Adviser (and later secretary of state) Condoleezza Rice.[57]

Siding more often than not with the neoconservatives, Bush embraced Israel and the lobby version of events at Camp David, a discourse in which the Israelis valiantly had "sought to end the conflict with the Palestinians through negotiations" only to "have been shocked and angered by the brutal campaign of violence launched by their supposed partners," as the *NER* put it.[58] AIPAC "warmly welcomed" Sharon at its annual Washington conference in April 2001 and followed up by mobilizing 87 of the 100 US senators and 189 House members to draft a letter to Bush blaming the collapse of the peace process on Arafat and the PA, whose actions therefore justified a "significant change in our relations with them." The *NER* noted approvingly that in response the "Bush administration backed Israel's stance that political negotiations cannot resume amid the continuing violence, which was launched by the Palestinians."[59]

With the Palestinians vilified and negotiations terminated, Sharon was free to indulge his passions for constructing new illegal settlements and unleashing the IDF on Palestinians. While condemning Arab terrorism, Powell also called for Israel to curb its indiscriminate violence, but he added that settlements were not to be "linked in any way" with the US position on the conflict and could be discussed later within the confines of "confidence-building measures."[60]

Pro-Israeli discourse blaming the failure of peace on Arab terrorism while enabling the expansion of Israel's illegal settlements and the separation wall dominated Washington. Think tanks such as the Washington Institute for Near East Policy (WINEP), whose founders in 1985 included Ross, featured regular reports and offered media access to "top Middle East experts," who were in actuality AIPAC-affiliated. Presenting the pro-Israel advocates Ross, David Makovsky, and Robert Satloff as objective social scientists, the *NER* reported, "Three top Middle East experts discuss how the Palestinian violence and Arafat's inability to make compromises—not the issues of settlements—have led to the current impasse."[61]

The September 11, 2001, terror attacks in the United States empowered the neoconservative faction within the Bush administration, further solidified the US-Israeli special relationship, and accelerated the fusion of their security policies. The traumatic attacks "recast the United States in Israel's image as existentially threatened," Amy Kaplan points out, and thus "joined the nations to each other as innocent victims of evil forces and bestowed moral righteousness on their pursuit of indomitability."[62]

AIPAC echoed the Bush administration's shallow explanation of the attacks having occurred because Al Qaeda and other terrorists "hate our freedoms." Anxious to deflect any suggestion that unstinting US support for Israel in the Palestine conflict may have been part of the motivation, the *NER* explained that the terrorists "hate America not because of what it does, but because of what it is."[63]

In actuality the September 11 attacks constituted blowback in response to a long history of US foreign policy intervention in the Middle East, including efforts to dominate oil supplies; support for dictators such as the shah of Iran as well as the Saud dynasty and other Arab monarchies; the presence of US military forces in Saudi Arabia (homeland of the majority of the 9/11 attackers); the deaths and deprivations of hundreds of thousands of Iraqis under the post-Persian Gulf War regime of sanctions; and not least the three-plus decade-long Israeli occupation, illegal settlements, culminating in efforts to establish the holy city of Jerusalem as exclusively the undivided capital of a Jewish state.[64]

Israel and AIPAC seized the opportunities offered by the September 11 attacks to forge unprecedented security collaboration with the United States. AIPAC's abundant allies in Congress supported the closer ties. "Israel has the experience, dedication and freedom that is absolutely necessary to prevail over these fanatics," Senator Mitch McConnell (R-KY) declared. "We must stand arm in arm with our ally."[65]

Amid the global war on terror, public opinion polls showed unprecedented popular US identification with Israel while lumping Palestinians with the Islamist terror groups, a narrative deliberately promoted by Israel and the lobby. Al Qaeda, Hizbullah, Hamas, Islamic Jihad and other terror groups, the *NER* averred, presenting no evidence, were "working together to help the Palestinians execute deadly terror attacks against Israelis."[66] In actuality considerable differences, ranging from religious views to strategies of resistance, divided the diverse Sunni and Shi'ite Muslim groups.[67]

The lobby mounted a massive propaganda offensive to counter expressions of concern about Israel's use of indiscriminate violence amid the largest Israeli military assault on the West Bank since the June 1967 war. Unleashed by Sharon, the attack came in the wake of the massive suicide bombing at the Passover Seder at the seaside resort of Netanya on March 27, 2002, which killed 30 Israeli citizens and injured 140 others. The devastating terror bombing, which killed mostly elderly people in the midst of a Jewish holiday dinner in a hotel dining room, enraged the Israeli public.[68]

The IDF response, replete with indiscriminate killing and wanton destruction, was intended to terrorize and humiliate the Palestinians. In April the IDF left the Jenin refugee camp in ruins and battered the historic city of Nablus with tanks, armored personnel carriers, and combat troops. Killing, detention, torture, destruction of property and civil infrastructure as well as blocking of medical and humanitarian relief ensued. Some 500 Palestinians were killed (to 29 Israeli soldiers) in the pre-planned operation "Defensive Shield" and thousands were left injured, homeless, hungry, and cut off from relief.[69] The full-scale military assault was calculated to destroy Palestinian civilian authority, including the main offices of the PA and Arafat's compound in Ramallah.[70]

Alarmed by the scope of Israel's retributive violence, Bush called for the IDF to withdraw, which ignited a massive lobby campaign and a public demonstration that clogged the nation's capital. On April 15, 2002, well more than 100,00 people--some claimed as many as 200,000--poured into the nation's capital from all over the country on less than a week's notice. "The crowd spilled from the front of the Capitol toward the Reflecting Pool on the Mall, packing the area between Constitution and Independence avenues." A blue and white Israeli banner enveloped the Civil War monument on the American National Mall.[71]

Major roads coming into Washington and the city's streets swarmed with traffic. Long lines awaited trains on the Washington Metro, which officials estimated carried 50,000 riders above the norm for a Monday on the subway system. The metro station closest to the Capitol Building was overwhelmed and had to be shut down. The number of buses entering RFK Stadium exceeded its capacity, prompting Abe Pollin, a Jewish philanthropist and the owner of two Washington professional sports teams, to allow buses to park in an US Airways Arena, which he also owned.

Featured speakers at the Solidarity for Israel rally, sponsored by Conference of Presidents of Major American Jewish Organizations, included representatives from a wide variety of Jewish and Christian Zionist organizations as well as Israeli and American politicians and officials. Officially sanctioned signs such as "Israel's Fight=America's Fight" and "US and Israel—United Against Terror" underscored support for Israel and for the special relationship.

The American rally mobilized support for an asymmetrical Israeli campaign of collective punishment targeting the infrastructure and civilians of the occupied West Bank. The rally, in other words, sought to safeguard Israel's ability to regiment and kill Palestinians with impunity. Most of the speakers at the rally, like Elie Wiesel, ignored that the vast majority of victims in the continuing violence were Palestinian, declaring instead, absurdly, that as in the Holocaust Israel was in the midst of a struggle for its very survival.

As the parade of speakers continued throughout the afternoon, the loudest cheers erupted at the mention of Sharon's name. When Paul Wolfowitz, a Jewish neoconservative and Bush's assistant secretary of defense, reminded the crowd, "Innocent Palestinians are suffering and dying as well. It is important that we recognize and acknowledge that fact," he was drowned out by jeers.[72]

Speaking at the rally, Netanyahu declared, "Yasser Arafat is nothing more than Osama bin Laden with good public relations." The crowd chanted, "No more Arafat!" in response.[73]

The mass demonstration included thousands of Christian Zionists and many speakers ended their talks with the invocation, "God bless America and Israel." The Christian Zionist groups inundated the White House with hundreds of thousands of letters and emails urging Bush to "end pressure" on Sharon enabling him to "complete the mission" of wiping out "terrorist cells and infrastructure from the West Bank territories."[74]

Later that same month, Senators and House members flocked to AIPAC's policy conference under the theme, "America and Israel Standing Together Against Terrorism." Israeli Ambassador David Ivry thanked the lobby for its support. "Just mentioning the name AIPAC on the Hill has a lot of value," he pointed out. "I must say that on the Hill there is no other lobby that can compare to AIPAC's efficiency."[75]

The lobby followed up with a letter signed by a whopping 88 senators and 321 House members demanding that prior to the resumption of any negotiations the "infrastructure" of Palestinian terrorism must be destroyed and Arafat dispensed with as an interlocutor.

Bush quickly backed off on pressuring Israel over Sharon's violent paroxysm. Like all American Presidents, Bush well understood that political security lay in siding with Israel, not in trying to restrain it. While Sharon had Arafat under house arrest in Ramallah, "he's had George Bush under house arrest in the Oval Office," wrote *New York Times* columnist Thomas Friedman. A combination of "Jewish and Christian pro-Israel lobbyists," backed by Cheney, "who's ready to do whatever Mr. Sharon dictates," were "conspiring to make sure the president does nothing."[76]

On June 24 Bush gave a major policy speech that acceded to Israeli demands, bolstered by the lobby, to cut off negotiations with Arafat. The European Union, by contrast, condemned the Israeli assault on the West Bank and maintained relations with Arafat, drawing sharp condemnation from Israel and its lobby. The *NER* charged, "US efforts to advance the peace process are being undercut by European leaders who continue to meet with Arafat" and continue to fund "terrorist groups."[77]

AIPAC had long displayed contempt for Arafat, who was reduced in its discourse to being nothing more than a terrorist and therefore "part of the problem, not the solution."[78] Arafat subsequently fell ill and died on November 11, 2004. It is possible but not certain that Israeli assassins poisoned the longtime Palestinian leader—Sharon had many times advocated just such a solution.[79]

Lobby Enthusiasm for the Iraq War

Israel and the lobby enthusiastically backed a war for regime change in Iraq. Dating to a favorite plan of Ben-Gurion's in the 1950s to install a Christian regime in Lebanon, Israeli elites had long been enamored with the idea of overthrowing and replacing hostile regimes on their borders. In 1996 American neoconservatives weighed in with "Clean Break," a proposal to terminate the peace process in deference to regime change and enhancing Israeli hegemony throughout the Middle East. Following the election of Bush and the September 11 attacks, they strove to implement this vision.[80]

Saddam Hussein, an inveterate foe of Israel, which reciprocated by depicting him as another Hitler, was an obvious target. The Bush administration insisted without evidence that Hussein possessed weapons of mass destruction. The neoconservatives received rhetorical support from Netanyahu, Sharon, Shimon Peres, and Barak, all of whom appeared on American television in support of the Iraq invasion. Declaring that Saddam was "as dangerous as bin Laden," Peres—who would be lionized as a "man of peace" at his death in 2016--told CNN at the time that the United States "cannot sit and wait" but should instead invade Iraq.[81]

When Bush launched the all-out invasion in March 2003, Israel and the lobby celebrated the drive for regime change in Iraq. AIPAC declared its "total support" for the "just war" in an editorial in the *NER*. As the war unfolded the newsletter followed up with a stream of articles and interviews with select "experts" justifying the Iraq campaign and the removal of Hussein.[82]

In concert with the war in Iraq, moderates in the Bush administration, hoping to remake the Middle East, attempted to revive the moribund peace process. Congenitally opposed to international involvement in the Palestine issue, Israel had no enthusiasm for the Quartet in which the UN, the EU, and Russia joined with the United States in floating a "Roadmap" for Middle East peace. Announced by Bush in 2003, the Roadmap called for an end to violence and restructuring of the PA, but also—and much to Israel's chagrin--a freeze on settlements and ultimately creation of an independent though reconfigured Palestinian state. "Sharon's government," as Khaled Elgindy notes, "refused to engage with either the plan or its sponsors."[83]

Resistance to the plan from Israel and the lobby prompted Bush to back off on the demand for a freeze on settlement construction. In an effort to secure Sharon's endorsement, the administration then caved in to the Israeli insistence that Israel's implementation of the Roadmap could be deferred until the Palestinians had fulfilled all of the demands made upon them. Rather than proceeding together incrementally, as the Roadmap had envisioned, Bush reverted to an embrace of a lopsided pro-Israeli approach.[84]

Sharon's acceptance of the Roadmap included the proviso that Israel would retain "control over all entry points to the territories." Backed by "overwhelming support" from the US Congress—including a House vote of 407-9 upholding the AIPAC-Israeli position—Bush acquiesced to Sharon's rejection of inclusion of the right of return of Palestinian refugees in any peace plan.[85] Bush's acquiescence to Israel and the lobby "cemented the Bush-Sharon alignment" and in the process delivered a fatal blow to the Roadmap as well as the multilateral Quartet.[86]

Having witnessed the mass demonstration in Washington that the lobby had orchestrated in 2002, Bush was careful not to arouse its opposition amid his reelection campaign. Speaking at the annual lobby conference in May 2004, Bush declared that AIPAC was "serving the cause of America."[87] During the campaign Bush distributed a 26-page booklet to the major Jewish organizations, entitled, "George W. Bush—A Friend of the American Jewish Community."[88] In his ensuing reelection Bush won a respectable 24 percent of the Jewish vote.

Standing up to the lobby was not an option for office-seekers, but Ernest "Fritz" Hollings (D-SC) was free to do so after announcing that he would not seek reelection after 38 years in the Senate. Citing the pervasive influence of Israel and the lobby over American politics, including the decision to go to war in Iraq, Hollings declared, "You can't have an Israel policy other than what AIPAC gives you around here."[89]

Chapter 7
AIPAC in Command

Israel's disproportionate projection of violence in the Occupied Territories and in Lebanon—vividly captured on video and circulated worldwide--posed a serious challenge to the lobby. In response AIPAC and other propagandists promoted a discourse emphasizing that Israel was legitimately defending itself against unprovoked attacks by fanatical Islamists, notably Hizbullah and Hamas.

In the years following the 1982 Israeli invasion of Lebanon, Hizbullah, which eventually allied with the Syrian-backed Amal faction, had eroded the authority of Israel's Christian proxy force, the South Lebanon Army (SLA). In April 1996, in an effort to salvage Israel's position, Labor Party leader Peres launched Operation Grapes of Wrath, a high-tech military assault on southern Lebanon, Beirut, and the Biqa Valley, which drove some 450,000 Lebanese from their homes. On April 18, in the midst of the conflict, Israel perpetrated a massacre of non-combatants, killing 102 people in the shelling of a UN compound at Qana.[1]

The second war in Lebanon further ensconced Hizbullah in Lebanese politics as a defender of the state against Israeli aggression and also a provider of social welfare to the long marginalized southern Shi'ite population. "Since its origins in the mid-1980s, Hizbullah has developed from its roots as a resistance militia into a full-fledged organization and party, which includes military, political and social welfare aspects," Laura Deeb points out. In 2000 Hizbullah's determined resistance, featuring Katyusha rocket attacks, roadside bombs, and kidnappings, prompted the dissolution of the SLA proxy force and an Israeli withdrawal to the international border.[2]

In July 2006 Israel seized upon the capture of two of its soldiers to launch a "shock and awe" campaign of indiscriminate bombing of Beirut, including the international airport, roads, bridges, schools, mosques, and entire neighborhoods. Israel carpet bombed Dahiya, a predominately Shi'ite suburb south of Beirut, killing 300 civilians but failing to score Hizbullah leader Hassan Nasrallah among the victims. An IDF general affirmed the "Dahiya Doctrine"—that Israel would make no distinction between civilian and military targets in the campaign to destroy its enemies. Overall Israel killed about 1,000 people in "Operation Just Reward."[3]

The Bush administration backed the special ally, as it fought off near-unanimous calls for a ceasefire from the UN, the EU, and world leaders. "This is no time for a ceasefire," declared the "moderate" secretary of state Condoleezza Rice. In concert with the lobby, the United States thus unilaterally enabled Israel to continue the onslaught for 34 days.[4]

Polls showed that most Americans embraced the AIPAC depiction of Israel as a besieged innocent under terrorist attack, though several thousand people did protest as the visually disturbing images appeared on their television screens. AIPAC'S friends in Congress reinforced the dominant discourse, passing resolutions "condemning Hizbullah and Hamas . . . and supporting Israel's exercise of its rights to self-defense" by unanimous consent in the Senate (98-0) and by a vote of 410-8 in the House. "The House and Senate recognize that Israel has been forced to respond to unprovoked attacks," an AIPAC propaganda missive declared, thus the "Jewish state" had merely exercised "the right and duty to defend its citizens."[5] An AIPAC press release asserted that "US support for Israel is at an all-time high and the resolutions are a reflection of the American people's desire to stand by Israel in this time of crisis."[6]

While Israel dominated the propaganda battlefield in the United States, it faltered on actual battlefield and essentially lost the war in southern Lebanon. The Shi'ite resistance forces endured the Israeli assault and ultimately prevailed in the asymmetrical conflict, adding salt to the wound by mocking "the myth of Israel's invincibility" in its own propaganda displays. An Israeli postwar investigation blamed the IDF leaders for the defeat and forced several high-ranking officers to resign.[7]

An international peace-keeping force anchored a ceasefire at the Israel-Lebanon border, but Hizbullah continued to gain strength and fortify its bunkers with rockets that could reach targets across Israel. Many Lebanese resented Hizbullah, backed by the foreign powers Iran and Syria, while others supported the Shi'ite group for its determined resistance. Overall, Israel's invasions had served to embed rather than to destroy the Shi'ite Islamists, who became ensconced in Lebanese national politics as well as its southern hills.[8]

Frustrated by their defeat in Lebanon, the Israelis "were ready for a redemptive war that would reestablish their national morale." They lashed out with a series of indiscriminate campaigns against a captive target, the Gaza Strip.[9]

Since taking control of Gaza in the June 1967 war, Israel had attempted to settle and pacify the Strip, a 146 square-mile-panhandle of the Sinai Peninsula. In 1972 Sharon orchestrated the summary expulsion of thousands of Gaza Palestinians from their homes, which were demolished. Israeli General Shlomo Gazit described the operation as "ethnic cleansing and a war crime," making it a typical Sharon operation.[10]

The return of the Sinai to Egypt, the failures in Lebanon, and the inability to subdue the Palestinians eroded Israel's commitment to retain the Strip, which was densely populated with refugees from the 1948 and 1967 wars. While Israel coveted the West Bank for its natural resources as well as its invocation of the biblical Israel, Gaza had come to be considered a "cancer" because of its teeming Palestinian population.

In 2005 Sharon decided to dismantle the settlements and disengage from Gaza. Only 8,000 Jewish settlers lived in the Strip compared with 400,000 by that time in the West Bank. By perpetuating the colonization of the West Bank, withdrawing from but still controlling access to Gaza, and branding the Palestinians as terrorists who refused to make peace, Sharon moved to bring an end to diplomacy without Israel having been compelled to recognize a Palestinian state--contrary to what the Oslo process and the Roadmap had envisioned.[11] "If, in a few months the Palestinians still continue to disregard their part in implementing the Roadmap," Sharon declared, "then Israel will initiate the unilateral security step of disengagement from the Palestinians."[12]

AIPAC endorsed disengagement from Gaza and successfully lobbied Congress for $2 billion in additional US aid for relocation of military facilities as well as the Gaza settlers. The ZOA, however, denounced the move to "throw Jews out of their home and give a terrorist regime more land." The ZOA's mounting extremism under the leadership of Morton Klein helped AIPAC depict itself as the reasoned and "centrist" component of the Israel lobby.[13]

Gaza disengagement had nothing to do with enabling genuine Palestine autonomy, as Israel demonstrated with its response to elections in Palestine. In 2006 Israel and the lobby sharply opposed participation by Hamas in the legislative elections, but the Bush administration wanted to stage a showcase of putative support for democracy as it had done amidst the US occupation of Iraq. However, when Hamas subsequently prevailed in what the US Congressional Research Service classified as a "free and fair election," the United States rejected the democratic outcome and joined Israel in an effort to overthrow Hamas and replace it with the loser in the election, Fatah, now led by Arafat's successor, Mahmoud Abbas.[14]

Hamas won the elections because the Palestinian people resented corruption within the PA, which had emerged from the Oslo process in its West Bank headquarters in Ramallah as a repressive security force collaborating with the Israeli occupation. After Hamas won the election, Israel and the Bush administration fomented an attempted coup by the PA. In 2007 Hamas again turned the tables, crushing the US-backed Fatah security forces in Gaza and taking control of the strip.[15]

Israel as well as the United States had long framed Hamas as nothing but a fanatical terror organization bent on the destruction of Israel, but in reality, it was "a complex movement rather than a mere terrorist bomb squad." Like the Islamic Republic of Iran and Hizbullah, Hamas embraced the intensely monotheistic Islamist worldview in which ultimate authority rested in God (the same God as recognized by Christians and Jews). Islamists owed loyalty to Allah and his messengers, notably the Prophet Muhammed, rather than to secular governments or the global nation-state system. At the same time, however, Hamas proved "capable of combining its militant activism and radical ideology with strategic thinking and pragmatism."[16]

Hamas opposed Zionism and the Oslo process in principle, but as a practical matter did not strive to sabotage the accords and also worked within the secular nationalist framework by participating—and winning—the legislative elections. Al-Qaeda and other more radical groups condemned Hamas for taking part in the elections, underscoring the fissures within radical Islamism. As Bjorn Brenner points out, Hamas "differed greatly from the dogmatism of groups like Al Qaeda and Daesh [ISIS]. There are enormous variations in how Islamist ideals such as the notions of 'Islamic state' and 'sharia rule' are understood and implemented by different Islamist actors."[17]

Just as the Islamists in Iran formed a government, and Hizbullah participated in Lebanese politics, Hamas had become "a nationalist movement that employs religious discourse to differentiate itself from secular competitors." Dependent on popular support from the Palestinian people, Hamas could not oppose a settlement under the Oslo framework if such diplomacy could bring an end to the occupation, checkpoints, and repression. However, as Israel refused to negotiate on these issues, the militant wing of Hamas embraced asymmetrical violent resistance, including the suicide bombings.[18]

Israel and the United States condemned Hamas as a terrorist group because it would not unilaterally renounce violence and recognize Israel. Hamas leaders pointed out that Israel would hardly renounce violence nor would it honor the results of the free elections by recognizing Hamas. The Islamic resistance group's leader Khaled Mishal did offer peace and recognition in return for an Israeli withdrawal to the 1967 borders.[19] Hamas also dropped language calling for the destruction of Israel dating to a statement made in 1988. Israel and the United States, however, remained adamantly opposed to viewing Hamas as anything but a ruthless terrorist organization.[20]

In 2007 the lobby weighed in by orchestrating a letter-writing campaign in which more than half the House and three-fourths of the Senate condemned conducting any negotiations with the Gaza Palestinians.[21] Israel, the lobby, and the neoconservatives who dominated the Bush administration propelled a demonizing discourse that provided a framework enabling Israel to unleash extreme violence against both Hamas and Hizbullah.[22]

Amid the clashes Hamas episodically fired homemade Qassam rockets, which did relatively little damage though they could and occasionally did kill Israelis. Israel killed Palestinians by a ratio of 15 to every one Israeli in sporadic clashes. In 2008 Egypt brokered a ceasefire, which Hamas honored but Israel deliberately violated in order to launch an indiscriminate assault.

On December 27, 2008, Israel unleashed Operation Cast Lead, an air and ground invasion that featured saturation bombing--another implementation of the Dahiya Doctrine. An estimated 300 Palestinians died in the first *four minutes* of the assault on the densely populated strip. "Much of the destruction," according to Amnesty International, was "deliberate and unnecessary demolition of property, direct attacks on civilian objects and indiscriminate attacks that failed to distinguish between legitimate military targets and civilian objects." Another report added, "Mosques, and more particularly minarets, had been deliberately targeted on the grounds that they symbolized Islam."[23]

Hamas fired hundreds of the homemade rockets and mortars in response but these "rudimentary projectiles" paled in comparison with Israel's sophisticated military hardware. Israel killed some 1,400 people, overwhelmingly civilians and including some 350 children, in Operation Cast Lead. Israel lost about a dozen people, some of those to friendly fire. As Norman Finkelstein notes, "The absurdly lopsided Palestinian-Israeli casualty ratio attested that Cast Lead was, in reality, not a war but a massacre."[24]

In September 2009 a UN fact-finding report provided abundant evidence of deliberate targeting and killing of civilians and other war crimes in Operation Cast Lead. The principal author of the report, Richard Goldstone, was a South African jurist, a Zionist, and member of the board of Hebrew University in Jerusalem where he had earned a doctorate. His daughter had emigrated to Israel.[25]

Despite Goldstone's Zionism and the overwhelming empirical evidence, Israel and the lobby launched a campaign to smear him as they denounced the report and blamed the conflict entirely on Hamas. As Finkelstein relates in a meticulous reconstruction, organizations such as Human Rights Watch amended their findings under relentless Israeli pressure. Then Goldstone, who originally responded that the Israelis were engaged in shooting the messenger, caved in and "effectively disowned the devastating UN report of Israeli crimes carrying his name."

Despite spurious claims, no new evidence existed that would justify calling into question the original report emphasizing the indiscriminate, disproportionate attack on civilians and other Israeli war crimes. The three other members of the UN investigating team that produced the original Goldstone Report issued a statement declaring, "Nothing of substance has appeared that would in any way change the context, findings or conclusion of that report."[26]

The Twenty-first Century Lobby

By the time of Israel's onslaught in Gaza, AIPAC's political clout as well as its physical presence had undergone another dramatic expansion. Thanks to a $10 million gift from the multi-billionaire Las Vegas casino owner Sheldon Adelson, AIPAC had moved out of its cramped quarters on Capitol Hill. In February 2008 Director Howard Kohr and Adelson presided at the ribbon-cutting ceremony as AIPAC moved into a sprawling seven-story structure at 251 H Street on the edge of downtown.

Kohr kept the lobby's engines humming, never losing its primary focus on the legislative branch. "We start our good relations with the incoming members" of Congress, Kohr emphasized. After every congressional election, the *NER* ran photographs and biographical sketches of new representatives and senators, which let them know immediately that AIPAC knew who they were and would be tracking their actions and voting behavior. Thereafter AIPAC closely monitored the voting record of each member throughout his or her tenure in Congress.

AIPAC-sponsored congressional trips to the holy land were having "a huge impact" as well, Kohr told the *NER*.[27] In 2003 Tom Delay (R-TX), the House majority whip, was so moved by the experience that he declared he was now "in solidarity, as an Israeli of the heart."[28] During that summer, "More than 60 members of Congress visited Israel during the August recess to learn first-hand about the US-Israel relationship and to see close-up the threats Israel is facing," the *NER* reported. "Most of the lawmakers visited the Jewish state on trips organized by the American Israel Education Foundation, a supporting organization of AIPAC."[29]

From 2000 to 2019 the American Israel Education Foundation spent $16 million on visits by more than 1,400 lawmakers and their staff members, according to the *Wall Street Journal*. By arranging the trips through its affiliated foundation, AIPAC evaded a 2007 law designed to eliminate congressional trips funded by lobbyists. The trips, valued at about $10,000 per person, were "a very successful lobbying tool" and popular among members of Congress. By routing the trips through its foundation, AIPAC "subverts the intention of the law," according to the congressional watchdog Public Citizen. An AIPAC spokesman insisted that the trips "strictly adhere to the spirit and the letter of all rules regarding congressional trips."[30]

The junkets to Israel were one of many means by which AIPAC's control over the Congress became increasingly institutionalized. As with other powerful lobbies on Capitol Hill, Kohr and other AIPAC executives prioritized the desired legislation or resolution that would most benefit Israel and then tapped key supporters in Congress to introduce it. At that point, AIPAC's registered professional lobbyists would descend on congressional offices, where they were already well known. Written communications and phone calls followed. Greeting each member by name, the lobbyists generated widespread approval for the measure in question. By efficiently carrying out the lobbying process, Israel and AIPAC nearly always got the legislation or congressional resolutions they wanted.[31]

The ability of AIPAC to support and indirectly finance congressional races was always implicit in these meetings—and especially effective with House members who had to stand for reelection every two years. Rep. Brian Baird (D-WA), a psychologist from Seattle, received about $200,000 from the Zionist lobby for each of his campaigns during his congressional service from 1999 to 2010. "That's two hundred thousand going your way, versus the other way: a four hundred-thousand-dollar swing," Baird explained years later.

By that time, Baird perceived that the AIPAC-affiliated sponsored trips to Israel had become "virtually obligatory" for new members of Congress. With first-class flights and accommodations provided, however, few members objected. AIPAC advised Baird as to its positions on issues as well as how to address them, including for example avoiding the term "occupied territories." Baird learned "a whole complex semantic code . . . After a while, you find yourself saying and repeating it as if it were fact."

When the time came to cast votes in Washington, Baird and scores of congressional representatives like him knew what positions to take. "When key votes are cast, the question on the House floor, troublingly, is often not 'What is the right thing to do for the United States of America?' but 'How is AIPAC going to score this?'"[32]

Mitch McConnell, who went on to become one of the most effective power brokers in the history of the US Senate, quickly became a reliable stalwart of Israel and the lobby. A narrow victory in his first Kentucky Senate election in 1984 made McConnell aware of the need to cultivate AIPAC, which had backed the Democratic incumbent. After the election McConnell met with AIPAC officials and said directly, "'Let me be very clear. What do I need to do to make sure that the next time around I get the community support?'" Lobby insiders assured McConnell that AIPAC would support Republicans who established themselves as "friendly incumbents." McConnell got the message, adopted the required uncritically pro-Israel stance, and received AIPAC support in six ensuing Senate campaigns.[33]

The lobby raised money for its efforts through its "Congressional Club," which encouraged AIPAC members--numbering some 100,000 by 2019—to contribute at least $2,500 a year to House or Senate candidates who were "clearly pro-Israel." Noting, "Congress has provided Israel with the strongest support of any institution in the world," AIPAC offered its members access to "special Congressional Club programming" such as briefings and conference calls in return for their "crucial" campaign contributions.[34]

As a result of these efforts, Israel and AIPAC dominated the US Congress as never before. The ability of the Congress to make an independent, interest-driven decision on the Israel-Palestine conflict was irretrievably "broken," as Kirk Beattie concluded after an in-depth field study. News that "an AIPAC vote" was impending ensured that whatever measure the lobby was supporting would win overwhelming approval. "You don't want to cross AIPAC," a Senate staffer explained to Beattie, "because to do so would be like the kiss of death."[35]

The Rising Tide of Christian Zionism

Further strengthening the lobby was the growing alliance with Christian Zionists. On the rise since the 1970s, fundamentalist support for Israel accelerated under Bush, who launched the global terror wars and decried the "axis of evil" linking the Muslim nations of Iran and Iraq with North Korea.[36] In 2006 the Rev. John Hagee, who presided over a fundamentalist megachurch in southeast Texas, propelled Christians United for Israel (CUFI), which rapidly emerged as the preeminent Christian Zionist lobby. To Hagee and his followers, unquestioned support for Israel and "Bible-believing Christianity" were inextricably linked. Recalling a trip with his wife to Israel in 1978, Hagee explained, "We went as tourists but came home as Zionists."[37]

Hagee was a "prosperity gospel preacher" who embraced a spirit-centered Christianity that took literally Genesis 12:3, which held that God would "bless those who bless" Israel. Hagee's Christian Zionism thus linked the achievement of personal financial success (he published books on the subject) with one's support for Israel. He explained, "God is going to judge us on how we treat Israel and the Jewish people."[38]

AIPAC readily embraced CUFI, inviting Hagee to speak at its annual Washington conference in March 2007. "It's a new day in America," the Texas preacher declaimed under the AIPAC banner. "The sleeping giant of Christian Zionism has awakened; there are 50 million Christians standing up and applauding the State of Israel . . . The roots of Christianity are Jewish."[39]

While AIPAC adopted CUFI, CUFI adopted AIPAC as its model for constructing a successful lobbying organization. "AIPAC has set an example of how a pro-Israel organization can and must be bipartisan," David Brog, CUFI's executive director, told the *NER* in 2007. "This is an example that CUFI is determined to follow."[40]

CUFI enjoyed spectacular growth in a country in which more than one in four Americans belonged to an evangelical church and 63 percent agreed with the statement, "The Bible says God gave the land of Israel to the Jewish people." CUFI reported that its membership soared from a little more than a million in 2012 to four million members in 2018.[41]

Christian Zionists demonized Muslims and ignored the plight of Palestinians under the occupation—including more than 50,000 *Christian* Palestinians. As Daniel Hummel has noted, the Christian Zionists viewed Israel and the United States as chosen peoples, but the "dark underside" of the movement was "the erasure of concern for Arab Christians in Israel and the fate of Palestinians."[42]

In concert with AIPAC, Christian Zionists provided hawkish support for the global war on terror against the "wicked" religion of Islam. AIPAC lobbyists and Christian fundamentalists alike approved as Congress stepped up military aid, security ties, and joint defense planning with the Zionist state. Since the mid-1980s Haifa had served as the principal Mediterranean port of call for the US Navy's Sixth Fleet. In the wake of the September 11 attacks, the two countries engaged in joint training exercises and exchange of information on "low-intensity" warfare as well as "shock and awe" campaigns and "homeland defense."[43] As the *NER* proudly noted, "American homeland security officials visit Israel to study first-hand how the Jewish state fights terrorism."[44]

Bush signed legislation strengthening American-Israeli security ties following passage in the House (371-40) and the Senate (85-8). "AIPAC supported these congressional efforts to expand US-Israel security cooperation," the *NER* noted.[45]

During the two-term Bush presidency the United States established an annual grant of $3 billion in direct military aid as the standard for Israel. Virtually without debate the Congress, closely monitored by AIPAC, thus doled out on uniquely favorable financial terms far more military assistance to the little Zionist state than to any other nation. The first ten-year, $30 billion agreement was signed at the end of 2007 and would be bolstered and renewed ten years later under Bush's successor, Barack Obama.[46]

Some AIPAC veterans had preferred the reliable GOP stalwart Sen. John McCain (R-AZ) over Sen. Obama (D-IL) in the presidential campaign. Obama's criticism of US foreign policy (he had opposed the Iraq War, which AIPAC had promoted), as well as his ethnicity—he became the first African-American president and his father was a native of Kenya, which had been colonized by the British—raised warning flags.

Both Obama and the lobby put a good face on relations at the outset. Having served in the Senate, Obama was fully aware of AIPAC's clout when he assumed the presidency.

For its part AIPAC acknowledged Obama's "historic victory," noting that the new president "has strong pro-Israel ties." The lobby newsletter quoted Obama's campaign speech before AIPAC in June 2008 in which he declared, "I know that when I visit AIPAC I'm among friends." In a typical fawning speech by an American politician before AIPAC, Obama embraced Jerusalem as Israel's undivided capital and concluded that the US-Israel bond was "unbreakable today, unbreakable tomorrow, unbreakable forever."[47]

Although like the vast majority of American politicians Obama had offered no direct criticism of Operation Cast Lead, the new president funded recovery efforts in Gaza in the wake of the devastating assault. [48] Moreover, Obama signaled that he intended to follow through on his campaign call for a two-state solution by appointing as special envoy to forge a Middle East peace former Senator George Mitchell (D-ME), who under Clinton had successfully negotiated the Good Friday Agreement on Northern Ireland.

On June 4, 2009, in a historic speech in Cairo, for which he would be awarded the Nobel Peace Prize, Obama called for a "new beginning" in relations with the Muslim world. Moreover, he condemned the historic mistreatment of Palestinians as "intolerable" and vowed that the United States intended to support their "aspiration for dignity, opportunity, and a state of their own." Obama's Middle East trip pointedly did not include a visit to Israel.[49]

Obama's efforts to placate the lobby, while at the same time promoting toleration of Islam and support for Palestinian aspirations, could not be sustained. His two-term presidency would ignite bitter conflict with Israel and the lobby, both of which were accustomed to having their way in American politics. The Obama administration thus presided over the death throes of the "peace process."

Netanyahu v. Obama

With the right-wing Likud firmly ensconced in power, Israel for the second time elected Netanyahu as prime minister in 2009. He worked in tandem with the lobby to circumvent the peace process. One of cardinal tenets of

Israel as well as the lobby, adhered to since the 1940s, was that it should curry favor with both parties and remain non-partisan. Netanyahu did not formally renounce the approach but the Likud leader, who had clashed repeatedly with Bill Clinton during his first term as prime minister, clearly preferred the Republicans.[50]

When Obama pressed the Netanyahu government to call a halt in settlement building in an effort to re-start negotiations with the Palestinians, Israel and the lobby responded with the usual propaganda blitz centered on Congress. In May 2009 AIPAC generated a letter signed by 76 Senators and 329 House members calling on the administration to abandon the call for a freeze on settlements and reiterating the standard Israeli line on the need for Palestinians to come to them for "direct negotiations."[51]

Confronted directly with the reality of the lobby's sweeping influence over the Congress, Obama backpedaled. He apologized to a longstanding lobby titan, the Anti-Defamation League executive Abraham Foxman, for pushing Israel too hard, and brought back as policy adviser the AIPAC retread Dennis Ross. An advocate for Israel rather than an honest broker, Ross "undercut Mitchell's efforts at the State Department to freeze Israeli settlements."[52]

In November Netanyahu claimed to offer a concession, a 10-month moratorium on new housing projects. It was largely an empty promise as the moratorium would not apply to construction of public buildings nor include any limitations on construction in the most sensitive site, Arab East Jerusalem, which was supposed to be the capital of the future Palestinian state. Underscoring his contempt for Palestinians in East Jerusalem, Netanyahu declared, "We do not put any restrictions on building in our sovereign capital."[53]

Four months later--amid a visit to Israel by Vice President Joe Biden, who was set to promote new peace talks spearheaded by Mitchell--the Netanyahu government announced approval of new construction in an existing settlement plus plans for construction of 1,600 new units in East Jerusalem. The action was a calculated insult, to which Biden reacted with a sharply worded statement in which he "condemned" both "the substance and timing of the announcement."[54]

Administration criticism of the provocative announcement of new settlements in defiance of Netanyahu's earlier promises brought another AIPAC-generated letter in defense of Israel's illegal annexation of Palestinian territory. It was again signed by 76 senators, including 38 Democrats, as well as 333 House members. The letter to Secretary of State Hillary Clinton expressed "deep concern over recent tension" and the need to affirm "the unbreakable bond" between the United States and Israel.[55]

A new generation of stalwart congressional supporters of Israel, representing both parties, sponsored the AIPAC-driven letter. They included Rep. Eric Cantor (R-VA), the Republican Whip; Rep. Steny Hoyer (D-MD); and Sen. Barbara Boxer (D-CA). The *NER* cheered the "decisive display of bi-partisan support for Israel on Capitol Hill."[56]

As other world powers moved to condemn Israel for the illegal construction boom in occupied Jerusalem, AIPAC's allies in Congress drafted a letter to Obama "asking him to pledge to veto any anti-Israel resolutions in the UN Security Council."[57] In February 2011 the administration complied by vetoing a resolution condemning the illegal Israeli settlements--the only SC veto cast during the two-term Obama presidency. While insisting, "We reject in the strongest terms the legitimacy of continued Israeli settlement activity," the United States nonetheless incongruously vetoed a resolution condemning that very action. UN Ambassador Susan Rice offered the tortured explanation justifying the veto on the grounds that the SC resolution would have undermined "negotiations," which in reality already were dead in the water because of Israeli intransigence and the settlement construction.

While acquiescing to continuing illegal settlements, the Obama administration also insulated Israel from any potential prosecution by the International Criminal Court for war crimes committed during Operation Cast Lead. Washington also helped deflect efforts to hold Israel to account for a piratical commando attack in international waters on the Turkish-flagged *Mavi Marmara*, killing nine people, one an American citizen.[58]

The ongoing air and sea Israeli blockade of Gaza, instituted in 2007, was a form of collective punishment and a violation of international law. Responding to the widespread suffering and desperate need of medical and other supplies in the devastated Strip, an international human rights flotilla was organized to "deliver humanitarian relief" in response to the "inhumane and unjust embargo on Palestine."[59]

On May 31, 2010, Israel carried out the commando assault in international waters on the Mavi *Marmara*, the lead vessel in the flotilla carrying 700 people and 10,000 tons of supplies for the residents of Gaza. The Israeli commandos boarded in a night raid and riddled the ship with bullets. A UN fact-finding commission judged the violence "disproportionate" and "totally unnecessary," reflecting "an unacceptable level of brutality." Israel condemned the report, exonerated itself, and confiscated all the photographic evidence of the unprovoked attack.[60]

The lobby sprang into action in order to distort the truth, mobilize the US Congress, and protect Israel's image amid worldwide condemnation over the maritime attack. "While most of the world rushed to condemn Israel after its soldiers defended themselves against a brutal assault by 'peace activists' aboard the Turkish-flagged *Mavi Marmara*," the *NER* declared, in one of its more creative historical reconstructions, "many members of Congress, despite being away on recess, stood up for the Jewish state's right to self-defense." In the attendant AIPAC letter-writing campaign, "More than three-quarters of the House and Senate signed bipartisan letters to President Obama that affirm America's support for Israel."[61]

In May 2011 Obama provoked another *hasbara* campaign when he tried to restart negotiations on a two-state solution with borders "based on 1967 lines with mutually agreed swaps." In town for an AIPAC policy conference, Netanyahu stormed into the Oval Office and "lectured" the American president over his endorsement of a two-state solution.[62]

In his speech before the AIPAC throng, Obama appeased Israel by parroting its position that the "parties themselves" unfettered by international forums like the UN, would have to agree on new borders, which would not be the same as in 1967. AIPAC had urged conference attendees not to boo the President, who received mostly tepid applause instead. Three days later, on May 24, 2011, Netanyahu received 29 standing ovations in his second address before a joint session of the Congress (the first had been in 1996).[63]

With Obama in the midst of retreating from his lofty pre-election rhetoric about pursuing justice in Palestine, a disgusted PLO sought to bypass the United States and Israel and appeal directly to the UN for statehood and full recognition. Lobbied by AIPAC, both houses of Congress, as the *NER* reported, "overwhelmingly passed resolutions calling on the administration to lead opposition to Palestinian efforts to seek statehood via the UN and urging the Palestinians to return to direct talks with Israel."[64]

At the AIPAC conference, Obama had received his loudest applause when he declared unequivocally, "No vote at the United Nations will ever create an independent Palestinian state."[65] The administration used its influence over foreign governments and in the UN to stymie the PLO bid for recognition, though in November 2012 the General Assembly did vote 138–9 (the United States voting with the minority) with 41 abstentions to grant Palestine permanent "non-member observer status."[66]

The Republican take-back of the House in the 2010 elections weakened Obama and forced him to be even more cognizant of the lobby as his own reelection campaign loomed. The *NER* found the mid-term election results encouraging, declaring, "The incoming 112th Congress is expected to be the most pro-Israel Congress ever. Many of Israel's strongest supporters were reelected." The publication proceeded with its regular profiles of new senators and House members.[67]

As the Republicans gained ground, congressional Democrats distanced themselves from Obama over his criticism of the settlements and his push for the Israelis to negotiate a two-state solution. Obama directed foreign policy adviser Ben Rhodes to telephone high-level Jewish donors to "reassure them of Obama's pro-Israel bona fides," Rhodes recounted. "Netanyahu had mastered a kind of leverage" working with the lobby "to demoralize any meaningful push for peace just as he used settlements as a means of demoralizing the Palestinians."[68]

At the 2012 Democratic National Convention, progressive Democrats sought to bring some balance to the uncritical pro-Israel positions on the party platform. The Party took a voice vote on a platform proposal, which required two-thirds approval, proclaiming that Jerusalem was an "undivided city" that should remain the capital of Israel. The voice vote from the floor was clearly contested, but the Party committee chairman summarily declared the motion had received the required two-thirds, prompting a chorus of boos.[69]

In the fall canvass Obama won reelection to a second term but his percentage of the Jewish vote dropped from 78 percent to 69 percent while GOP candidate Mitt Romney received 30 percent of the Jewish vote, a sharp increase over McCain's 22 percent.[70]

Far removed from the determined calls for Palestinian rights of his pre-presidential years, Obama all but gave up in his second term on negotiations, which had no chance of success in view of Netanyahu's intransigence. Placed in charge of the talks, the AIPAC-spawned think-tank partisan Martin Indyk contemptuously dismissed the Palestinians for attempting to "sign conventions and appeal to international bodies in their supposed pursuit of 'justice' and their 'rights.'"[71]

Visiting the holy land for the first time in March 2013, Obama placated Israel with a speech emphasizing the "unbreakable alliance" while doing little to advance the "peace process." Obama urged Netanyahu to restart negotiations and orchestrated the Israeli leader's telephone apology to the Turkish government, which had cut off relations in response to the assault on the *Mavi Marmara* in 2010.[72]

Replacing Hillary Clinton as secretary of state, John Kerry tried to revive the moribund negotiations. Kerry was serious and knowledgeable about the conflict but his proposals ran headlong into Netanyahu's obstructionism, which Kerry abetted by embracing the Israeli leader's demand that Israel be recognized as a "Jewish state." The proposed recognition—which had not figured into previous Israeli peace treaties with Egypt and Jordan—would define Palestinians, including those who comprised 20 percent of Israel's population, Christians as well as Muslims, as aliens in their native land. The call for a Jewish ethnic state exposed the hollow core of Israel's claim to be a democracy representing all of its people.[73]

Although Israel continued to build illegal settlements and stonewall negotiations, the Obama administration nonetheless acceded to the unprecedented Jewish state designation that only widened the gulf with the Palestinians. Netanyahu claimed he would support a two-state solution if such an agreement included recognition of the "Jewish state," but he knew the Palestinians had already disengaged from the "peace process" over the relentless settlement construction. The Israelis "were never sincere in their commitment to peace," Rhodes observed in 2018. "They used us as a cover . . . killing time, waiting out the administration."[74]

Once again, the United States ended up demanding new concessions from the Palestinians while Israel stonewalled the moribund peace process. Abbas was asked to sign off on a "state" dissected into enclaves and checkpoints, demilitarized, with control over Jerusalem and "security" left in the hands of Israel. While the Palestinians would be required to recognize a "Jewish state," nothing was to be done about Gaza or Palestinian refugees.

By March 2014, as the proposed talks went nowhere, Kerry acknowledged that it had been a "mistake" to infuse the demand for recognition of Israel as a "Jewish state" into the two-state framework. The next month he warned ominously that in the absence of a two-state solution, "a unitary state winds up either being an apartheid state with second-class citizens—or it ends up being a state that destroys the capacity of Israel to be a Jewish state."[75]

Enabling Slaughter in Gaza

In the summer of 2014, following the lead of the AIPAC-policed Congress, the Obama administration slavishly defended Israel as it carried out another military onslaught in Gaza. Frustrated by the survival of the Hamas government, Netanyahu responded to the deaths of three Israelis in the West Bank in June 2014 by launching Operation Brother's Keeper, an attack that resulted in five Palestinian deaths, scores of homes and businesses demolished, and 700 arrests. Most of those arrested were members of Hamas, which not coincidentally had by this time entered into a unity agreement with Fatah, thus undermining Israel's divide and conquer colonial strategy.

Hamas responded to the repression by launching some of its crude rockets against the Israelis, which provided Netanyahu with the opportunity to unleash on July 8 another indiscriminate war. The ferocious

117

51-day assault featured US-manufactured bombs and Hellfire missiles that helped kill some of the more than 2,000 Palestinians who died in Operation Protective Edge. More than 10,000 Gazans were injured, more than a third of them children, and about 1,000 people were left permanently disabled. Some 18,000 homes were destroyed. Israel reported 67 soldiers and five civilians killed.[76]

While "deeply concerned about the consequences of Israel's appropriate and legitimate efforts to defend itself," as Kerry torturously put it, the United States declined to use its power and influence to stop the indiscriminate slaughter and destruction.[77] AIPAC put its domination of the US Congress on full display amid the asymmetrical military campaign in Gaza. By the summer of 2014 the Israeli-AIPAC narrative depicting Hamas as purely and simply a "terrorist" organization, one that posed an actual threat to Israel and thus had to be pummeled until it was "demilitarized," had become virtually monolithic in mainstream media.[78]

Israel lobby groups launched a broad-based propaganda campaign emphasizing that in Gaza Israel was merely engaging in "the right to defend itself." Friends in Congress quickly picked up on the corollary claim that Hamas "has been using civilian populations as human shields by placing their missile batteries in densely populated areas and near schools, hospitals, and mosques."[79] In-depth analysis found more evidence of international monitors parroting Israeli claims regarding Hamas' alleged use of human shields than verifiable evidence of incidents in which this occurred. The actual incidents of the people of Gaza functioning as human shields were few and even these may have been incidental cases in which Hamas batteries were located near civilian sites in the densely populated Strip.[80]

Backed by an overwhelmingly compliant news media--as vividly demonstrated in the acclaimed documentary film, "The Occupation of the American Mind"--AIPAC spurred a congressional resolution depicting the events in Gaza as a campaign of self-defense against terroristic efforts to destroy the Jewish state.[81] "During the Gaza conflict," as Connie Bruck reported in *The New Yorker*, "AIPAC has made a priority of sending a message of bipartisan congressional support for all of Israel's actions." In addition to rhetorical support, Israel and AIPAC also demanded additional funding for the Iron Dome defense system, which the United States had developed and provided to Israel to enable it to intercept the homemade rockets that Hamas episodically launched into Israel as a symbol of resistance.[82]

Israel-AIPAC domination of Congress was palpable in July 2014, as both houses *unanimously* passed resolutions affirming, as the Senate version put it, "support for Israel's right to defend its citizens and ensure the survival of the State of Israel." The resolution, co-sponsored by 79 senators, blamed Hamas for the carnage and demanded that Abbas renounce a unity agreement with Hamas, which had been a key factor igniting the renewal of Israel's rage against the captive Strip.[83]

AIPAC thanked the Congress before turning to the matter of "emergency funding" for the Iron Dome system. An allocation of $351 million for the system was already scheduled for October but Israel and AIPAC exploited the Gaza assault to request immediate funding. Israel's bipartisan friends, led by Majority Leader Harry Reid (D-NV) and Minority Leader McConnell, stayed overnight into the congressional recess to overcome concern by budget hawks and in the end to assure an immediate $225 million infusion into Iron Dome.[84] "Not only are we going to give you more missiles," declared lobby stalwart Sen. Lindsey Graham (R-SC)—"we're going to be a better friend. We're going to fight for you in the international court of public opinion. We're going to fight for you in the United Nations."[85]

Despite its indiscriminate violence and contempt for the now-moribund "peace process," AIPAC was thus fully in command of the US Congress. "Anybody who pretends like AIPAC isn't hugely responsible for the positions that are taken by Congress is just sticking their head in the ground," a chastened Ben Rhodes declared. As an Israeli filmmaker would acknowledge in the title of her documentary in 2020, the pro-Israel lobbyists had secured their perch as "the kings of Capitol Hill."[86]

Chapter 8
Demonizing Iran, Cashing in on Trump

While Israel laid waste to Gaza, Netanyahu and the lobby kept up a steady drumbeat essentializing Iran as a relentlessly expansive terrorist regime bent on dominating the Middle East and accessing nuclear weapons in order to annihilate the Jews.

Demonization of Iran had prevailed since the hostage crisis in 1979, but the campaign accelerated amid the war on terror. Even as Iran attempted to enact reforms, vilification of the regime persisted. In January 2002 Bush's "axis of evil" speech, which targeted Iran along with Iraq and North Korea, undermined the strongly reformist government of Mohammad Khatemi, who was elected as president of Iran in 1997 and thereafter had pursued domestic reforms and a rapprochement with the United States.[1]

"Ever since President Bush designated Iran part of an international terrorist network open to American attack, conservatives in Iran have been buoyed," the *New York Times* reported in February 2002. "This has made it harder for President Khatemi to preserve his reformist agenda for promoting democracy." In elections culminating in 2005, reactionaries came to power under President Mahmud Ahmadinejad, terminated the reforms and sharpened confrontation with the West.[2]

The Israeli and AIPAC propaganda campaign targeted not only Iran but also its ally Hizbullah, ensconced in southern Lebanon, and the regime of Bashar al-Assad in Syria. Since the collapse of negotiations over return of the Golan Heights under Rabin, Israel and the lobby had reinforced a staunchly anti-Syrian stance. Israel, supported by AIPAC, the Jewish Presidents' Conference, and far-right Jewish groups led by the ZOA, thus condemned all the neighboring Islamic forces--Iranian, Syrian, Lebanese, and Palestinian.[3]

Paralleling Israel's failed intervention in Lebanon, the American war in Iraq became a debacle, thus eroding public support for wars of regime change that Israel and AIPAC members often called for against Iran. An effort to reassert congressional war-making powers led to inclusion of a provision in a funding bill that would have precluded the president from going to war in Iran absent explicit congressional authorization. In 2007 AIPAC, once again putting its clout in Congress on full display, interceded against the effort to preserve congressional war-making powers with a propaganda campaign that got the provision removed.[4]

With regime change wars out of favor, Israel and the lobby focused on containing the Iranian nuclear research program. In 2004 the *NER* had the *chutzpah* to condemn the International Atomic Energy Agency—which Israel had flaunted for decades in constructing and secreting its own arsenal of nuclear weapons—for allegedly failing to arrest Iran's "pursuit of nuclear arms."[5]

By 2008 AIPAC had worked into both major political party platforms provisions "emphasizing the need to stop Iran from acquiring nuclear weapons." With Congress fully mobilized by 2010, Obama signed into law the Comprehensive Iran Sanctions Accountability and Divestment Act, which the *NER* applauded as "the toughest sanctions on Iran ever passed by the United States Congress."[6]

In December 2011 AIPAC cheered as all members of the US Senate voted to sanction the Central Bank of Iran, which it accused of "financing global terror" and carrying out "various illicit activities." Months later the lobby lauded the "increasingly aggressive array of sanctions on Iran," which "exerted a powerful impact on the Iranian economy." The *NER* warned, however, that sanctions were not sufficient and failed to impede Iran's ability to "make rapid progress in its quest to achieve a nuclear weapons capability."[7]

The AIPAC propaganda offensive propelled a perfervid worst-case scenario that a nuclear-equipped Iran would pose "a grave threat" to the United States and not just to Israel. Armed with nuclear weapons, Iran would "have unprecedented leverage over our economy, enable terrorist groups to act with impunity around the world, and endanger America's position of leadership in the Middle East and its sway around the world."[8]

Netanyahu spoke out repeatedly on Iran, threatened a unilateral Israeli raid reminiscent of the 1981 attack on Iraq, stepped up assassinations of Iranian scientists, and urged the United States to take military action against the Islamic Republic.[9] Netanyahu's obsession with Iran was deadly serious, but nevertheless reached a level of comic absurdity in September 2012, as he attempted to bolster his dire warnings at a press conference by holding up a cartoonish picture of a nineteenth-century, bowling ball style anarchist bomb replete with burning fuse.[10]

The Diplomacy of Assassination

Since World War II, Israeli journalist Ronen Bergman has pointed out, "Israel has assassinated more people than any other country in the Western world." Mossad has killed several Iranian scientists mostly by means of car bombs. In one operation Israel took out an Iranian general in charge of missile development along with 17 of his men.[11] On November 27, 2020, Israel assassinated Mohsen Fakhrizadeh--typically described as "the Robert Oppenheimer" of the Iranian nuclear program--when his car was riddled with bullets east of Tehran.[12]

In 1975 Americans had been shocked when the Senate Church Committee uncovered revelations of a history of top-secret CIA assassination plots against Cuba's Fidel Castro and other foreign leaders.[13] In the new century, however, amid the global terror war, assassination became routine for the United States, as it was for Israel, which thus served as a role model for its benefactor.

The Bush administration initiated the American mirroring of the Israeli approach to the "war on terror." In 2000, when Israel stepped up its assassination policy against alleged terrorists, the United States condemned the actions as "too aggressive." In the wake of the September 11, 2001 attacks, however, the United States embraced extrajudicial assassination as a tool in the terror war and engaged in joint planning with Israel on such actions. The US-Israel Joint Counterterrorism Group began to convene annually "to formally review the full range of counterterrorism issues."[14]

Obama relished lethal drone technology, as he authorized more than 560 drone strikes—more than ten times the number approved by his predecessor—and worked to provide legal justification for targeted killings. He even approved the assassination of a US citizen, Anwar al-Awlaki, in Yemen. Awlaki's 16-year-old-son, a US citizen, was killed in a follow-up drone strike two weeks later.[15]

On January 3, 2020, the Trump administration provocatively took credit for the assassination of Iranian general Qasem Soleimani, commander of an elite force of the Islamic Revolutionary Guard, which had orchestrated myriad foreign attacks of its own. Nine other people died in the US drone strike near the Baghdad International Airport.[16]

By embracing targeted killings, replete with "collateral damage," the United States collaborated with Israel in normalizing actions that had been considered illegal and atrocious before September 11, 2001. As a result of the US "adoption of the assassination policy," as Noura Erakat explains, "Israel's violations steadily escaped the zone of brazen violations and moved into the scope of legitimacy. Assassination shifted from being the policy of one rogue state to being a policy of targeted killing by the world's superpower in what it called the Global War on Terror."[17]

While the Obama administration drone strikes overwhelmingly targeted Pakistan, Somalia and Yemen, rather than Iran, Israel and lobby kept up the drumbeat for war with Iran. Christian Zionists joined Israel and the lobby in demonizing Iran. Deploying language from the Book of

Revelation, CUFI's Hagee described Iran as "the beast of radical Islam in the Middle East." As the time drew near for the "biblically prophesied end-time confrontation with Iran," the United States "must join Israel in a preemptive strike against Iran to fulfill God's plan for both Israel and the West."[18]

Throughout the Obama years Netanyahu, AIPAC, and Christian Zionists lobbied relentlessly in opposition to the administration's quest to achieve an international diplomatic solution by easing economic sanctions on Iran in return for restraints on Iranian nuclear development. The *NER* featured dire warnings from "experts" in its affiliated think tanks as well as members of Congress opposed to Obama's ultimately successful efforts to negotiate a diplomatic resolution of the confrontation with Iran.[19]

In the fall of 2013 negotiations progressed in Geneva between Iran and the world powers—the United States, Britain, France, China, Germany and Russia. Obama administration efforts to secure Israel and AIPAC acquiescence to the impending accord failed completely. In November Kerry met in Jerusalem with Netanyahu, who denounced the proposals as "very, very bad." The agreement would be the "deal of the century for Iran."[20]

The Netanyahu/AIPAC demonization of Iran as a Nazi-like aggressor bent on "gobbling up" the Middle East belied the realities of the region's geopolitics. The Saudi monarchy, strongly supported by the United States, spent more than five times Iranian spending on its military. The Gulf Cooperation Council as a whole, comprised of Kuwait, Qatar, Bahrain, Oman, and the United Arab Emirates as well as Saudi Arabia, outspent the Iranian military by a ratio of 8-1. To be sure, Iran backed Hizbullah, Syria, and various Shi'ite insurgencies, but the idea that Iran was approaching or even seeking hegemony over the region was ludicrous in view of the preponderant military power possessed by its rivals in the Arab world, not to mention Israel, the predominant military power in the region.[21]

Undercutting the American President

Republican House and Senate leaders colluded with Netanyahu, the head of a foreign government, in an effort to embarrass the sitting US president and undermine his effort to contain the Iranian nuclear program through diplomacy. Netanyahu directed his close adviser and the Ambassador to the United States, Ron Dermer, to spearhead an effort to undercut Obama and torpedo the proposed Iran nuclear agreement. Dermer was ideally suited to make the United States Congress the pivot of the campaign by Israel and the lobby to sabotage an American-led international nuclear arms control accord. A former Miami businessman and architect of Newt Gingrich's "Contract with America" campaign to neuter the Clinton presidency, Dermer subsequently emigrated to Israel and entered politics and right-wing journalism before being tapped by Netanyahu. Dermer now colluded in secrecy with the Speaker of the House John Boehner (R-OH) to arrange another address by Netanyahu before a Joint session of Congress.[22]

The Obama administration was livid when it learned of the Israeli-GOP plan to have Netanyahu go before the US Congress to derail multilateral international peace negotiations led by the American chief executive. Certainly nothing like the campaign had ever been orchestrated by a foreign government and its domestic American lobby. "The gravity of that was shocking," a senior administration official declared.[23]

The day before his congressional speech condemning Iran, Netanyahu appeared before a record 16,000 people at the annual AIPAC Conference.[24] Dubiously professing his "great respect" for Obama, Netanyahu insisted that despite his impending speech arranged by the opposition party without the president's knowledge he was not siding with the Republicans or intruding in American partisan politics. "Israel has always been a bipartisan issue," he declaimed, "and Israel must always remain a bipartisan issue." He thanked "members of Congress, Democrats and Republicans," for their "steadfast support, year in and year out. You have our boundless gratitude."[25]

On March 3, 2015, Netanyahu appeared before "the most important legislative body in the world" to urge the US Congress to oppose the president, as well as the UN, the EU, and the world community, and to instead side with Israel. Vice President Biden and 57 House and Senate Democrats—more than half of them African-American or Latino—boycotted the session. Adopting the tone of a declaration of war, Netanyahu declared Iran, led by a "Persian potentate," had a "voracious appetite for aggression" that menaced the entire Middle East. Netanyahu asserted that the proposed accord "paves Iran's path to the bomb" and would produce "a Middle East littered with nuclear bombs." He did not of course mention that Israel—acting in defiance of its special ally as well as the international community--had been the country actually responsible for developing and introducing nuclear weapons to the Middle East while refusing to sign the NPT.

"No matter on which side of the aisle you sit, you stand with Israel," he thundered--"year after year, decade after decade!" After pointing up to the relief portrait of the Hebrew prophet Moses high on the wall of the House chamber, Netanyahu concluded, "May God bless the State of Israel and may God bless the United States of America!"[26]

The Israeli leader nodded and waved from the dais in the midst of a prolonged standing ovation that followed his address. The applause, shouts and whoops of approbation continued for more than two minutes, even as Netanyahu stepped down and began shaking hands across the floor. Not even Winston Churchill in the midst of World War II could rival the fawning reception accorded the right-wing Israeli leader, who received 39 bursts of applause and 23 standing ovations. The applause alone consumed more than a quarter of Netanyahu's 40-minute address.

While seething over the Israeli and Republican-led stunt, the Obama administration forged ahead with the multilateral Iran nuclear agreement. On July 14 the United States joined other members of the Security Council and its EU allies—in other words, all the major nations in the world-- entering into with Iran the Joint Comprehensive Plan of Action (JCPOA), which included rigorous verification provisions in return for sanctions relief.

The *NER* relentlessly condemned the multi-lateral JCPOA, insisting that it allowed Iran to continue to make progress toward building a bomb. In reality the treaty precluded Iran from pursuing levels of uranium enrichment that would enable weapons development. The newsletter declared the treaty had emboldened Iran in its "attempts to dominate the Middle East." The *NER* editorial noted that "members of Congress from both sides of the aisle are rightly speaking out" against the treaty but had thus far been unable to alter Obama's "weak" policy on Iran.[27]

In the end Israel and the lobby could not overcome the support of the entire international community as well as the American president—though they did lay the groundwork for the future revocation of the treaty by the succeeding Trump administration. Ironically, as Obama and the international community spokespersons emphasized, the JCPOA ultimately enhanced Israel's security through its safeguards against Iranian nuclear proliferation. "The day the agreement was reached with Iran should have been a holiday celebrating the prevention of the next war, the worst of them all," wrote *Haaretz* columnist Gideon Levy, a courageous journalist who regularly called attention to Israel's repressive policies. "When a country claims to face a threat to its survival, what should make it happier than a chance to prevent war?" But instead of celebrating the treaty, Levy noted, Israel chose to depict a nuclear arms control agreement as "another holocaust."[28]

After exploiting its pervasive influence in Congress in an effort to sabotage US foreign policy, Israel and the lobby welcomed the release of an American traitor who had sold US secrets to Israel for profit. The convicted spy was Jonathan Pollard, a former civilian analyst for the US Navy who in the 1980s turned over highly classified documents to Israel, ultimately costing the United States billions of dollars to replace compromised intelligence-gathering systems. Pollard was the latest in a long line of little publicized spies for Israel, many of them unpunished or lightly punished.[29] In the years following his arrest and conviction in 1987 for conspiracy to commit espionage, Pollard launched "a brilliant public relations campaign from his jail cell" that succeeded in igniting the support of "a huge network of supporters in Israel as well as a substantial following in the United States." Israel and the lobby rallied behind Pollard, who had become an Israeli citizen. Whereas Americans who spied for Russia and other countries typically received life without parole, Pollard gained his release after serving 30 years.[30]

Business as Usual

Despite Netanyahu's contemptuous treatment of his administration, Obama had little choice in view of the lobby's clout other than to advance American security ties and affirm US financial support for Israel. In 2014 he signed the "United States-Israel Strategic Partnership Act," sponsored by AIPAC's allies in Congress. The action advanced security linkages, facilitated military assistance, and mandated the President report to Congress every two years to ensure that Israel maintained its "Qualitative Military Edge" (QME)—military superiority--in the region.[31]

The AIPAC-generated measure passed unanimously in the Senate and by a vote of 410-1 in the House. "By declaring in legislation that Israel is a 'major strategic partner' of the United States," AIPAC noted in satisfaction, "the measure lays the foundation for expanded US-Israel cooperation in a wide variety of spheres, including defense, intelligence, homeland security, cyber security, energy, water, agriculture, and alternative fuel technologies."[32]

Despite Israel's efforts to sabotage the signal foreign policy achievement of his presidency, Obama showed no hesitation in renewing the expiring decade-long military aid program to the special ally. In 2016 he and Netanyahu agreed on a new 10-year, $38 billion assistance agreement.[33]

Afforded regular opportunity to offer extensive "expert" testimony before Congress, AIPAC's Kohr made a pro forma appearance before a House subcommittee on March 25 to request the already assured "robust annual security assistance to Israel." No Israeli could have more patriotically represented the Zionist state before the US Congress than Kohr, an American from Cleveland.

Reiterating the theme of a small, persistently besieged democratic state, the AIPAC chief executive argued that Israel's "survival and security" were imperiled as a result of "an unprecedented array of threats stemming from the growing instability gripping the Middle East. These challenges require Israel to spend significantly more on its defense" in order to maintain its QME.[34]

Contrary to AIPAC's claims, American military-security assistance enabled Israel not merely to defend itself but to become a major arms exporter and global leader in the development of new weapons systems and sophisticated surveillance technologies. Neighboring states but especially the West Bank and Gaza had long since become testing grounds—their residents in effect serving as guinea pigs—for a variety of new weapons and surveillance technologies, all of which could subsequently be marketed internationally as "battle-tested" in the wake of Israel's regular military assaults.[35]

Glossing Israeli cross-border aggression, Kohr depicted a Zionist state under siege from an ongoing "Palestinian wave of terror" as well as threats posed by Iran, Hizbullah, Hamas, and Syria. Facing "unprecedented strategic threats on all its fronts," Israel urgently needed the continuing US military assistance under the terms that "it has historically been provided," including the "early disbursal" arrangement that Israel and no other country in the world enjoyed.

Kohr testified that massive US military aid benefited the United States as well as Israel, citing the myriad joint military maneuvers, anti-terrorist operations, military research and development, and intelligence-sharing programs that were "saving American lives on the battlefield." He trumpeted the missile defense programs Iron Dome as well as David's Sling, the latter jointly "developed by the US defense company Raytheon and Israel's Rafael Advanced Defense Systems." But "the centerpiece of the US-Israeli cooperative defense relationship" was the Arrow "exo-atmospheric defense system designed to counter long-range conventional and unconventional strategic threats to Israel."

Kohr wrapped up his testimony by condemning the UN, thereby underscoring the Israeli and AIPAC deeply rooted contempt for international law and universal human rights. The AIPAC executive dismissed the UN General Assembly as "an unalterably hostile forum," while giving thanks for the 42 vetoes of Israel-related UN Security Council resolutions (out of 76 total vetoes) issued by the United States over the 70-year history of the international peacekeeping organization. Confirming that the United States was the chief obstacle to the pursuit of international justice in the Palestine conflict, Kohr acknowledged, "Without this crucial American support—and only American support . . . dozens of binding anti-Israel resolutions would have undercut Israel's international standing."[36]

During his final days in office, Obama turned the tables on AIPAC by abstaining rather than vetoing UNSC 2334, which stated that Israeli settlements in "Palestinian territories occupied since 1967, including East Jerusalem," constituted a "flagrant violation" of international law. The resolution passed 14-0 with the lone American abstention.

Israel, the lobby, and most members of Congress were apoplectic about the abstention, which Obama had delayed until after the 2016 presidential election, which the Democrats lost anyway. "AIPAC is deeply disturbed that the Obama Administration did not exercise America's veto," the *NER* declared, "allowing this destructive resolution to pass. This move came despite overwhelming bipartisan majorities of Congress urging the Administration to maintain its longstanding policy of vetoing such measures."[37]

Obama no doubt enjoyed exacting a measure of revenge at the expense of Netanyahu and AIPAC, but the president of "hope and change" had presided over the collapse of any actual hope for a two-state solution and had declined to attempt to rein in Israel's brutal assaults on Gaza. Immediately upon taking office Obama ran headlong into the most powerful lobby representing the interests of a foreign nation in American history and he ultimately bowed before it.

AIPAC lined up unqualifiedly pro-Israel platforms for both political parties in the 2016 election, but Sen. Bernie Sanders (I-VT) amassed enough support to put up a fight in the Democratic platform committee meetings. Hillary Clinton's unambiguously pro-Israel proposals eventually won out over more critical language proposed by Sanders' representatives. The final document made no mention of settlements, avoided the term "occupation," and condemned pressuring Israel through a boycott or sanctions.[38]

The Gift of Trump

The election of New York real estate tycoon and reality television star Donald J. Trump in November 2016 was the perfect storm for Israel and the lobby, which had a free rein to pursue all of their dreams and ambitions with an accommodating White House backed by the AIPAC-controlled Congress.

Trump catered to the far right of the Israel lobby—billionaire Sheldon Adelson, CUFI, the ZOA and like-minded groups that were positioned from AIPAC to the right. Adelson gave at least $21 million to Trump's 2016 campaign and provided an additional $113 million to right-wing Republican causes in 2018.[39]

The lobby extremists won Trump administration backing for cutting off funds to the PA, whereas AIPAC supported continuing support of the PA as a means of maintaining the fiction of an ongoing "peace process."[40]

In March 2018 Trump signed the Taylor Force Act, named for an American killed in a terror attack in Israel, which cut off aid to the PA, citing its Martyrs Fund, which authorized payment to families of Palestinians who engaged in resistance or were imprisoned by Israel.[41]

While crippling the PA financially, the Trump administration also withdrew US economic support for the United Nations Relief and Works Agency, which previously stood at about $300 million annually. The action was another blow at international law, which mandated UNRWA support for the dispossessed refugees, who by this time numbered some six million people.[42] In December 2017, the Trump administration continued the onslaught by recognizing Jerusalem as Israel's capital, thereby reversing seven decades of official US policy, though AIPAC and Congress had paved the way with passage of the Jerusalem Embassy Act in 1995.

In March 2019, with Syria crippled by a devastating civil war and US-sponsored sanctions, Trump signed a presidential proclamation recognizing Israel's annexation of the Syrian (Golan) Heights. Under Obama the United States had collaborated with Israel in calling for the overthrow of the Assad regime, a goal they failed to achieve. Syria was left devastated and disgorging streams of refugees as a result of the actions of Assad and a host of foreign intruders, including Turkey and Russia along with the Americans and the Israelis.

The strategically significant high ground of the Golan Heights, about 40 miles long and 12 miles wide, had been seized from Syria and illegally occupied by Israel since the 1967 war. Overlooking Syria and the Jordan Valley, the Golan Heights also possess valuable water resources, fertile soil, and possibly significant oil deposits.[43]

The Syrian Heights had never been part of the Palestine mandate or the biblical Israel, but in 1981 Menachem Begin had proclaimed the territory part of the Zionist state. Settlers and tourists followed. The UN and the rest of the world, including the United States until Trump, had for 50 years rejected Israel's illegitimate usurpation of the territory. As with Jerusalem, Trump ignored law and history in deference to bolstering Netanyahu and recruiting Zionist voters into the Republican Party.

No one appreciated Trump's accommodationist policies more than Netanyahu, who cultivated Trump's support for the crowning annexationist project—a call amid his 2019 reelection campaign for incorporation of a large swath of the West Bank into Israel. Netanyahu's election opponent Bennie Gantz cried foul, insisting that *he* was the first one to suggest annexation of "Judea and Samaria." Thus, consistent with Israel's congenitally aggressive and historic settler state expansionism, the Israeli public voted overwhelmingly in this and subsequent tightly contested elections for two candidates who both advocated the extension of the illegal occupation.

The State Department condemned Netanyahu's Likud Party for "promoting hatred" against Arab Israelis amid the election campaigns. The report noted that a chat box on Netanyahu's Facebook page during the campaign claimed, "The Arabs want to destroy all of us, women, children, and men." Facebook temporarily shut down the page and the message was removed.[44]

The racially based contempt for Palestinians fueled calls for Israel to carry out cleansing operations, which in fact were already under way with home demolitions and deportations from East Jerusalem. Right-wing politicians such as Avigdor Lieberman openly advocated "transfer" operations targeting the Palestinian population.[45] Former post-Zionist, turned court historian Benny Morris lamented that Ben-Gurion had failed to carry out a "full expulsion" of Palestinians in the original ethnic cleansing of 1947-1948.[46]

In November 2019 the Trump administration opened the floodgates to Israeli chauvinism by issuing a historic statement declaring that the United States no longer considered the West Bank settlements illegal. The pronouncement was bereft of any legal foundation and was an interpretation rejected by virtually every other nation in the world outside Israel and the United States.[47]

Obsessed with Obama, whose birth in the United States and legitimacy as an American citizen he had publicly questioned for years, Trump culminated a broad-based assault on his predecessor's legacy by announcing unilateral US withdrawal from the Iran nuclear accord. Trump reinstituted sweeping sanctions and dispatched B-52 bombers, Patriot missile batteries, an aircraft carrier, and troops to the allied regime in Saudi Arabia, which was also embroiled in conflict with Iran. Trump continued to bolster the Saudi regime despite its brazen murder of a *Washington Post* journalist Jamal Khashoggi. Trump then authorized the US assassination of Soleimani.

Trump placed his son-in-law Jared Kushner, a right-wing Zionist dedicated to maximalist Israeli expansionist goals, in charge of devising a Middle East peace plan. Announced in January 2020, the "deal of the century" accommodated Israeli plans to annex the Jordan Valley and other areas of the West Bank while offering financial assistance to the Palestinians in return for accepting colonialism, as they would be relegated to a disconnected rump state, divided and slashed by checkpoints and bypass roads and with no control over borders and security.[48]

The Trump administration made no pretense of maintaining a multi-lateral "peace process," as the President and Netanyahu jointly announced the "deal" without the presence or consultation of Palestinian representatives. Despite the lopsided imperial character of the plan— which sanctioned an illegal occupation and continuing war crimes--

Kushner channeled Abba Eban's comment from 1973 in preemptively blaming Palestinians for the dead-on-arrival rejection of the "deal." Kushner declared of the Palestinians, "If they screw up this opportunity, which again, they have a perfect track record of missing opportunities, if they screw this up, I think they will have a very hard time looking the international community in the face, saying they're victims, saying they have rights."[49]

In the last months of the Trump presidency Kushner orchestrated cynical accords with four Arab regimes--the United Arab Emirates, Bahrain, Sudan and Morocco—which agreed to move toward recognition and normal relations with Israel in return for US weapons sales, financial incentives and other desiderata. Trump and Kushner claimed the much-ballyhooed "Abrahamic accords" had popular support in the Arab world and would bring peace to the Middle East, but neither claim was true. The region remained roiled by dissatisfaction and suffering in the wake of decades of brutal violence in which the United states and Israel were deeply implicated.[50]

By the end of 2020, "America's war for the Greater Middle East" had ended in abject failure.[51] The United States had armed and supported reactionary Arab regimes and worked with them and with Israel to pummel and punish those that would not follow its dictates in the region. Under the American superpower watch, the Middle East became increasingly unstable, wracked by horrific violence in Libya, Syria, and Yemen, and was more undemocratic than ever. Israeli repression of Palestine remained the bleeding wound in the heart of a tumultuous region.

Chapter 9
Resistance to Israeli Apartheid

On November 14, 2017, Rep. Betty McCollum (D-MN) made history. She became the first person in Congress ever to introduce legislation aimed specifically at protecting Palestinian human rights.[1]

In collaboration with the human rights organization Defense for Children International-Palestine, McCollum crafted a bill that would prevent US tax dollars from supporting ongoing Israeli practices of detention and mistreatment of children.[2] Since 2000 more than 10,000 Palestinian children, most between 11 and 15 years old, had been detained and subject to abuses such as chokeholds, beatings, coercive interrogation, and in some cases torture. The UN Children's Fund reported children were frequently detained for extended periods without access to their parents much less an attorney.[3]

"This legislation highlights Israel's system of military detention of Palestinian children and ensures that no American assistance to Israel supports human rights violations," McCollum declared. "Peace can only be achieved by respecting human rights, especially the rights of children. Congress must not turn a blind eye to the unjust and ongoing mistreatment of Palestinian children living under Israeli occupation."[4]

Myriad church groups and international human rights organizations endorsed the Promoting Human Rights by Ending Military Detention of Palestinian Children Act. Co-sponsors of the bill included Rep. Rashida Tlaib (D-MI)—the first Palestinian-American woman to hold office in the Congress--and Rep. Ilhan Omar (D-MN), who along with Tlaib became the first Muslim women to hold congressional seats.

Israel and the lobby sharply opposed the bill. Israel also pressured Belgium to withdraw its invitation to a representative of Defense of Children International-Palestine to present a briefing on the abuses before the UN Security Council.[5]

Given lobby opposition, McCollum's bill to protect children had no chance of passage in the Congress but her introduction of it underscored the rise of human rights-based resistance to Israel's repression of Palestinians. McCollum's action and the outspoken opposition to Israeli policies by the two Muslim-American congresswomen, backed by several others, revealed that even within the citadel of AIPAC power—the United

States Congress—contestation over the unquestioning US support for Israel was beginning to percolate.

Human rights-based resistance gained momentum as the Oslo paradigm collapsed amid the extreme violence of the Second Intifada. The turn to an approach centered on human rights and international law was thus "a strategy of last resort" owing to the failure of the Oslo process, which had succeeded only in reinforcing Israeli settler colonization.[6]

The rights-based approach sought to revitalize resistance and take the Palestine struggle beyond the Middle East and to center it within a global emancipatory framework emphasizing decolonization and racial equality. The historic campaign against apartheid South Africa provided a model for the rights-based approach.

Parallels with Apartheid

While not wholly analogous, Israeli and South African settler colonialism shared much in common. Both Israel and South Africa were setter colonial states rooted in racial hierarchy, political exclusion, displacement of indigenous people, restrictions on movement, intimidation, incarceration, and torture. Israel relegated Palestinians to South African-style Bantustans policed and cut off from Jewish settlements as well as from East Jerusalem—which was supposed to be the capital of a Palestinian state. And like the Reagan administration policy of "constructive engagement," which had discouraged pressuring South Africa over apartheid, the US-brokered and dead-ended "peace process" enabled the ongoing occupation and repression in Palestine.[7]

Furthering the parallels, Israel and South Africa had long been close allies in world politics. Herut, the political party originally founded by Menachem Begin and "unabashedly racist toward Arabs," received "the bulk of [its]funding from South Africa." Begin made repeated fundraising trips to the Jewish communities in South Africa, which backed apartheid as well as the vision of the Greater Israel. Israel became the top supplier of weapons to South Africa, as a "thriving arms trade" flourished between the two exclusionary regimes. Israel and South Africa secretly collaborated on nuclear weapons and long-range ballistic missile research as both cultivated the weapons of mass destruction.[8]

With the collapse of the apartheid South Africa in 1994 the Israelis thus lost a key ally. The international boycott of South Africa, which helped bring an end to the white supremacist state, coincided with the rise of human rights consciousness and other tectonic global political shifts, including the end of the Cold War. One of the heroes of the liberation struggle, Bishop Desmond Tutu, embraced the call for a boycott and sanctions movement targeting Israeli apartheid, citing parallels with the transformation he had helped to orchestrate in South Africa.[9]

Despite Israel's long history of intimate economic, political, security, and identity-based relations with apartheid South Africa, Zionists bitterly resented the drawing of parallels between the two settler states. In 1975 Israel and the lobby were apoplectic when the UN General Assembly passed a resolution equating Zionism with racism.[10] Similarly, they reacted with outrage in 2006 when Jimmy Carter published *Palestine: Peace, not Apartheid,* which warned that Israel's failure to negotiate a two-state solution would lead inevitably to an apartheid state. Lobby apologists publicly labeled the former president and champion of human rights a "Jew-hater" who had advanced "traditional anti-Semitic canards."[11]

Despite its efforts to shoot down the parallels with South Africa, Israel's own actions affirmed racial and ethnic bias. In 2003 Israel passed and later upheld through the courts a discriminatory marriage law that forbids non-Jews from the Occupied Territories, Gaza, and the "enemy states" of Iran, Iraq, Syria, and Lebanon, from gaining citizenship and residency through marriage to an Israeli citizen. By contrast, any Jew from anywhere in the world can become an Israeli citizen.[12]

In July 2018 the Knesset affirmed Israel's embrace of apartheid through passage of the new nation-state law, which defined Israel as a "Jewish state" in which Hebrew was the official language. The law declared "the right to national self-determination" was "unique to the Jewish people" and embraced "Jewish settlement as a national value." The Jewish state law thus undermined the citizenship and language of already long marginalized Palestinian citizens, Christian as well as Muslim--20 percent of the population--and made Israel, legally and officially, an undemocratic state.[13]

The new law "puts an end to the farce about Israel being 'Jewish and democratic,'" *Haaretz* columnist Gideon Levy explained. "If the state is Jewish, it cannot be democratic, because of the lack of equality; if it is democratic, it cannot be Jewish, because democracy does not bestow privilege based on ethnicity. So now the Knesset has decided: Israel is Jewish." By rejecting the option of acting as a state with equal respect for all the citizens living within it, Israel had "ceased to be an egalitarian democracy, not just in practice but also in theory. That's why the law is so important," Levy concluded. "It is a truthful law."[14]

The 12 Palestinian members of Knesset (out of 120 total)—known as the Joint List—attempted to introduce an alternative law stressing "the principle of equal citizenship for every citizen." The Knesset rejected their attempt even to participate in parliamentary debate within the "sole democracy" of the Middle East by disallowing introduction of the measure on grounds that no bill could be proposed that denied "the existence of the State of Israel as the state of the Jewish People."[15]

Discrimination against non-Jews extended beyond political participation into housing, education, employment, access to water and other vital resources. Israel cultivated an unequal society with a sharp disparity of wealth and living conditions between Jews and Palestinians, as well as Ethiopian immigrants, who encountered racial hostility and discrimination. More than half of the Arab citizens of Israel live in poverty. "The unspoken but intended effect of this de facto discrimination," Ali Abunimah argues, "is to create conditions so dire that Palestinian citizens of Israel will find no option but to leave."[16]

While Israel formally forbids discrimination based on race, Palestinians can be denied choice of residence based on "social suitability." Some 900 towns in Israel's segregated society have no Arabs or Palestinians living in them. Israelis employ an expansive interpretation of "social suitability" to deny residency to non-Zionists, or people who do not send their children to Hebrew-language schools, or those who did not serve in the IDF. Unlike Jews and other groups, Muslim Arabs and the vast majority of Palestinian Christians do not serve in Israel's armed forces.[17]

Israeli discourse routinely references the Palestinian minority as a "demographic threat" whose *very existence* undermines the "Jewish state." As advocates of the marriage law openly proclaimed, all Arabs were potential terrorists and thus could not be allowed into Israel. "Muslims that arrive here," Israel's minister of Interior explained in 2012, "do not even believe that the country belongs to us, to the *white* man."[18]

Israel's racist and xenophobic policies resonated with Trump, who condemned Muslims, ripped migrant children from their families on the US Southern border, and defended the good heartedness of white supremacists. As Israel became increasingly reactionary, Trump's anti-Palestinian policies capped off decades of US appeasement of Israeli settler aggression.

Growing Public Awareness

By the twenty-first century Israel and the lobby confronted a growing challenge from a rising and increasingly interconnected global peace and justice movement. Israel faced unprecedented damaging publicity from a variety of new media sources over its violent repression of Palestinians in the Second Intifada as well as the indiscriminate assaults on Lebanon and Gaza. Since the 1980s scholars led by Noam Chomsky had begun to expose Israel's aggressive actions as well as American complicity. Published in 1983, Chomsky's book *The Fateful Triangle: The United States,*

Israel and the Palestinians condemned Israeli aggression in Lebanon, repression of Palestinian rights, and US support for Israel as an outpost of corporate capitalism and a "strategic asset."[19]

Other critical scholarly and journalistic accounts illuminated the role of the Israel lobby.[20] AIPAC and other lobby groups typically ignored critical accounts, or if they became popular, as with Chomsky's book, which went into multiple editions, they attacked the author. In 2007 Norman Finkelstein, an accomplished scholar and withering critic of Israeli aggression, was forced out of his political science teaching position at DePaul University in Chicago in a move "reminiscent of McCarthy era academic purges" of the early 1950s.[21]

That same year a smear campaign was mounted against the authors of *The Israel Lobby*, the book that condemned the lobby for promoting unrealistic and unproductive US policies in the Middle East. Co-authored by two distinguished political scientists, *The Israel Lobby* generated widespread publicity, particularly as the Iraq War--which as the book pointed out the lobby had supported--became an ongoing foreign policy disaster. *The Israel Lobby* was a powerful critique of AIPAC's overweening influence, yet despite the authors' impeccable credentials the book was widely and falsely dismissed as inaccurate or arbitrarily anti-Israel, a propaganda campaign promoted by the lobby itself and widely reflected in journalistic as well as scholarly assessments.[22]

Mainstream American media and especially network television remained reluctant to criticize Israel or provide air time to consider Palestinian perspectives and otherwise critical narratives. While the *Nation* and other progressive magazines offered episodic critical coverage of Israeli policies, the only sustained source of critical reporting on the Palestine conflict and the systemic role of the lobby was the *Washington Report on Middle East Affairs*. Launched in 1982 by former US diplomats, who had extensive personal experience with Israeli and lobby efforts to impede a more balanced US diplomacy in the region, the full-color magazine compiled a long track record of evidence-based critical reporting on the Middle East, US policy, and the role of the lobby.[23]

In addition to the journalistic and scholarly accounts, the worldwide web of the Internet played a pivotal role in the mounting twenty-first century challenges to lobby efforts to regiment media coverage. In 2001, Ali Abunimah, a Palestinian-American journalist, was among the co-founders of the influential web site The *Electronic Intifada*, which featured critical reporting on Israeli policies while advocating a one-state democratic solution to the Palestine issue.[24] Founded in the 1990s, Antiwar.com condemned US military intervention around the globe, including support for Israeli militarism.[25]

In 2002 Juan Cole, a distinguished historian at the University of Michigan specializing in the Middle East, launched *Informed Comment*, another web site that became well known for critical accounts of the Israeli occupation and US complicity in the repressive policies and instability in the region. In 2006, as Cole was on the verge of being offered a position in the History Department at Yale, the lobby launched a smear campaign that succeeded in prompting the Ivy League university cravenly to withdraw the offer. Cole later sued the FBI and the CIA, which allegedly spied on him and collaborated with the George W. Bush administration to scotch the Yale appointment.[26]

Formed by Grant F. Smith in 2002, the Institute for Research Middle Eastern Policy (IRmep) established a web site featuring in-depth research into the history and activities of the Israel lobby. The non-profit unearthed and published online and in books and reports a wealth of information on the history and previously secret activities of the Israel lobby. In collaboration with the *Washington Report on Middle East Affairs*, IRmep in 2014 began sponsoring an annual Israel lobby conference--deliberately coinciding with the annual AIPAC meeting--which featured an array of international experts on the role of the lobby and Israel's repressive policies. The venerable public affairs reporting network C-SPAN typically televised the annual Israel Lobby and American Policy Conference, which was held annually at the National Press Club in Washington.[27]

In 2007 another influential blog and web site was initiated by Philip Weiss, a journalist and non-Zionist Jew, who added collaborators in the creation of *Mondoweiss*. The site was another source of critical analysis, including regular accounts illuminating the entrenched liberal media bias in favor of Israel, notably on the part of the *New York Times*. Weiss, who kept a close watch on AIPAC and lobby activities, was at the forefront of a growing movement of progressive Jews offering public condemnation of Israeli repression.[28]

Through the determined activism of these and myriad other sources, the Israel-Palestine conflict was being hotly contested in cyberspace as well as on the ground. In the age of Google, Facebook and Twitter, Israel and the lobby could not contain or control critical knowledge on the conflict, however much the lobby's media-focused attack groups such as CAMERA and FLAME might regularly assail the opposition. The concern on the part of Israel and the lobby only grew when the quest for justice in Palestine began to coalesce behind a coordinated international campaign aimed at forcing Israel's hand.

The BDS Campaign

An international campaign of boycott, divestment and sanctions (BDS) became the centerpiece of efforts to resist Israel's race-based repression in the twenty-first century. Following the collapse of diplomacy amid the Second Intifada, the grassroots movement to promote BDS emerged as an alternative to the mythical "peace process."

In 2005 scores of Palestinian civil society organizations issued a call--modeled on the resistance to South African apartheid as well as the historic campaigns launched by Mahatma Gandhi in India and Martin Luther King, Jr. in the United States--for a BDS campaign targeting Israel. BDS did not endorse either a one-state or two-state solution, focusing instead on specific demands for justice. Citing the occupation, the separation wall, unequal treatment under the law, and rejection of the refugees' right of return, the organizers called for isolating Israel until these policies were changed and the injustices addressed.[29] In tandem with BDS, the Palestinian Campaign for the Academic and Cultural Boycott of Israel (PACBI) urged artists, musicians, and academics to refuse to perform in Israel.[30]

Several mainstream religious groups debated sanctions and some endorsed BDS. Endorsements came from the Presbyterian Church USA, the United Church of Christ, the United Methodist Church, and several Quaker groups.[31] Famous musicians and writers including Roger Waters, Elvis Costello, Carlos Santana, Alice Walker, and Naomi Klein endorsed the BDS call while others canceled planned appearances in Israel.[32] Although Israel and the lobby asserted that only marginalized, left-wing groups supported BDS, polls showed at least 20 percent and possibly as much as 40 percent of the American public endorsed the idea.[33]

The BDS campaign condemned but had little impact on multi-national corporations doing business with Israel, many of them "defense" industries such as Northrup Grumman, which supplied Israel with cluster bombs, and Raytheon, a partner in Israeli missile development. Another major target was Caterpillar, whose bulldozers razed Palestinian homes and villages and in 2003 crushed to death an American college student, Rachel Corrie, in Rafah, as she protested Palestinian home demolitions in the Gaza Strip.[34]

The academic and cultural boycott made an important distinction between Israeli institutions and individuals. Institutions, including the seven major research universities in Israel, which in myriad ways helped anchor and support colonialism, were held to account but individuals, such as a student or professor at those universities, were exempt.[35] "The BDS movement, including PACBI, rejects on principle boycotts of individuals based on their identity (such as citizenship, race, gender, or religion) or opinion," the official policy explained. "Mere affiliation of Israeli cultural workers to an Israeli cultural institution is therefore not grounds for applying the boycott."[36]

Ironically, some of Israel's most celebrated critics rejected or offered only limited support to BDS. Chomsky endorsed a boycott limited to products produced in the occupied territories, but not those made inside Israel's borders.[37] Finkelstein, though a relentless critic of Zionist militarism and exploitation of the Holocaust, opposed BDS. Chomsky and Finkelstein thus rejected the tactic of a punitive boycott designed to pressure the Zionist state into abandoning an occupation that both Jewish men had long and vigorously condemned.

Finkelstein took his opposition a step further, dismissing BDS as a "cult" that he believed detracted from efforts to resolve the Palestine question through a focus emphasizing international law. Moreover, Finkelstein charged, BDS had a hidden agenda to drive Israel completely from Palestine. Israel and the lobby frequently leveled this charge as well.[38]

These otherwise radical critics thus sided with Democrats and liberals who declined to back the human rights-based initiative. Consistent with their general support for Israel and trepidation about opposing the lobby, liberals joined in the effort to delegitimize BDS, thereby affirming a derisive acronym created for them—PEP, or "progressive except for Palestine." Those fitting the description included Obama, who responded to lobby pressure by denouncing BDS in his 2012 address before AIPAC wherein he vowed to "stand against" the movement.[39]

While Israel, the lobby and many liberals charged that BDS was out to destroy Israel, the BDS call did not advocate such a position. Many BDS supporters, including its Palestinian progenitor Omar Barghouti, rejected an exclusionary *Jewish* state in Palestine, yet the BDS call did not demand nor encompass the elimination of Israel. Barghouti advocated a democratic state in which Jews could live but not dominate based on their ethnicity.[40]

While some BDS proponents reject Israel's "right" to have a Zionist state in Palestine, such a position is not tantamount to advocating the elimination of Israel. Individuals might reject Israel's "right" to occupy Palestine—just as they might reject the "right" of the United States to occupy the Black Hills, which under the terms of a lawful treaty upheld by federal court rulings should belong to the indigenous band known as the Sioux—but this does not mean that they expect that the occupiers will leave.[41]

The first point of the formal BDS call emphasized ending the "occupation and colonization of all Arab lands," which can be read to mean occupied territories beyond the 1949 "green line." Such a reading seems logical, as the second point of the BDS call acknowledged Israel's existence by demanding recognition of "the fundamental rights of Arab-Palestinian citizens *of Israel* to full equality" [emphasis added]. The third point supported the "rights of Palestinian refugees to return to their homes and properties as stipulated in UN resolution 194," leaving open and potentially negotiable the question of just how many refugees might seek to return or otherwise receive compensation.[42]

While the BDS call did not embrace either a one- or a two-state solution, many of its advocates argued that as a result of Israel's illegal expansion into the Occupied Territories only a one-state solution was any longer possible to achieve. Under such a solution Israel--or Israel-Palestine--could function as a genuine plural democracy and therefore not as a theocratic Jewish state. To reiterate, a Jewish state is an apartheid state because it privileges one religious-group over masses of people, ethnicity over democracy, and thus stands in contradiction to internationally sanctioned democratic values.

Cleavages Within the Jewish Community

A small but influential minority, American Jews had long played a crucial role in the rise of the Israel lobby and in generating popular support for Zionism. "Although it is often overstated, sometimes ludicrously and sometimes maliciously," Dov Waxman has pointed out, "American Jewish political power cannot be denied." Jews are "very well represented in the US government and in think tanks, journalism, and academia."[43]

Since its foundation in the 1940s Israel and the lobby had been able to rely upon the largely uncritical support of an overwhelming majority of American Jews, but in the new century that was no longer the case. For decades "American Jews were often cast by Israelis into the role of a rich but distant uncle," Theodore Sasson pointed out in 2014. "Their job was to write checks and not ask too many questions—knowing that the money was 'going to Israel' was enough. This is less often the case today."[44]

While there had always been Jews who were either indifferent or overtly non-Zionist, disaffection from Israel grew in the 1980s and 1990s amid Israel's aggression and the failure of the "peace process." The growing divisions among American Jews reflected a generational and religious divide, as many older, wealthier, more politically conservative, and often Orthodox Jews continued to embrace Israel virtually without question. Younger, more middle class, and often Reform or non-religious Jews were more inclined to be troubled by Israeli repression in Palestine.

Many American Jews rejected Zionism yet continued to "care deeply about the future of Judaism and the Jewish people."[45] A large number of

American Jews remained "either reasonably satisfied or simply unaware and apathetic" about Israeli policies.

Establishment Jewish groups including AIPAC, the Anti-Defamation League, the American Jewish Committee, B'nai B'rith, Hadassah, the Zionist Organization of America, local Jewish Federations, among others, continued overwhelmingly to back Israel without question. "Almost instinctively, the major organizations in the American Jewish establishment are reluctant to criticize Israeli policies," Waxman notes, hence "their support for Israel is automatic and unconditional."[46]

Many of the Jewish establishment organizations were "dependent on a small number of very rich people." Many of the executives of the major organizations served for decades, thus ensconcing right-wing, uncritically pro-Israeli policies. Malcolm Hoenlein headed the Conference of Presidents of Major American Jewish Organizations for more than 30 years; Abraham Foxman headed the ADL for nearly 30 years; Morton Klein has headed the ZOA for nearly three decades as well. Howard Kohr became director of AIPAC in 1996 and still held the position in 2021. These and other executives receive generous annual salaries in the hundreds of thousands of dollars and munificent benefits packages in return for their unquestioning pro-Israel advocacy.[47]

Throughout the history of the lobby, as J.J. Goldberg noted years ago, "Big givers have played a key role in setting policy in every Jewish organization." The casino magnate Adelson, one of richest men in world, donated millions of dollars to Israel, the lobby, and the Republican Party. "The organized American Jewish community is not a democracy," Waxman points out. "It is run by an oligarchy."[48]

Israel and the lobby's uncritical supporters thus represent an elite, wealthy minority of American Jews. In addition, "many of the active participants in major Jewish organizations are politically conservative and religiously Orthodox." As older, wealthy, and politically well-connected Jews "exercise a disproportionate influence," the establishment organizations have become "more right-wing and religious than the majority of American Jews."[49]

Orthodox Jews, "generally right-wing" and uncritically pro-Israel, were becoming an ever-greater percentage of American Jewry as a result of higher birth rates. In New York, the heartland of American Jewry, from 1981 to 2011 the percentage of Orthodox among Jews rose dramatically from 13 percent to 32 percent. It was "safe to say that the predominantly secular, liberal American Jewish community of today is endangered," Waxman notes.[50]

While right-wing, wealthy, and often Orthodox Jews dominate the pro-Israel lobby in the United States, their uncritical support of Israel increasingly is being contested by the younger generation. "Angry arguments" and "ugly" debates erupt within families and in "many Jewish communities."[51] The gulf between majority liberal American Jewish sentiments on one side and Israeli aggression backed by a right-wing minority of American Jews on the other constitutes an ongoing "crisis of Zionism."[52] With the consensus unraveling, it seems apparent that the right-wing, uncritically pro-Israeli elite of the American Jewish establishment will become "smaller and weaker," thus offering a genuine opportunity for change emanating from a crucial base—American Jews.[53]

In addition to divisions over Israel and the injustice in Palestine among American Jews, a growing divide separated Israeli public opinion from American Jewry as a whole. According to in-depth Pew Research Center polling in 2017, a majority of American Jews viewed Israeli settlements in the Occupied Territories as an impediment to peace with the Palestinians, which they believed could be achieved. A majority of Israelis, by contrast, favored the settlements and doubted that Israel and the Palestinians would find their way to a peace settlement. This divergence mirrored divisions between Republicans, toward which Israel and the lobby were increasingly gravitating, and Democrats, who still commanded majority support of American Jews. "In many respects," as Steven M. Cohen, an expert on Jewish public opinion, succinctly put it, "Israel is a red state and American Jews are a blue country."[54]

In the twenty-first century, increasing numbers especially of younger and non-Orthodox Jews began to dissent from Israeli policies and moreover, to organize. To be sure, an overwhelming majority of American Jews remained Zionist, endorsed a two-state solution, opposed BDS, and rallied behind Israel whenever it was engaged in military conflict, yet at the same time the support for Israel among many Jews was "no longer unquestioning and uncritical."[55]

J Street Challenges AIPAC

J Street, founded in 2008 as a "pro-peace, pro-Israel movement," strove to create an alternative to AIPAC, yet the new organization remained part of the broader matrix of the Israel lobby. The Washington-based group worked closely mainly with liberal and centrist pro-Israeli Democrats in emphasizing the urgency of achieving a two-state solution. Unlike AIPAC, J Street strongly condemned Israeli settlements in the Occupied Territories, lobbied in favor of the Iran Treaty, and opposed the Israeli plan to annex portions of the West Bank.

Like AIPAC, however, J Street was a strongly Zionist organization that lobbied in favor of the outsized and uniquely favorable congressional funding of military assistance for Israel. J Street thus cultivated the special relationship, Israeli militarism and the strategic partnership with the United States. Like AIPAC, J Street condemned the general BDS call but unlike AIPAC did not rule out boycotting companies engaged in settlement activity beyond the 1949 Green Line.[56]

Growing rapidly amid Israel's brutal assaults on Gaza, J Street formed a PAC, which raised millions of dollars and built a national network of followers. J Street's budget grew from $1.5 million in 2008 to about $10 million in 2019. Like AIPAC, J Street held an annual conference, which attracted headline figures including Israeli politician Tzipi Livni and Vice President Joe Biden. J Street spent $5 million advertising its support for the Iran nuclear agreement--about a quarter of what AIPAC spent opposing it.[57]

The mainstream Israel lobby condemned the rise of a liberal Jewish lobby. In 2014 the Conference of Presidents of Major American Jewish Organizations, interlinked with AIPAC throughout its history, rejected a proposal to admit J Street even though it clearly had become a major Jewish organization. "People whose views don't fit with those running longtime organizations are not welcome, and this is sad proof of that," J Street President Jeremy Ben-Ami said in response to the vote of exclusion. "It sends the worst possible signal to young Jews who want to be connected to the Jewish community, but also want to have freedom of thought and expression."[58]

Although J Street embraced Israel as a "Jewish homeland," the liberal group unlike AIPAC condemned the Nation-State Law that officially proclaimed Israel as a "Jewish state" with Hebrew as the official language. Expressing "deep sadness, anguish and fear for the future," J Street condemned the 2018 law as unnecessary and discriminatory. "The new law asserts the primacy of Jews in the nation at the expense of the equal status of other citizens," J Street declared, "and it erodes the very foundation of democracy on which the country was built seventy years ago."[59]

At its annual conference in fall 2019, J Street hosted Democratic presidential hopefuls including Bernie Sanders, a Jew and persistent critic of Israeli policies who clearly would not have been welcomed at an AIPAC meeting. "The Palestinian people have a right to live in peace and security," Sanders declared, adding, "It is not anti-Semitism to say that the Netanyahu government has been racist. That is a fact." Sanders said the United States should "leverage" its $3.8 billion in annual military aid to "demand" Israel respect "human rights and democracy" and "negotiate an agreement that works for all parties," a position J Street and of course AIPAC opposed.[60] When Sanders emerged as a serious threat to compete for the nomination, the Democratic Majority for Israel, an AIPAC-affiliated "super PAC," launched a television advertising campaign attacking the Vermont senator.[61]

In December 2019 J Street lobbied heavily for a congressional resolution affirming that "only" a two-state solution could ensure "Israel's survival as a Jewish and democratic state and legitimate the aspirations of the Palestinian people for a state of their own." The non-binding resolution also affirmed "ironclad commitments" of US military assistance, which Sanders had called into question. Republicans, by now committed to permanent Israeli colonial occupation of "Judea and Samaria," opposed the measure, which passed 266-188. Rep. Tlaib and other progressives also opposed it. Appearing in the House with a *kuffiyeh* draped around her neck, Tlaib denounced the two-state framework as an "unrealistic, unattainable solution, one that Israel has made impossible, but also one that legitimizes inequality, ethnic discrimination, and inhuman conditions."[62]

Like J Street, Americans for Peace Now (APN)--sister to the eponymous Israeli organization--opposed the occupation and settlements and advocated a two-state solution while otherwise supporting Israel and Zionism. Like J Street, APN rejected BDS for targeting the nation of Israel with economic boycotts but did not oppose those focused solely on campaigns targeting economic links to Israeli settlements beyond the 1967 lines.[63] While opposed to BDS, both J Street and APN condemned the campaigns aimed at repressing free speech critical of Israel (see next chapter).[64]

Jewish Voice for Peace

To the left of the mainstream J Street as well as APN was Jewish Voice for Peace (JVP). Unlike J Street and APN, JVP was a thoroughly progressive Jewish organization that in no way functioned as part of the Israel lobby. JVP was sharply critical of Israel and fully supportive of the BDS campaign.

Founded in 1996, JVP rejected equating Jewishness with unquestioned support for Israel, called for withholding all US military aid to Israel until the occupation and settlements ended, and declared it could support either a one-state or two-state solution. JVP advocated "progressive Judaism for Palestinian rights" and backed up the claim by publicly endorsing BDS in 2015.[65] In 2019 the organization boasted 18,000 members in more than 70 chapters, youth, cultural, and advisory groups, and some 250,000 online supporters. Despite this growth the organization brought in only $3.7 million according to 2019 tax declarations, a paltry sum in comparison with AIPAC.[66]

JVP rejected "trying to be an alternative AIPAC" and instead emphasized "claiming our space" as a grassroots movement outside the uncritically pro-Israel mainstream. The "coming out moment" for JVP arrived in November 2010 with a coordinated disruption of a speech by Netanyahu before the Jewish Federation General Assembly meeting in New Orleans. JVP protesters reversed lobby propaganda by shouting, "The occupation delegitimizes Israel!" and "Loyalty oaths delegitimize Israel!" The outbursts stunned Netanyahu, accustomed to fawning support from American Jews. The protesters were quickly escorted from the hall only to be followed moments later by another orchestrated interruption of the Israeli leader's speech. The protesters were shut down with increasing vigor and had the banners they unfurled torn to shreds, one by a man using his teeth.[67]

JVP also launched Deadly Exchange, a campaign against a rapidly growing number of law enforcement exchange programs in which US police personnel, immigration officers, border patrol, and FBI met primarily to learn from their Israeli counterparts—accustomed to dealing with "terrorists." JVP condemned the collaboration for encouraging the "worst practices" in which both countries engaged, including racial profiling, repressive policing, shoot-to-kill policies, deportation and detention, and surveillance and spying.[68]

The routine exchanges "completely whitewash Israel's occupation and apartheid," JVP charged. The group was "disturbed to learn" that "many Jewish organizations" including Jewish Federations, the ADL, and the Jewish Institute on National Security of America (JINSA) supported the "deadly exchange" of thousands of security officials annually.[69] JVP's critique of police violence and linkage with Israeli repression resonated in the wake of the nationwide demonstrations that erupted following the Minneapolis police killing of George Floyd in May 2020.

Another grassroots group, IfNotNow, arose in the midst of Israel's 51-day military assault on Gaza in 2014. "While the out-of-touch establishment claims to speak for our community, we know that American Jewry is eager for change," the group declared. IfNotNow called for an end to the war on Gaza as well as the occupation, but distinguished itself from JVP by stopping short of endorsing BDS.[70] Still other small Jewish grassroots organizations emerged as the new century brought "an expansion and proliferation of Jewish social justice and environmental groups."[71]

Although the dissident Jewish groups had minimal funding in comparison with AIPAC and its allies, they were making an impact on popular discourse nonetheless. The increasing numbers of American Jews speaking out against Israeli repression underscored that AIPAC and its cohorts could no longer rely on unquestioned support from its onetime core constituency. Jewish dissidence, conjoined with continuing Palestinian resistance, thus posed a potential threat to the Israel lobby's mission to command a hegemonic discourse.

Chapter 10
Repressing Free Speech

The growing human rights-based resistance to Israeli policies provoked a predictably fierce reaction from Israel and its American lobby. Leveling baseless charges of anti-Semitism, the lobby attempted to undermine freedom of speech in the United States and to criminalize opposition to Israel's repression of Palestinian human rights. Unquestioning support for Israel abroad thus began to erode American freedom at home.

By highlighting Israel's repression of Palestinians, the BDS movement posed a potentially lethal challenge to the signature Zionist propaganda theme, namely that Israel was the peace-seeking "sole democracy" of the Middle East. Israel and its supporters reflected this concern when they charged that BDS sought to "delegitimize" Israel.

AIPAC and affiliated lobby groups intensified their campaigns as BDS began to mount "a robust and sustainable response to longstanding orthodoxy in the United States that excuses, justifies, and otherwise supports discriminatory Israeli government policies," the New York-based Center for Constitutional Rights (CCR) reported. Rather than contend with the advocacy on its merits, the Israel lobby deployed its financial resources and political influence to pressure universities, government actors, and other institutions to "to censor or punish advocacy in support of Palestinian rights."[1]

In 2010 the Reut Institute, an influential Israeli think tank, advocated a campaign of "attack" and "sabotage" against the rising movement for justice in Palestine. The Institute's reports emphasized that traditional Israeli strategic doctrine, focused on military threats, was outdated. In its place the global "delegitimization network" now posed the primary "existential threat" through efforts to promote a political "implosion" in Israel, modeled on the end of apartheid and the collapse of the Soviet empire. The report found particularly menacing the threat of a "coalescence behind a 'one-state solution' as a new alternative framework."[2]

Israel thus approached the BDS movement through "the language and metaphor of war," as Sunaina Maira notes. The lobby unleashed "ferocious, well-funded, and highly orchestrated campaigns opposing the boycott and BDS, relying on strategies of defamation, intimidation, and lawfare." The effort became a focal point for virtually every lobby affiliated pro-Israeli group and organization, from the ADL and AIPAC to the ZOA.[3]

The CCR uncovered hundreds of efforts to "intimidate activists for Palestinian human rights, chill criticism of Israeli government practices, and impede fair-minded dialogue." Such actions often had the "desired effect" of spurring punitive responses, sanctions, censorship, cancellations of events, intrusive investigations, even criminal prosecutions. Activists and their free speech "were routinely maligned as uncivil, divisive, antisemitic, or supportive of terrorism."[4]

Israel and the lobby unleashed attacks and smears against BDS proponents but at the same time stepped-up propaganda depicting Israel as a tolerant, forward-looking society. Israel trumpeted its toleration of gay, lesbian, and transgender people, which critics derided as "pink-washing"; cultivated allies among American Indians ("red-washing"); depicted the society as a global leader in science, technology, engineering, and math ("STEM-washing"); and claimed to be a leader in environmental consciousness ("green-washing").[5] All of these claims were designed to emphasize that Israel was a progressive society and thus far from a reactionary apartheid regime. Some, notably the claim to high-level environmental consciousness, were blatantly false, as Israel was in a reality a heavy polluter of the promised land.[6]

In March 2017 Israel's Mission to the UN hosted an "Ambassadors Against BDS" summit in New York. Gidi Grinstein, an Israeli government adviser and founder of the Reut Institute, declared, "Our community invested 20 times" the resources in 2016 as in 2010, yet he asked, "Why are we not winning?" Israel's UN Ambassador Danny Danon conceded that the BDS movement was "still active and still strong" and called for a united effort to "eliminate BDS on our campuses."[7]

The Battle on Campus

BDS activism as well as the reaction to it centered on college campuses, which the lobby had for decades identified as a crucial arena for its pro-Israel advocacy. The campaign, often with willful support from university boards and administrators, struck blows against free speech and freedom of expression at colleges and universities across the country.

Lobby organizing on campuses dated to the 1940s and gained momentum over the years. In 1993, in conjunction with the AIPAC annual conference, the lobby had launched a new "Young Leadership Program" in which "AIPAC-trained activists at colleges and universities" throughout the United States received instruction on how to combat "efforts by Israel's detractors . . . to intensify their attacks on the Jewish state."[8]

In the twenty-first century, the lobby stepped up its activism to "reposition" the debate on Israel amid rising criticism of the repression of the Second Intifada. "AIPAC campus activists recently came to Washington to explore how to make their schools assets to the American pro-Israel movement," the *NER* reported in 2005.[9] The lobby also began to sponsor the "AIPAC Campus Allies Mission to Israel," which provided 10-day trips taking "non-Jewish campus political activists to Israel to experience the Jewish state firsthand."[10]

The lobby brought selected college students to its yearly conference in Washington for the "annual Campus Awards Dinner, during which AIPAC presents awards recognizing the most accomplished AIPAC-trained student activists and supportive campus professionals in the nation."[11] The lobby also targeted high schools, conducting three-day "summits" in Washington for "pro-Israel high school students and education professionals." In 2010, the NER reported, "More than 500 teenagers, facilitators and advisors from 131 high schools across the country came to Washington, D.C., for AIPAC's sixth annual Schusterman Advocacy Institute High School Summit."[12]

The lobby stepped up its involvement on campuses in 2013 when the academic boycott scored a victory as the American Studies Association voted to endorse BDS. Other small academic subgroups, such as the Association for Asian American Studies and the Native American and Indigenous Studies Association, endorsed BDS but several major academic groups considered and rejected the call, including the Modern Language Association, the American Anthropological Association, and the American Historical Association.[13]

The historic champion of academic freedom, the American Association of University Professors (AAUP)--which had supported the boycott of South Africa--reversed itself when the focus was on Israel. Insisting that its opposition was rooted in "academic freedom and the free exchange of ideas," AAUP ignored the absence of academic freedom—or freedom in general—in occupied Palestine. As two scholars noted in opposition, the AAUP formulation was "inconsistent with past policy and practice," reflecting an "exceptional exoneration that the AAUP grants to Israel alone among states."[14]

The AAUP opposition to BDS cemented under Cary Nelson, who served as president from 2006 to 2012. Nelson was a dedicated Zionist who equated BDS with anti-Semitism and delegitimization of Israel. After his tenure at AAUP Nelson advocated the decision by his home institution, the University of Illinois, to withdraw a commitment to hire

Steven Salaita, a professor and outspoken critic of Israel's indiscriminate campaign in Gaza. Nelson subsequently edited a tendentious, 500-page anthology entitled, *The Case Against Academic Boycotts of Israel.*[15]

The Israel lobby also "captured" Hillel, the world's largest campus Jewish organization, in an effort to ensure that it reflected exclusively Zionist and uncritically pro-Israeli discourse. Founded in 1923 and with some 550 chapters in North America and a few dozen in other countries, Hillel had long provided a presence on college campuses emphasizing a commitment to Jewish religion and culture.

In 2010 Hillel International adopted a new "Standards of Partnership" policy that forbade hosting or partnering with organizations deemed anti-Israel or, specifically, those in support of BDS.[16] The next year the casino mogul Adelson and his wife pledged $1 million for a program placing Zionists in Hillel throughout North America "to assist with Israel education and advocacy."

The lobby-controlled Hillel parent organization forced cancellations of speakers and events and threatened lawsuits against universities. Hillel thus transitioned from "a religious and cultural organization in which a variety of opinions were tolerated, to a wing of a hardline pro-Israel lobby" intolerant of dissent. In 2015 at Swarthmore College, when Jewish students tried to discuss BDS and Palestine issues at the campus Hillel, the parent organization declared it would sue the university if the event were held on site. Organizers relocated the discussion to another venue on campus.[17]

Liberal Jews fought back through Open Hillel, which sought to eliminate the exclusionary practices of campus Hillel out of respect for "the diversity of viewpoints found in the communities that they serve." Open Hillel emphasized that "events, programs, membership, and leadership" should be "open and accessible to all," adding, "We are united not by a shared perspective on Israel/Palestine, but by a shared commitment to Jewish values of open discussion and debate."[18]

The right-wing Republican Adelson collaborated with Democratic Party pro-Israel donor Haim Saban and CUFI in the campus campaign to shut down critical speech on Zionist repression. The two Jewish billionaire lobby donors pumped $50 million in startup funds for the new anti-BDS group, the Campus Maccabees, and named as its head David Brog, the leader of CUFI. Brog, a Harvard Law School graduate who had been credited with reining in the apocalyptic Hagee and making CUFI more amenable to a broader range of evangelicals, was married to an Israeli-American and was a cousin of former Israel prime minister Ehud Barak.[19]

The media watchdogs CAMERA and FLAME kept up a steady drumbeat of vitriolic attacks on academic and other critics of Israel, but the lobby stooped to new depths with the launch of Canary Mission, a web site dedicated to anonymous cyber-stalking and harassment of college students and faculty. While the BDS campaign deliberately exempted individuals, the anti-BDS movement deliberately targeted them. Beginning in 2014, the site showed the names, photographs, and biographies of scores of students and academics who had been critical of Israeli policies. Adopting the shopworn cliché of the canary in the coal mine, the site claimed it was "created to document the people and groups that are promoting hatred of the USA, Israel and Jews on college campuses in North America."[20]

An undercover mole posing as an uncritical Zionist but actually working for the Al-Jazeera television network infiltrated and exposed by means of a repressed but covertly leaked film, "The Lobby—USA," the virulent tactics of lobby extremists, including financier Adam Milstein's lead role in funding Canary Mission.[21] The "fear-mongering McCarthyesque agenda of Canary Mission," which attempted to sully the career prospects of college students, let alone professors, was too much even for a group of pro-Israeli opponents of the BDS movement, who denounced it. The AAUP also condemned Canary Mission.[22]

Attacks on Student Groups

From 2014 to 2019 Palestine Legal, an organization founded in 2012 and dedicated to protecting the legal and constitutional rights of advocates of justice in Palestine, responded to some 1,500 incidents of attempted suppression of US-based Palestinian advocacy. Most of these centered in college campuses. Tactics included urging donors to threaten to withdraw funding from schools that did not attempt to stifle pro-Palestinian activism, as well as threats to spread publicity that might weaken community support for universities.[23]

While the nationwide lobby campaign to demonize BDS, suppress free speech, and exercise a chilling effect on student activism failed to bring a halt to initiatives, the leveling of "baseless accusations of anti-Semitism" could succeed in "diverting activists, students and professors from their work of advocating for Palestinian rights," Amira Mattar of Palestine Legal pointed out. "The more time an activist spends having to respond to baseless charges, the less time they have to focus on such issues as settlements, diversion of water, and human rights in Palestine." Noting that many of the legal challenges against Students for Justice in Palestine (SJP) and other activists were baseless, Maria LaHood, deputy legal director of CCR noted, "It doesn't always matter if they win, they still succeed in disrupting the efforts of the advocacy groups."[24]

At the same time, however, the avalanche of attacks on free speech revealed the lobby's insecurities over the extent to which Palestinian advocacy has entered into mainstream organizations and especially college campuses. "As the movement grows in the United States, so does the effort at suppression," LaHood pointed out.[25]

Palestine Legal, CCR and other defenders of free speech on college campuses stymied a lobby-inspired effort by Fordham University to deny the startup of an SJP chapter at the private university in New York City. In August 2019 a New York Supreme Court judge rejected as baseless Fordham University's claim that an SJP chapter would create "polarization" on campus. The jurist concluded Fordham's "disapproval of SJP was made in large part because the subject of SJP's criticism is the State of Israel" and came "in spite of the fact that SJP advocates only legal, nonviolent tactics aimed at changing Israel's policies."[26]

In November 2019 a lobby campaign tried but failed to shut down the National Students for Justice in Palestine meeting in Minneapolis. An Israeli government-sponsored App advised people to complain of an unsafe environment at the meeting site, the University of Minnesota (UMN) campus, while anonymous websites smeared the organizers with groundless accusations of support for terrorism. UMN rejected calls to cancel the conference, which went ahead, attracting 350 participants.[27]

In October 2019, Chancellor Robert Jones of the University of Illinois at Urbana-Champaign--a campus that had proven hostile to free speech on Palestine in the Salaita case--dispatched an email equating a Palestinian student presentation on Israel with anti-Semitism. The Student Government responded by voting overwhelmingly to condemn the chancellor's false conflation of criticism of Israeli repression with anti-Semitism.[28]

On March 6, 2020, just before the Corona virus shut down the campus, Columbia University President Lee Bollinger condemned a student referendum calling on Columbia to divest from companies complicit in Israeli human rights violations. Bollinger parroted Israel and lobby propaganda equating BDS with anti-Semitism by declaring without citing any evidence or examples that BDS reflected a "mentality that goes from hard-fought debates about very real and vital issues to hostility and even hatred toward all members of groups of people simply by virtue of religious, racial, national or ethnic relationship."[29]

Pro-Israel lobby groups sponsored a follow-up petition signed by more than 70 Columbia faculty members applauding "our president's condemnation of anti-Semitism in its many forms." The letter-signing campaign was initiated by the Academic Engagement Network (AEN), a lobby watchdog group created to oppose efforts to "delegitimize" Israel. It seeks to muzzle groups like SJP and proponents of BDS while at the same time claiming it supported "campus free expression and academic freedom." As evidenced by its website, AEN has sponsored scores of letter-writing and smear campaigns on campuses across the country.[30]

In early March 2020 at Bard College two SJP students were cleared of baseless charges of anti-Semitism sparked by their criticism of a panel discussion featuring a Harvard emeritus professor, Ruth Wisse, who once declared, "Palestinian Arabs are people who breed and bleed and advertise their misery." Palestine Legal came to the defense of the two students, pointing out that they "disagreed with the speakers' viewpoint that Palestinians are undeserving of equal human rights." The two students underwent an investigation by a panel of Bard professors, who in the end cleared them of any wrongdoing. Bard's President Leon Botstein acknowledged the students had done nothing wrong and were in compliance with the campus policy on free speech.[31]

In April 2020 the SJP chapter at Tufts University in Boston received the Collaboration Award from the Office of Campus Life in recognition of a campaign it waged in support of Deadly Exchange, a program that condemns Israeli training of US police forces in methods of repression. The Tufts SJP chapter had collaborated with some 20 other groups to call into question the campus police chief traveling to Israel for training at a "counter-terrorism seminar," which SJP argued represented a larger pattern of militarization of the campus police and mistreatment of people of color.

The day after the announcement of the award, Tufts administrators—the president, the provost, and deans—declared, "We strongly disapprove of this award," citing SJP support for BDS. The administrators proceeded to parrot lobby propaganda equating BDS with anti-Jewish prejudice. Lobby influence clearly lay behind the Tuft's administrators' *smearing of their own students*, as their action came on the same day that "a barrage pro-Israel groups released condemnation of the award," Mattar pointed out. "This explains why the university president and the provost, who normally would never have gotten involved in a student award decision, took such a direct and active role."[32]

Weaponizing Charges of Anti-Semitism

By the time of Trump's election, the Israel lobby already "routinely equate[d] anti-Zionism with anti-Semitism," but the election of the right-wing president spurred efforts to outlaw free speech on the subject.[33] Beginning in 2016 the lobby's congressional supporters introduced the Anti-Semitism Awareness Act, legislation that would enable the Department of Education to stifle campus free speech on Israel. The legislation, backed by scores of lobby organizations, was rejected in 2016 but continually reintroduced in subsequent years. Under the proposed law, charging Israel with having racist policies or applying "double standards" by singling out Israel for criticism would be tantamount to anti-Semitism.[34]

Although the Anti-Semitism Awareness Act was blatantly unconstitutional, and presumably therefore could never be enacted into law, merely proposing it advanced the lobby agenda of tarring critics of Israel and proponents of BDS with anti-Semitism. The proposed law exercised a chilling effect on individuals as well as activist groups such as SJP. With Trump issuing a series of executive orders tightening border control and putting into effect bans targeting select Muslim immigrants, the political pressures closing in on Muslim students and professors were palpable. The threat of lobby-orchestrated smears presumably discouraged many professors and students from taking up research on Israel-Palestine. Clearly it was much safer for students, career-minded academics, and timid university presses to bypass the subject altogether.

Proponents of the assault on free speech—AIPAC, the Simon Wiesenthal Center, the ZOA, and Christian Zionist groups, among scores of them—insisted that criticism of Israel and support for BDS amounted to an anti-Semitic discourse that was creating a hostile climate for Jewish students and citizens. The liberal groups J Street and APN, though opposed to BDS, also condemned the campaigns against the movement and efforts to repress freedom of speech.[35]

Evidence on campuses and in communities of BDS supporters intimidating Jewish students or citizens was minimal, whereas *actual* anti-Semitism had exploded at the Charlottesville, Virginia, rally in May 2017—wherein marchers chanted, "You Jews will not replace us!"—and in the massacre of 11 worshippers at a Pittsburgh synagogue the following year, as well as an attack on Jews in the Bronx in December 2019.

Analysis of the testimony of the backers of the Anti-Semitism Awareness Act suggested they "care very little about combating white supremacy, for that would put them at odds with the current administration and its supporters in Congress. It's not what the legislation addresses," Jewish history scholar Barry Trachtenberg pointed out. "It's primarily concerned with curbing political speech that threatens the continuing occupation of Palestine."[36] In January 2019 the spate of unconstitutional assaults on free speech in deference to Israel continued as Republicans introduced a bill—dubbed the "Strengthening America's

Security in the Middle East Act"—which backed legislation denying contracts or investments with individuals or companies either supporting or refusing to renounce BDS.[37]

With the legislation pending in Congress, Trump's Department of Education launched investigations of academic programs intersected with the Palestine question. Trump's appointees probed the program at Rutgers University and ordered Duke University and the University of North Carolina to recast their joint Middle East Studies program, citing alleged anti-Israel bias.[38] Such overt intrusions on academic programming on campuses were virtually unprecedented.

Efforts at the state as well as the national level to repress free speech critical of Israel were so plentiful that Palestine Legal created a separate web site to track them. By the end of 2020 the legal advocacy group counted 202 bills introduced, about a quarter of which had passed. Thirty states passed legislation criminalizing support for BDS as equivalent to anti-Semitism.[39]

Beginning with Illinois in 2015, states passed laws blacklisting foreign companies that supported BDS and outlawing the signing of contracts with them. Dismissing the legislative process as "tedious," New York's Democrat Gov. Andrew Cuomo issued an executive order to create a blacklist of institutions and companies and ordered the state to divest from them. In some states, individuals, churches, foundations, trade unions and other groups could be blacklisted for boycotting or divesting from corporations complicit in Israel's violations.

Lobbied by a wide range of Jewish and Christian Zionist groups, several states proposed laws that would punish individuals and institutions, including colleges and universities, for advocating a boycott of Israeli products, thereby defining political action and free speech as anti-Semitism. All of these actions were blatantly unconstitutional but nonetheless mounted a chilling effect on dissent before court challenges could come to fruition.[40]

By the summer of 2019 Israel and the lobby had pumped more than $100 million into the campaign to combat BDS and their efforts were beginning to make an impact. "Our efforts are producing results," declared Israel's "Strategic Affairs" Minister Gilad Erdan. Noting the spurt of state and national anti-BDS legislation, Erdan added, "Let's give a hand to all the governors and state legislators who supported" the new laws.[41]

In Fall 2020 the anti-free speech campaign expanded into the international online social media platforms Facebook, YouTube and Zoom. Responding to direct pressure from Israel and lobby groups, the three tech giants censored online seminars, which featured Palestinian and other activists, at San Francisco State University, the University of Hawaii and British and Canadian institutions. "This is a dangerous attack on free speech and academic freedom from Big Tech," warned Dima Khalidi, director of Palestine Legal. The effort to "stamp out discussion of Palestinian freedom comes in response to a systematic repression campaign driven by the Israeli government and its allies."[42]

The threat of online censorship loomed large, as webinars and web sites had long played a critical role in the BDS and Palestinian rights campaigns. Indeed, the effort to suppress these sources of information—directly instigated by lobby groups—underscored their effectiveness and the importance of the online platforms that were now being targeted for censorship in the campaign against free speech.

In addition to mounting the campaign of online censorship citing individual participants, Israel precluded hundreds of critics and BDS supporters from traveling to Israel or the Occupied Territories, while the Trump administration denied many Palestinians and Muslims entry into the United States. Among those prevented from entering the United States were the distinguished Palestinian diplomat Hanan Ashrawi and the BDS proponent Omar Barghouti. Both previously had freely traveled for many years and had family members residing in the United States.[43]

The effort to equate criticism of Israel with anti-Semitism profoundly influenced media coverage, including continuing exclusion of Palestinian voices and critics of Zionism. In December 2018 the "liberal" network CNN summarily dismissed commentator Marc Lamont Hill when he called during a speech at the UN for a "free Palestine from the river to the sea," by which he meant a one-state solution and a genuine democracy in Palestine. Had Hill called for a *Jewish* state between the Jordan River and the Mediterranean Sea "he would safely have continued holding down his job," Gideon Levy pointed out, but "in the heavy-handed reality that has seized control over dialogue in the United States, there's no room for expressions that may offend the Israeli occupation."[44]

Smearing Rep. Omar

Under the prevailing discourse, baseless charges of anti-Semitism were quickly transformed into established fact in the American national media. The most striking example was the vilification of Rep. Ilhan Omar, who won election to Congress in 2016 and proceeded to discuss Israeli repression and the actual double standards pertaining to the Israel lobby and US media.

In February 2019 Omar tweeted, "It's all about the Benjamins [$100 bills]" in reference to lobby influence in Congress. In another tweet she incorrectly referenced AIPAC campaign contributions. In fact, AIPAC is not allowed under its IRS designation to make direct contributions but instead oversees how much and on whom to spend money in congressional races, leaving to other Zionist PAC the routine task of doling out the dollars to the candidates.

Israel's vocal partisans in Congress, backed by the lobby, launched an Orwellian assault on Omar when she declared that she opposed Israel lobby efforts to promote "allegiance to a foreign country." The statement was purely factual insofar as AIPAC's *raison d'etre* was to raise revenue and work tirelessly to promote unquestioning public and congressional support for the foreign nation of Israel. Nonetheless, Omar apologized for her tweet, explaining that her intent was to emphasize the power of the lobby and not to "offend my constituents or Jewish Americans as a whole."[45]

While Omar never used the term "dual loyalty," her critics deployed the trope and charged that she had wielded it as an anti-Semitic slur against American Jews. Unreflective journalists including the supposedly liberal news media jumped on the bandwagon, affirming and spreading the word to the point that a canard effectively became the "truth," namely that Omar had trafficked in anti-Semitic discourse. What she had done in actuality was attempt to criticize Israel and illuminate the role of the lobby. These were the reasons for the campaign to smear and silence her.

While the lobby routinely condemned the alleged "double-standard," by which it charged Israel was held to higher standard than other nations by its critics, the Omar vignette illuminated the actual double standard that insulated Israel and the lobby from harsher criticism. As Omar pointed out, criticism of the "gun lobby," "big Pharma," and other lobbies was accepted as legitimate, but criticism of "Big Israel" remained subject to vituperative policing.

A double standard also prevailed pertaining to religious discourse. While Omar, whose family had emigrated from Somalia when she was a child, received a slew of death threats over the chimera of her anti-Semitism, her own religion of Islam was routinely demonized in twenty-first century America. Since the neoconservative-dominated George W. Bush administration, the trope "Islamic terrorism" had been deployed, equating the world's second largest religious tradition, with millions of law-abiding adherents in scores of countries all over the globe, with terrorism. No one invoking "Islamic terrorism" would be targeted for vilification or subjected to an attack led by a powerful nationwide lobby. Condemning Islam as an "evil" religion was widespread in American evangelical discourse, yet unacceptable was any suggestion that Israel might benefit from a powerful lobby—especially when the suggestion emanated from a brown-skinned, head-scarf wearing Islamic congresswoman.

Christian Zionists embraced the demonization of Islam and of Omar, as CUFI and other fundamentalists continued to bolster the Republicans and the Israel lobby. Selected by Trump to shore up his support among evangelicals, Vice President Mike Pence, a fundamentalist from Indiana, delivered. According to exit polls in 2016, 81 percent of "evangelical Christians" voted for Trump to 16 percent for Hillary Clinton.[46] In 2018 polls by the Pew Research Center showed a widening gap between Democrats and Republicans, with the latter far more likely to offer uncritical support of Israel and show little sympathy for Palestinians. More than a quarter of the voters in the midterm elections were white evangelicals, the vast majority of which were uncritically pro-Israel and voted Republican.[47]

Pence, who regularly deployed the trope "radical Islamic terrorism," took up the campaign of vilification against Omar, dubbing her an anti-Semite and calling on her to resign from Congress or at a minimum be removed from the House Foreign Affairs Committee—a position notably that would deny her a forum to comment on foreign policy issues. At the March 2019 AIPAC annual conference, Pence reiterated the slurs against Omar, receiving a standing ovation.[48]

In August 2019 Israel denied Omar and Tlaib, the two Muslim congresswomen, entry into the country. Tlaib had hoped to visit her grandmother in the occupied West Bank. The unprecedented restraint on travel to Israel by members of Congress aroused widespread condemnation, including even a modest protest from AIPAC.[49]

Quick to disassociate themselves from Omar's comments, Democrats announced they were preparing a resolution condemning anti-Semitism. The move provoked the Congressional Black Caucus to mount a defense, declaring that Omar was being vilified because she was brown-skinned and Muslim. There was evidence to back the charge. In 2018 the Jewish Democratic Council of America rebuked three Democratic candidates—Omar, Tlaib, and Rep. Alexandria Ocasio-Cortez (D-NY), who had referred accurately to an Israeli "massacre" in which unarmed protesters were shot to death at the Gaza border. Rep. McCollum also used the term massacre in reference to Gaza and condemned Israeli "bigotry, racism and segregation," but she was not rebuked by the Jewish Democrat monitoring group. McCollum is white while the other three women are brown-skinned and two are Muslim.

The intervention of the Black Caucus prompted the Democrats to revise the resolution to condemn anti-Muslim discrimination as well as anti-Semitism, angering several Zionist Democrats in the process. Trump maliciously weighed in, declaring the Democrats had become an "anti-Israel party. They've become an anti-Jewish party."[50]

Thoroughly aligned with the lobby, the Trump-led Republican Party denounced BDS as "anti-Semitic" in its 2020 reelection platform. Under some pressure from the progressive wing of the party, the Democratic National Committee platform upheld the right to free speech on BDS, though it opposed the boycott itself. Centrist Democrats prevailed over the Bernie Sanders-led progressive insurgency, which had called for linking US financial support of Israel to its compliance with international law and negotiations for a just peace. Instead, the platform committee upheld an "ironclad" US commitment to funding Israel--in spite of its pending plan to annex the Jordan Valley--and defeated proposals to confront the Zionist state over its illegal settlements and denial of Palestinian rights. Sanders delegates condemned the "unwavering support for a country that continues to thumb its nose at international law" even as "pro-Israel lobbyists openly bragged about their ability to strip out language critical of Israel."[51]

Clearly unnerved by the growing threat posed by the progressive Democrats, AIPAC lashed out with baseless charges of anti-Semitism. In early 2020 AIPAC ran Facebook advertisements picturing and labeling Omar, Tlaib, and McCollum as "anti-Semitic" and "maybe more sinister" than the extremist Islamic group ISIS (*Daesh*). McCollum put out a blistering response, condemning AIPAC as a "hate group" that was "weaponizing anti-Semitism and hate to silence dissent." AIPAC "wants its followers to believe that my bill, H.R. 2407, to protect Palestinian children from being interrogated, abused, and even tortured in Israeli military prisons is a threat more sinister than ISIS," McCollum responded. "This is not empty political rhetoric. It is hate-speech."[52] AIPAC offered a tepid apology and took down the ads but said it remained concerned about efforts to "undermine the US-Israel relationship."[53]

AIPAC also pledged that it would not target or attack members of Congress who criticized Israel's drive to annex portions of the Palestinian West Bank, actions that would affirm the death of the two-state solution, as long as the representatives stopped there and did not offer a broader critique or advocate any limitations on continued funding for Israel.[54] "The message is unusual," *The Times of Israel* acknowledged, as normally AIPAC "assiduously discourages public criticism of Israel."[55] Whether the pledge was sincere, however, was another matter. When a group of Democratic congresspersons criticized Israel for a demolition operation wiping out a West Bank village in November 2020, leaving 11 Palestinian families homeless, AIPAC's affiliate, the Democratic Majority for Israel, condemned the representatives.[56]

Trump's carte blanche enabling of Israel and the lobby created anxiety among Democrats, who feared that criticism of the Israeli excesses that

Trump supported would alienate wealthy Jewish Democratic donors. "Of the dozens of personal checks greater than $500,000 made out to the largest PAC for Democrats in 2018," the *New York Times* reported, "around three-fourths were written by Jewish donors." The "donor class," as one Democratic insider put it, was positioned politically "profoundly to the right of where the activists are, and frankly, where the majority of the Jewish community is."[57]

During the 2020 campaign the liberal wing of the lobby, J Street, reported raising more than $9 million in grassroots funding for Democrats, including some $2 million for Joe Biden.[58] By contrast, Sheldon Adelson and his Israeli-born wife alone reportedly contributed to the Republican cause more than $250 million, some $100 million directly to the Trump campaign.[59]

As he launched his campaign for reelection, Trump had declared that American Jews would be guilty of "great disloyalty" to Israel if they failed to support the Republican party.[60] Yet the Democrats not only prevailed under Biden in the 2020 campaign, they commanded the Jewish vote despite Trump's unprecedented support for Israel and efforts to depict the Democrats as hostile to the Zionist state. Even partisan Republican polls crediting Trump with a respectable 30 percent of the Jewish vote showed a 2-1 Democratic margin for Biden. A poll commissioned by J Street, however, concluded that Biden swamped Trump in the Jewish vote 77 percent to 21 percent. In either case, Jewish votes helped Biden prevail in close contests in pivotal states such as Arizona, Nevada, and Wisconsin.[61]

Trump "might have thought he was going to lure Jewish voters to the Republican Party with his lock-step alliance with the Israeli right," Michelle Goldberg pointed out. "Instead, by attempting to use American Jews as mascots for an administration that fills most of them with horror, he has spurred a renaissance on the Jewish left."[62]

While the administration's pro-Israeli propaganda and policies did not sway a once-dependable core constituency, American Jews, the Trump-Pence team won eight of every 10 votes cast by the much larger constituency--American evangelicals.[63]

Chapter 11
Conclusions

In the first half of the twentieth century, the Zionist movement spawned a massive migration of European Jews to Palestine. Determined to establish a state with as many Jews and as few indigenous residents as possible, the Zionists drove hundreds of thousands of people from their homes in the *Nakba* of 1948.

Proclaimed that same year, the new nation of Israel shared much in common with other settler societies, but what distinguished the Zionist state from them--in addition to the powerful driving force of historic anti-Semitism--was its late arrival on the stage of history. Unlike the earlier settler societies, including the United States, the birth of Israel coincided with the post-World War II era of decolonization, rising human rights consciousness, and recognition of the historic victimization of indigenous people. The late arrival of Zionist settler colonialism in Palestine thus established Israel's core identity as a *reactionary* settler colonial state.

As the quest for a Jewish state accelerated during World War II, the Zionist movement sought political support and funding from the most powerful country in the world, the United States. In the ensuing years, the Zionist lobby grew rapidly, became more assertive, and increased its influence over the US Congress. Israel and its American lobby fended off State Department diplomats and a series of presidents who attempted to rein in Israel's settler colonial aggression, violations of international law, and to negotiate a just peace. Time and again, as analyzed in this book, the Israel lobby effectively mobilized Congress and public opinion to contain political threats posed by a range of sources, including non-Zionist Jews, progressive human rights advocates, and politicians of both political parties.

In order to secure funding and political support, the Israel lobby—spearheaded by AIPAC and the Conference of Presidents of Major American Jewish Organizations, but also mobilizing scores of additional Zionist advocacy groups--had to obscure Israel's identity as an aggressive settler state that was running roughshod over indigenous Palestinians. Instead, Israel and the lobby framed Israel as a small and vulnerable democracy surrounded by hostile Arabs, much as Americans had confronted hostile Indian tribes in their own much romanticized frontier history.

Lobby propaganda went on to promote Israel as a Cold War ally and national security asset of the United States, paving the way for the continuous flow of massive US military assistance, which has far exceeded that provided to any other nation and is dispensed on uniquely favorable terms as well. After September 11, 2001, the lobby depicted Israel as an indispensable ally in the "global war on terror." As collaboration grew, the United States began to mirror the practices of the smaller security state, as it instituted increasingly militarized methods of policing as well as targeted assassinations.

As this book has shown, for decades the lobby played a pivotal role as the United States enabled all of the following: Israel's disdain for a negotiated settlement of the Middle East conflict; its contemptuous dismissal of the plight of Palestinian refugees; its cultivation of nuclear weapons in defiance of the global nuclear non-proliferation movement; its profusion of palpably racist, illegal and destabilizing Jewish-only settlements; its takeover of Jerusalem, much of the West Bank, and the Golan Heights; and its ongoing violent aggression, which has victimized Palestinians in the West Bank and the Gaza Strip as well as neighboring states notably Lebanon.

In more recent years the Israel lobby launched a campaign to criminalize political engagement and freedom of speech by equating criticism of Israel with anti-Semitism. Not content to repress Palestinian rights, the lobby now seeks to take them away from their fellow Americans.

Through disinformation campaigns, Americans are being coerced to embrace the founding myths and inherent racism of a reactionary settler colonial state. Americans are being pressured to roll back centuries of support for freedom of speech to comply with the demands of Israel and the lobby. The United States, which has struggled mightily to combat its own historic racism and acknowledge removal policies targeting indigenous North Americans, is now providing unfettered support to a state that embraces these reactionary policies.

Challenges Ahead for the Israel Lobby

Today Israel and the lobby are increasingly being called to account. They face unprecedented critical challenges worldwide. Israel has undermined its own much-vaunted claim to be the "sole democracy" in the Middle East. By formally proclaiming itself to be an exclusively "Jewish state," repeatedly reelecting a racist leader in Netanyahu, and extending its political boundaries deep into the West Bank as well as over the Golan Heights, Israel has become a de facto apartheid state. With its military assistance and security needs guaranteed by the most powerful nation in the world, Israel continues down the apartheid path as it roots out indigenous people in order to constructs roads, towns and settlements exclusively for Jews and to the isolation and immiseration of Palestinians.

At the beginning of the twenty-first century, Palestinians launched the BDS movement to mobilize worldwide economic and moral pressure against Israel's annexationist and apartheid policies. The campaign for Palestinian rights triggered a fierce reaction from Israel and the lobby, replete with intimidation and lawfare. But the growing grassroots opposition, fueled by global public awareness and the demand for human rights and international justice, is not receding. It seems clear that an increasingly broad constituency will continue to demand change and call into question unfettered US support for Israeli policies of occupation, exclusion and repression.

Under the ever-watchful eye of the lobby, nearly all Republicans as well as mainstream or centrist Democrats led by President Biden and Speaker of the House Nancy Pelosi maintain virtually unquestioned loyalty to Israel and the lobby. By contrast, a 2019 Center for American Progress poll found that 71 percent of Democrats and more than half of Americans as a whole favored conditioning US aid to Israel if it continued to construct illegal settlements and followed through with plans to annex portions of the West Bank.[1] The split between Democratic party elites and their base is fast reaching unsustainable proportions. By 2020 progressive elected representatives advocating justice in Palestine were entering Congress and holding on to their seats backed by growing public support.

For decades AIPAC flexed its muscle by targeting and defeating incumbents who criticized Israeli policies, but increasingly the tables have turned. In July 2020 Jamaal Bowman, a middle school principal from the Bronx, upset one of the lobby's perennial stalwarts, 16-term incumbent Rep. Eliot Engel, in the Democratic primary in New York's 16th congressional district. The chairman of the influential House Foreign Affairs Committee, Engel once declared that he would sit down with AIPAC on "every piece of legislation coming out of the Foreign Affairs Committee."[2] The Democratic Majority for Israel, an AIPAC affiliate, spent an estimated $2 million and launched a smear campaign against Bowman, but when the votes were tallied, he won by a landslide.[3] The lobby also targeted Rep. Ilhan Omar and heavily funded her Democratic primary opponent, but in August 2020 she also won in a landslide.[4]

In addition to confronting a loosening of their vice-grip on Congress, Israel and the lobby are increasingly alienating a core constituency: American Jews. Traditionally politically progressive, more and more American Jews are acknowledging that Israel's rejectionism has precluded a just peace. In July 2020 Peter Beinart--a longtime bellwether of liberal Jewish opinion who first commanded attention in 2012 with his pronouncement that Israeli repression in Palestine was precipitating a "crisis of Zionism"—provoked another "earthquake" within Jewish public opinion when he declared that the quest for a two-state solution was dead. In its stead he called for a one-state solution and transition to a genuinely democratic Israel. As Philip Weiss noted, "Beinart's apostasy has been a bombshell" in the American Jewish community.[5] Israel and the lobby thus face a future of growing grassroots Jewish opposition combined with the passing of aging Jewish megadonors personified by the casino mogul Sheldon Adelson who died at age 87 in 2021.

Most lobby fundraising continues to emanate largely from a relatively small number of right-wing, wealthy, and mostly Orthodox Jewish donors, but Israel and the lobby have also cultivated the ready support of Christian Zionists. Indeed, the metastasizing phalanx of right-wing evangelism, emanating from the grassroots and mobilized by organizations such as Christians United for Israel, has become a powerful underlying base of support for the lobby.

Continuing struggle over Palestine thus lies ahead and may well pivot on what happens in the United States rather than in the Middle East itself. AIPAC and the scores of other groups that comprise the Israel lobby understand this reality. That knowledge alone gives them an advantage over those who continue to downplay the political power of the lobby.

For decades the lobby has been successful not only in generating lopsided support for Israel but also in deterring analysis of its role in manipulating the political process. The Israel lobby became the most powerful lobby advancing the interests of a foreign country in all of American history, yet its pivotal role in the conflict is typically either willfully denied or naively downplayed.

Despite the high visibility of its annual conferences, AIPAC and other lobby organs do most of their propaganda work behind the scenes and especially in the halls of Congress. When critics including scholars call attention to the lobby's overweening influence, the pro-Israel advocacy groups invariably malign the works as fatally flawed if not anti-Semitic. The lobby thus routinely responds to critical analysis on the Israel-Palestine issue with disinformation and smear tactics. As a result, mainstream media, many scholars, and university presses steer clear of critical analysis of the Israel lobby.

Surprisingly, even some radical and pro-Palestinian scholars buy into the narrative that the lobby influence is exaggerated. Noam Chomsky and Norman Finkelstein, for example, have long downplayed the role of the lobby.[6] In a recent book the eminent Palestinian-American scholar Rashid

Khalidi acknowledged "the formidable power of the Israel lobby" and the absence of "an effective countervailing force in US politics. Any semblance of an Arab lobby," he added, "has never been more than a collection of high-priced PR shops, law firms, consultants, and lobbyists paid handsomely to protect the interests of the corrupt, kleptocratic elites that misrule most of the Arab countries." Nonetheless, Khalidi argued that the Israel lobby exercises influence "*only*" [his emphasis] when US national security elites "do not consider vital US strategic interests to be engaged." He argues that examples such as Obama's ability to secure the Iran nuclear agreement in 2015 (reversed by Trump three years later) and the US decision to sell AWACS to Saudi Arabia in 1981, show that when vital strategic interests are perceived as at stake the American executive will defy lobby opposition.[7]

It makes little sense to focus on rare and ephemeral defeats suffered by Israel and the lobby when they have prevailed for decades on far and away the most significant issue: precluding a comprehensive Middle East peace accord while enabling the relentless expansion of illegal Jewish-only settlements, which now number some 700,000 residents in the occupied Palestinian territories. Even if it were true, as Khalidi suggests, that American elites did not consider political stability in the Middle East a "vital strategic interest," some "credit" for that attitude must be attributed to Israel lobby disinformation campaigns.

In the final analysis, it is absurd to downplay the influence of a lobby that has made Israel--a small nation of less than nine million people--the most heavily subsidized foreign country in American history. Since the creation of Israel in 1948, the Congressional Research Service notes, "the United States has provided Israel $146 billion (current, or non-inflation-adjusted, dollars) in bilateral assistance and missile defense funding."[8]

While few people question that the gun, pharmaceutical and elderly person lobbies are highly influential, applying the same logic to the Israel lobby is somehow derided as hyperbolic if not a conspiracy theory. Academics and mainstream media have not done nearly enough to explain these realities to the public. Analysis of the special relationship and criticism of Israel are heavily policed by the lobby. Academic and journalistic timidity enables the Israel lobby to continue to vilify and marginalize critics even as AIPAC expands its ability to dish out distortion.

In February 2008 AIPAC christened its seven-story, 89,000-square-foot headquarters on H Street in Washington. A mere seven years later the lobby announced plans to add an additional two stories on top of the existing structure and a new 11-story attached office building. The multi-million dollar-expansion of the lobby headquarters would produce "a signature building . . . in a high-demand area," AIPAC told the Washington, D.C. Planning Commission.[9]

AIPAC anticipated dramatic growth in personnel and programming, thus the need for the expanded physical facilities. The lobby, which employed 125 people at the time of its 2008 expansion, had grown to 220 people in just seven years and was nearing 500 employees in 2020.[10]

By 2019 AIPAC was raising more than $100 million annually from donors, according to the lobby's tax returns, thus it had ample capitalization for its expanded programs and physical facilities.[11] Prior to the cancellation of its 2021 Washington conference owing to the Corona virus pandemic, the AIPAC annual event was attracting more than 18,000 people, including a majority of the members of Congress sitting alongside members of the Israeli Knesset.

One AIPAC-affiliated group started in 1996 by Eric Cantor, who championed Israel and the lobby while representing Virginia's seventh congressional district from 2001-14, illuminates growing Israel lobby efforts at the state level. In Virginia, as Grant F. Smith has revealed, a state agency known as the Virginia Israel Advisory Board (VIAB) has secured millions in taxpayer and other state funds to support the entry of Israeli companies into energy, defense, packaged foods and other industries. Some of the companies built their business in the illegally occupied territories. Propelled by the state's Jewish federations, the VIAB is building the wealth and lobbying resources of Israel advocates and has engaged in campaigns to rewrite the state's textbooks and otherwise stifle, through new laws, speech perceived as critical of Israel.[12]

AIPAC, which mobilizes the collective power of all the Israel affinity organizations, claims well over 100,000 members and has regional offices all over the country. In 2020, the broader lobby "ecosystem," taking into consideration scores of groups, was projected to consist of some 14,000 employees, many more thousands of volunteers, all backed by some $6.3 billion in revenue.[13]

Is it rational to suppose that the Israel lobby invests such effort and resources, yet has little impact on US public opinion and policy on Middle East affairs? AIPAC and its allies know better. They are waging an ongoing propaganda battle—and they are accustomed to winning. "Our detractors think we are vulnerable, that we will fold when we're pushed," AIPAC Director Howard Kohr recently declaimed. "But they don't know what we are made of!"[14]

The stakes are high in the struggle for justice in Palestine and for understanding of the power of Israel and the lobby within the United States. In addition to the financial costs to the American taxpayer—money that could and should go to the benefit of Americans--there are political, moral and national security costs and consequences as well.

The United States has undermined its oft-proclaimed commitment to liberty and democracy through its support of Zionist repression in Palestine and through its obeisance to a lobby serving the interests of a foreign power. The United States has also undermined the United Nations as a forum for peacemaking and the promotion of international justice. The repression of Palestinians through violence and discrimination undermines the essential principles of universal human rights and international law that the United States originally championed in the wake of World War II. Israel and the lobby have worked tirelessly and nearly always successfully to garner American favoritism in the UN—sometimes against the wishes of virtually every other country in the Security Council or the General Assembly—while at the same time eliminating even humanitarian support for Palestinians.

Unstinting support for Israel, along with controlling oil supplies and propping up Arab dictatorships as bulwarks against populism and radicalism, have been at the center of American foreign policy in the modern Middle East for decades. Throughout the postwar era, settler colonization of Palestine, encompassing the expulsion and continuous repression of the indigenous residents as well as the takeover of Jerusalem, has been the overriding geopolitical issue in Middle East politics and a source of continuous anger and unrest in the Arab-Muslim world. Though often elided, Israel's aggression and the occupation were a major impetus behind the September 11, 2001 attacks. Those assaults brought the Middle East conflict back home to the United States, which subsequently became mired in a series of failed "forever wars" in the region. American foreign policy in the Middle East--anchored by unbalanced support for a regional aggressor in Israel--has been a disaster of death, destruction and displacement, arguably commensurate in scope with the US debacle in Vietnam, and it should be acknowledged as such.

Propelling Change from the Bottom Up

Grassroots efforts are coalescing behind a much-needed new US policy in the Middle East—one that will embrace American values of justice and democracy and reject subservience to a lobby that serves the interests of a foreign country. Under a new paradigm of Middle East diplomacy, the United States should use its power and influence to pursue a balanced policy rather than financing and enabling Israel's racism and repression. The United States could still maintain a special relationship with Israel and could continue to guarantee the security of its residents while at the same time, however, rejecting the outsized funding for militarization as well as the pro-apartheid stance demanded by Israel and the lobby. The United States can and should become the driving force behind a peace accord that ensures the rights of the Palestinian people to live as equal citizens in their own homeland.

The United States should take these steps not only because they promote human rights, justice and equality but because they promote American national security as well. If Americans take these steps, the illegal and repressive occupation would cease to be a rallying point for millions of frustrated Arab and Muslim people who in the past have made the United States itself a target for their wrath. If Americans ceased to support settler colonialism and apartheid, the US role in the Middle East and the world would be strengthened rather than serving as motivation for terror groups.

It remains possible to create a unified state or some form of negotiated political entity in which Jews, Muslims, Christians, and others would be free to live, work, and worship in a shared space, with Jerusalem and its special places open and accessible to all. Israel is located in the Middle East, many of its citizens are Sephardic Jews who migrated from other Middle East countries, and Israel therefore has the potential to become a decolonized Middle Eastern nation.

Under US and international sponsorship, a one-state solution in which all citizens of Israel and Palestine would be equal could be put into effect. Jewish settler colonists are not going to leave Israel any more than American settlers will return Arizona or the Black Hills (or indeed the entire North American continent) to indigenous people. But no one would be required to leave their homes under a one-state democratic solution. Instead, Israelis could remain, and Palestinians could be enabled to return or alternatively if they chose, to receive compensation, as has been proposed many times in the past. Such a state or federation could serve as a powerful example for the world of post-colonial liberation. A decolonized, integrated, and less militant Israel would have tremendous potential to contribute to the technological advance, economic growth, and even political stability in the Middle East. With American and international support, an Israel transformed into a genuine multi-ethnic democracy could thus serve as a forward looking rather than a violently reactionary force in Middle East politics.

The above scenario may appear to be a tall order, yet history shows that dramatic change can occur with little warning at decisive historical moments. The Soviet Empire, riven with internal and external contradictions like the Israel of today, collapsed and transitioned with stunning rapidity from 1989-91. A few years later South Africa, like Israel an apartheid state facing a growing movement of boycott, divestment and sanctions, finally abandoned apartheid and transitioned to democracy. After decades of frustration, LGBTQ (lesbian, gay, bisexual, transgender and questioning, or queer) in much of the world, including Israel and the United States, have successfully demanded and achieved greater rights and inclusion.

The rise of the Black Lives Matter (BLM) movement, especially in the wake of the George Floyd murder in Minneapolis in May 2020, ignited a growing demand for meaningful racial reform. The wave of the anti-racist demonstrations in the United States, and all over the world, is in the process of ushering in meaningful social change and enhanced understanding of systemic racism and its legacies. The symmetry between historic American racial oppression and the suffocating occupation of Palestine and severe marginalization of Palestinians living inside Israel is palpable. Progressive forces and segments of the BLM movement have embraced full solidarity with the battle for justice in Palestine as well efforts to expose the distorted perspectives that are churned out by Israel and its lobby.[15]

The dramatic changes that are required in Middle East politics depend to a great extent on Americans coming to grips with the irrefutable facts of Israeli racial repression and the lobby's distortions and assaults on free thought and free speech. Once a critical mass of Americans understands that they are financing racial repression and aggression, Israel and its lobby will be called to account. At a minimum, the United States should make all future financial assistance and political support of Israel dependent upon a just solution in Palestine. In order to make this approach a reality, the lobby's grip on Congress must be publicized, condemned, and broken. The liberation of Palestine—and of Americans from an oppressive lobby—is on the agenda of humanity.

Appendix

The Biblical Narrative and Jewish Monotheism:

A Brief History

At a meeting of the UN Security Council on April 29, 2019, Danny Danon, Israel's UN representative, held aloft the Bible and declared, "This is the deed to our land." The 47-year-old Likud politician and former IDF official averred, "The Jewish people's rightful ownership of *Eretz Israel*, the land of Israel" was "well documented throughout the Old Testament and beyond." The Bible thus provided the modern state of Israel an "everlasting covenant" to "all the land of Canaan."

Danon's dramatic reading—at one point he paused, attached a *kippah* to his head, and read from the Bible in Hebrew—went viral on the internet, but it was not the first time an Israeli invoked biblical sanction in an effort to justify Israeli ownership of the "Jewish communities of Judea and Samaria." The notion of the "return" to ancient Israel—following, as Danon put it, a "2,000-year exile"—long has been inextricably linked with the Zionist movement and notably with the Christian Zionist movement as well.[1]

In 1936 Israel's patriarch, David Ben-Gurion, though an agnostic, had declared, "The Bible is our mandate."[2] AIPAC went biblical in the aftermath of the June 1967 war, justifying Israel's retention of the occupied territories by explaining, "Jews have lived in *Eretz Israel* since the days of Abraham, about 2000 B.C." Israel thus had a legitimate claim to the land "going back to the Bible. And no state has such an impressive international birth certificate."[3]

Asked in 2019 why he condemned American advocates of ethnic white supremacy in the United States, while justifying the "Jewish state" in Israel, Morton Klein, head of the ZOA, responded, "Israel is a unique situation" because it was "a Jewish state given to us by God." He added, "God did not create a state for white people or for black people." Klein was a right-wing conservative, but Sen. Chuck Schumer, a liberal Democrat from New York, speaking at the AIPAC Conference in 2018, declared: "Of course, we say it's our land, the Torah says it."[4]

Jews were not alone in invoking the Bible as evidence of divine authority for the creation of Israel. In 2013 extensive polling by the Pew Research Center found that 44 percent of the American public answered affirmatively to the question, "Was Israel given to the Jewish people by God?" Eighty-two percent of white evangelicals said Yes.[5]

With such large numbers of Jews and Christians, Israelis and Americans, citing the authority of the Bible, the issue is clearly relevant to the history of the Israel-Palestine issue. The biblical narrative of "the land of Israel" therefore must be interrogated rather than dismissed as a distant and no longer relevant "ancient history." Clearly it remains relevant to a lot of people.

Historical analysis shows that the evolution of Jewish monotheism was a cultural rather than a divine project. It is also a remarkable story of a people, the powerful religious tradition that they made, and the persecution they suffered.

At the core of the Hebrew Bible is the existence of a single, all-powerful god, as told in the first five books, or the Pentateuch (Genesis, Exodus, Leviticus, Numbers, and Deuteronomy). The deity, Yahweh, designated the Israelites as his chosen people and they entered into a covenant with him. The relationship was fundamental: the Israelites agreed to be his chosen people and in return Yahweh agreed to be their god for all eternity.

The biblical covenant of the ancient Hebrews subsequently emerged as arguably nothing less than "the single most powerful cultural construct yet built by humankind," as Donald Akenson avers. The Covenant acted "as a romantic magnet to later generations of diaspora Jews and as an ethical and moral justification of Jewish actions in the Holy Land." For Covenant societies, "the scriptures have acted culturally and socially in the same way the human genetic code operates physiologically," Akenson suggests, adding: "The great code is about right, and the inevitable biblical concomitant, might."[6]

Within Western culture the biblical narrative centering on ancient Israel provided a framework for Zionist settler colonization by overshadowing a broader history of ancient Palestine or the southern Levant. Through reification of ancient Israel, the Bible took command of the past, a form of "theocratic colonialism" that served as prelude to asserting control over the region. "Arabs and Muslims were left outside the realm of professional historical writings." Accordingly, efforts to "decolonize the history of ancient Palestine" require complicating and contextualizing the biblical narrative.[7]

For centuries belief in the veracity of the biblical narrative of the land of Israel dominated not only popular opinion but scholarship as well.[8] Skepticism surfaced during the Enlightenment, but it was not until the late nineteenth century that Julius Welhausen established a foundation for scholars to call into question the biblical narrative. The German scholar's research "largely eliminated an acceptance of the historicity of the referents of the Pentateuchal narrative, which includes not only the origin narratives of Genesis but also the patriarchal stories and the Mosaic traditions." Welhausen suggested that the biblical stories should be seen as "literary documents" and "that nothing historically dependable about earlier periods in Israel's history could be gained from them." This analysis became "the dominant critical interpretation by the end of the century."[9]

From the beginning the critical biblical scholarship pioneered by Welhausen encountered determined opposition in the academic world as well as popular opinion. Religion and Theology departments of universities and religious institutions throughout the Western world ensured the domination of "biblically inspired histories and archaeologies of ancient Israel."[10] Beginning in the last two decades of the twentieth century so-called "biblical minimalists" demonstrated the absence of historical foundation for many of the biblical stories, including the story of creation, the great flood, the wandering of the Jews, the exodus from Egypt, and the conquest of Canaan. Some of these scholars were driven from their academic positions.[11]

In order to assess the veracity of the Bible, it "must be analyzed historically without preconception just like any other document from antiquity."[12] Such analysis reveals that the Bible was less an effort to faithfully record historical events than a response to theological, allegorical and identity-driven motivations. Biblical narratives of ancient Israel, steeped in folklore, legend, and mythology, were purposefully constructed and reconstructed over the course of centuries. "It is obvious that the Bible's authors used old sources during the forming of the Old Testament text and that at a certain moment they selected some stories that were considered to be canonical, and removed others," Lukasz Niesiolowski-Spano points out.[13]

In recent years scholars in the disciplines of history, archeology, geography, and ethnography have employed a broader lens bringing into focus "the rest of Palestine's ancient polities, traditions and stories from the southern Levant."[14] Historical, archeological, and anthropological research has largely disproven the biblical narrative. British theologian Michael Prior alludes to the "virtually unanimous scholarly skepticism concerning the historicity of the patriarchal narratives." Israeli scholar Shlomo Sand declares that the saga of the ancient Jews has been "relegated to the status of fiction, with an unbridgeable gulf gaping" between the biblical stories and what is known of the actual history.[15]

Archeological excavations and historical reconstructions--the collection and assessment of writings, artifacts, bones, and chemical analysis of soil samples--have unearthed no evidence of the Israelites either living in Egypt or marching out of it "through the heavily guarded border fortifications into the desert and then into Canaan." Such a massive exodus would have been halted or in any event recorded in the extensive Egyptian records. Moreover, the exodus would have left behind remnant of encampments and other archeological evidence, yet none exists. According to the Israeli scholar Israel Finkelstein and the US scholar Neil Silberman, "The conclusion--that the Exodus did not happen at the time and in the manner described in the Bible--seems irrefutable when we examine the evidence at specific sites."[16]

Outside of the biblical narrative there is "no explicit mention of the man Moses in any ancient Egyptian or other texts," Thomas Romer points out.[17] No evidence supports the biblical account that the children of Israel wandered in the deserts and mountains of the Sinai Peninsula, where Moses was said to receive the Ten Commandments directly from God. There was no conquest of Canaan, which remained firmly under Egyptian control at the time of the supposed takeover. Scholars have (literally) uncovered myriad additional contradictions between biblical narratives and verifiable history. For example, research demonstrates that no walls existed at Jericho to come tumbling down, as recounted in the Book of Joshua when the Israelites were said to have defeated the Canaanites.[18] Kings David and Solomon may have existed yet, "The idea of a great kingdom, united under David and Solomon, comes more from the imagination of the authors of these books of the Bible than from any historical reality."[19]

While the Bible thus "cannot be used as a straightforward historical source," it nonetheless is not entirely fictional.[20] Many of its references to geographic sites and features as well as peoples (Egyptians, Canaanites, and the Israelites themselves) are verifiable. "The point at issue is not whether an ancient Israel ever existed," Nur Masalha points out, "but whether the historical ancient Israel was like the portrait in the Bible."[21]

Geographically situated within the Levant (modern-day Israel/Palestine, Jordan, Lebanon and Syria), Israel first appears in Egyptian records in 1210 BCE. As part of the "Fertile Crescent," an area with ample rainfall for productive agriculture, the Levant was perennially contested by surrounding empires. By the end of the thirteenth century Israel had established itself as a distinct clan or tribal grouping on the basis of material culture and cult rituals such as circumcision and refraining from raising or consuming pork. Israel remained under Egyptian authority until the pharaohs lost control of the Levant amid a series of upheavals of the late Bronze Age.[22]

The Israelite cult or kingdom (there is no historical evidence of the "twelve tribes" of biblical lore) thus arose within the indigenous communities of the Levant rather than as a result of a divinely sanctioned external invasion. Rather than conquering the "Canaanites," as per biblical mythology, the Israelites *were* the Canaanites, that is, they were among the "multiplicity of ethnic identities" within ancient Canaan. Prior notes, "Israel's origins were within Canaan not outside it." Romer adds, "The opposition we find in the Bible between 'Israelites' and 'Canaanites,' was in no way based on an existing ethnic difference, but is a much later theoretical construction in the service of a segregationist ideology."[23]

The invented tradition of distinct ethnic groups of Israelites and Canaanites became central within Zionist ideology to a mythical history of the Jews that is still taught today in Israeli schools and other Jewish and some Christian religious institutions. Until its refutation by Welhausen and his successors, the school associated with William F. Albright dominated both popular and scholarly views of ancient Israel, including an emphasis on drawing invidious comparisons in which a superior race of Israelites invariably displaced Canaanites, Philistines, and Amelkites. In his *From Stone Age to Christianity*, for example, first published in 1946, Albright explained it this way: "It often seems necessary that a people of markedly inferior type should vanish before a people of superior potentialities."[24]

In describing the supposed conquest of Canaan, Albright thus simultaneously alluded to and yet glossed the violent settler colonization of ancient Israel. As Pekka Pitkanen points out, maximalist interpretation of the Bible must confront the fact that "the early history of ancient Israel was defined by settler colonialism." The biblical narrative sanctions righteous violence, retribution, and slaughter, acts of ethnic cleansing and genocide that are characteristic of settler colonies and constitute war crimes under modern definitions of the terms. For example, in Deuteronomy 20: 16-18 God commands the Israelites to "save alive nothing that breathes" and to "utterly destroy" the Canaanites as well as the Hittites, Amorites, and Jebusites, among other groups. "Even if historically true," Pitkanen notes, "surely an ancient genocidal settler colonial process that relates to the birth of ancient Israel should be considered as ethically problematic." Adherents to maximalist biblical interpretation, Albright for example, thus engage in disavowal—another prominent characteristic of settler colonization—to elide the extreme violence sanctioned by the biblical narrative.[25]

The Israelites and Monotheism

By the ninth century BCE Egyptian authority had receded and the people who constructed an identity as Israelites grew in strength. They carried out numerous construction projects notably in the city of Samaria. In the next century the Levant came under control of the Assyrians, a militaristic empire known for its pitiless siege warfare. The Assyrians conquered Israel, sacking Samaria in 722 and deporting many of its residents while reducing the kingdom to vassal status. The Assyrian conquest scattered the Israelites to the south toward another small kingdom, Judah, and the modest settlement of Jerusalem. The Assyrians did not directly assault Jerusalem, but only because Judah acquiesced to vassal status.[26]

Traumatic events continued to plague the residents of Israel and Judah along with many other settlements and kingdoms, as powerful empires grappled for control of the Levant. Early in the sixth century the Babylonian Empire displaced the Assyrians as the new masters of the Near East. In 587 the Babylonians occupied Jerusalem, destroyed the temple, and carried out mass deportations from the kingdom of Judah.

The destruction of Jerusalem by the Babylonians, on top of the Assyrian conquest, created an existential crisis at the core of Judean and Israelite identity, as the king, the temple, and the God that it housed all had been destroyed. At this point major parts of the Bible notably Deuteronomy, which likely originated in the seventh century BCE, were revised with an emphasis on Jerusalem as a revered site and its temple at the center of an emerging monotheism.[27] Prior argues that "the fabricated myth of origins" emerged as part of a "process of 'nation'-building in the wake of the Babylonian exile, and perhaps later in the Persian period."[28]

The crafting of the biblical stories was a literary project, probably undertaken by priestly aristocratic elites, and intended to promote unification of the separate northern and southern kingdoms of Israel and Judah. These peoples had been conquered and scattered through the Egyptian and Assyrian conquests culminating in the "Babylonian captivity."

The term "Bible" stems from a Greek plural for books hence it can be viewed as a library or a collection of books that evolved over some 500 years in a complex process of drafting, revising, and redacting the various stories. The essence of the project remained consistent, however: the unification of a people with a powerful sense of destiny centered in the kingdom of Judah and free to worship in the rebuilt temple of Jerusalem. "Thus, the pan-Israelite idea, with Judah at its center, was born," Finkelstein and Silberman explain.[29]

The Bible constituted an epic anthology comprised of myths, legends, and heroic tales centered on a prophecy of the redemption of a chosen people in the wake of terrible hardship. But how could a people be "chosen" and yet subjected to such repeated conquests and traumas? Why did their god not protect them and instead allow them to succumb to other peoples with by implication palpably more powerful gods? The Bible provided the answers to these troubling questions with the creation of a single and all-powerful monotheistic god, a god who had not failed the peoples of Israel and Judah—rather they had failed him. Through their own lack of faith and failure to adhere to his commandments, the Israelites had shattered the covenant with Yahweh who therefore unleashed the Babylonians to chastise them.[30] Far from being weak, the God of Israel was almighty and willing to severely punish as well as liberate his chosen people.

The monotheistic god of Israel broke with the traditional practice in the ancient Mesopotamian world of polytheism or multiple gods. Reverence for a unitary god or a single deity above other gods, however, has been identified in ancient Egyptian and Persian traditions notably with the ancient prophet Zoroaster. Originating around Judah, Yahweh, the single god presented in the Bible was not unlike warrior and storm gods within other kingdoms and cults. The monotheistic god, represented for a time with an icon in the form of a bull, had gradually displaced multiple gods including a sun god. In addition, "It is highly likely that Yahweh had a goddess associated with him in Judah and consequently also in Israel," but she may have absorbed the blame for the catastrophic loss of the temple and in any event was cast aside.[31]

The Bible attests to the prior existence of other deities through God's many proscriptions against worshipping or representing them. Warning that he is a "jealous God," He commands in Exodus 20, "You shall have no other gods before me." Similarly, in Deuteronomy 17 God calls for death by stoning of anyone found "transgressing his covenant" by worshipping other gods of Israel, mentioning specifically those of "the sun or the moon."[32] Worshipping of solar and especially sun gods permeated Egypt and Mesopotamia at the time.[33]

The Bible stories responded to the existential crisis by unifying Israel to the north with Judah in the south as a single chosen people. By infusing the debacle that they had suffered with powerful theological meaning, the Israelites laid the foundation for recovery and redemption. The genius of the Bible, as the collection of epic stories began to cohere over centuries of revision and redaction, was the construction of an inspirational saga of origins, trials and tribulations, defeat, destruction, and finally redemption and recommitment to the covenant with an all-powerful monotheistic god. Biblical scholars believe the bondage in Egypt represented the actual bondage in Babylon, which had forced the Israelites to wander the desert. Abraham "functions as the unifier of Northern and Southern traditions bridging north and south."[34] Moses powerfully represents the diaspora of the Israelites, the miracle of liberation, and perpetual striving for the Promised Land.

Historic events facilitated the recovery of Jerusalem and rebuilding of the faith. In 539 BCE the Persian King Cyrus seized the city of Babylon bringing an end to the Babylonian empire and the captivity of Jerusalem.

Cyrus instituted a liberal policy permitting reconstruction of destroyed temples and allowing deported populations to return to their homes. Around the turn from the sixth to the fifth century the Israelites rebuilt the Temple of Jerusalem. Many Judean exiles remained in Babylon while others spread across the Levant and gradually filtered into the Mediterranean world as well.

Under the Persian Empire, Judah became the province *Yehud* and Judah-ites became *Yehudim*, or Jews. They began to reference the Pentateuch as the Torah, a term reflecting priestly revisions and redactions of the "Five Books of Moses." Jews and Judaism as a codified religious system thus came into existence only after the Babylonian captivity and were not firmly established until the subsequent Hellenistic era in the wake of conquests of the Levant by Alexander the Great of Macedon, culminating in 331 BCE.[35]

Even as Greek influence spread across the Near East, Jewish religious tradition coalesced around the shared origins, exile, destruction and redemption of the Jews, as well as their covenant with the all-powerful monotheistic god. Jewish worship as well as administrative affairs centered on the temple at Jerusalem while rituals such as circumcision, animal sacrifice, and observance of the Sabbath and Passover took hold. By the second century BCE synagogues (from the Greek word for "assembly") expanded throughout the Hellenistic world. The Torah continued to evolve, as fragile scrolls required constant recopying, which provided opportunity for revisions and redactions hence the Bible "received the present form only in the Hellenistic period."[36]

The translation of the Pentateuch into Greek, probably beginning in the third century BCE, was the crucial event in the evolution of Yahweh as a *universal* god for all humanity, not just the Jews. To be sure, the cult of Yahweh spread with the Jews, as they migrated into the Mediterranean basin and built synagogues for their worship. Yahweh transcended the Jews, however, as other religions notably Christianity and Islam adopted the concept of a unitary almighty god. A single god need not have a name to distinguish him from other gods hence Yahweh gave way to an unnamed deity, the Lord or simply God.

As Alexander's empire receded, Israel fell under control of the Persian Seleucid Empire. A revolt led by a prominent family secured independence of Judea from the Seleucids, a triumph commemorated by the eight-day celebration of *Hanukkah* (rededication) of the desecrated temple in 164 BCE. Internal conflict among Jews also undermined the Judean dynasty, prompting the arrival of the Roman general Pompey to arbitrate the clash in 63 BCE. Pompey decided to settle the matter by annexing Judea thus turning it into a vassal state of the Roman Empire.[37]

Jews frequently clashed with Roman imperial authorities and with non-Jewish residents of the empire. Gentiles criticized Jews for their monotheism and rejection of multiple Roman gods and for celebrating their own Sabbath as well as Jewish holidays. As the Roman historian Tacitus (56-117 CE) observed, the Jews "are distinguished from the rest of mankind in practically every detail of their life, and especially in that they honor none of the other gods, but show extreme reverence for one particular deity."[38]

In 38 BCE in the Egyptian city of Alexandria, vicious rioting erupted over the Jewish Passover celebration, as many Egyptians resented the story celebrated by the Jews of Moses leading them to liberation against the hated pharaoh. "Whole families, husbands with their wives, infant children with their parents, were burnt in the heart of the city by supremely ruthless men who showed no pity for old age nor youth, nor the innocent years of childhood," the Jewish philosopher Philo recounted. He and others appealed to Rome for protection and in 41 Roman Emperor Claudius directed the Alexandrians "to behave gently and kindly toward the Jews who have inhabited the same city for many years, and not to dishonor any of their customs in their worship of their God but to allow them to keep their own ways."[39]

Popular resentment of Jews combined with Jewish resistance to Roman authority caused ongoing political instability, which erupted anew and with dramatic consequences in 70 CE. The Romans summarily crushed a Jewish revolt, causing widespread damage in Jerusalem culminating in destruction of the Temple. The destruction left only the Western Wall or "Wailing Wall" of the temple, which endures to this day as a sacred place for Jews and others. Whether a group of Jews held out against the Romans at Masada in 73 CE is uncertain, but the narrative of their martyrdom became integral to the Jewish symbolic past.[40]

The Roman repression in 70 brought a decisive end to the so-called "second Temple" period in Jewish history. The Romans put down another revolt from 132-35 CE, which brought increased destruction and repression in and around Jerusalem. In the wake of the second rebellion the Romans instituted punitive policies against Jews, including prohibition of circumcision and other religious rituals, though the right to engage in these practices was later restored.[41]

The Romans incorporated Judea and Samaria into "Syria Palaestina," which became a regularly functioning imperial province until the Arab conquests of the seventh century CE. In addition to changing the name to Palestine, the Emperor Hadrian forced thousands of Jews into slavery. The Romans did not single out the Jews for repression, as they treated other recalcitrant minorities equally harshly. Nonetheless, stereotypes and resentment of Jews proliferated in the Roman Empire.[42]

Around 33 CE the crucifixion by the Romans of the apocalyptic Jew, Jesus Christ of Nazareth, inspired the rise of a new monotheistic cult that took his name. Followers believed that Christ, which means "chosen" in Greek, was the son of the monotheistic god who had been sent to redeem humankind for its sins in breaking his commandments. Jesus was thus perceived as the messiah, which is the Hebrew term for "chosen." Believers avowed that the martyred Jesus had been resurrected from the tomb following his crucifixion and had ascended to God in Heaven.[43]

After a revelation, the apostle Paul (Saul of Tarsus) did more than anyone else to promote the new faith. A primary author of the New Testament, Paul was a Jew who thus led others in promoting conversion to Christianity. The new religion flourished, as Paul and others circulated the teachings of Christ throughout the Mediterranean world. Christianity emphasized that individuals could worship God through Jesus and not, as the Jews insisted, exclusively through the Torah. Many Christians interpreted the destruction of the second temple in 70 CE as a sign from God and that Christianity now represented the true Israel. God, many Christians believed, had allowed the temple to be destroyed to punish the Jews for having rejected Jesus as the Son of God. Christians and Jews thus began to define themselves by emphasizing their differences, including days of worship and holidays, while both retained faith in the monotheistic god.

The conversion of the Roman Emperor Constantine to Christianity in 312 followed by his conquest of the eastern Roman or Byzantine Empire after civil war in 324 solidified Christian monotheism. The spread of Christianity further marginalized Judaism as a minority religion. Constantine called Judaism "dangerous" and "abominable" yet toleration coexisted with bursts of hostility toward Jews.[44] Synagogues became ever more important sites for preservation of Jewish tradition and communal organization. Jews emphasized endogamous marriage, or Jews marrying within the faith, and also promoted conversion as means of preserving the community. Despite their minority status, "Jews had wide latitude in organizing their religious lives and, it seems, aspects of their economic lives as well."[45]

Meanwhile, the rise of Islam under the Prophet Muhammad ushered in a new religious order affecting the lives of Jews, Christians, Zoroastrians, and all peoples of the ancient Near East. Born around 570 CE in Mecca, Muhammad claimed to be a prophet in a long line of succession from the Old to the New Testament, from Abraham and Moses to Jesus. The new religion became known as Islam, or submission to the will of the universal God. Rejected in Mecca, Muhammad removed to the oasis community of Medina where he attracted converts and led a coalition that repeatedly clashed with Mecca, which eventually surrendered to his authority.[46]

During the early years of preaching Muhammad showed a positive view of Judaism by calling for renewed purity of worship of the already revealed monotheistic god of the Jews. Like the Jews the Arabs were Semitic peoples who traced their lineage to Abraham's son Ishmael and his second wife Hagar. However, Medina had a substantial Jewish population, which largely rejected Muhammad's claim to be a prophet in the Hebrew tradition. The Prophet declared that the Jews had broken their covenant with God whereas he had been sent to purify the relationship with the Almighty that had lapsed since the time of Abraham. "Conflict with the Jews led to the redefinition of Islam as a new confessional religion," Ira Lapidus points out, "and led to new laws and rituals to provide Muslims with a separate identity."[47] Despite these clashes neither Muhammad nor Islam was inherently violent. The religion spread widely through conversion and soft power rather than militancy.[48]

Muslims adopted a new form of prayer characterized by recitations and prostration and instituted rituals such as the month-long fast of Ramadan. Nonetheless, Islam shared much in common with Judaism and Christianity, including monotheism, written revelations, divine guidance, prophets sent to redeem and enlighten, and the possibility of salvation in an afterlife.

Islam was thus self-consciously a continuation and renewal of existing monotheistic traditions. The Quranic teachings forged the *umma* or brotherhood of all Muslims through adherence to the faith and its communal rituals and practices. Emphasis on submission to the will of an utterly transcendent god, conjoined with emphasis on Muslims constituting a community of believers with an obligation to spread the faith, distinguished Islam albeit still within the monotheistic tradition.[49] Following Muhammad 's death in 632 Muslims flowed out of Arabia and the Middle East, establishing authority over a vast area with large Christian, Jewish and Zoroastrian populations. Islamic society required religious minorities to pay tribute in return not only for tolerance but also for protecting their right to follow their own faiths.

During the first half of the Middle Ages, roughly from the 6th through 10th centuries, the overwhelming majority of Jews lived in the Islamic world. The second largest number lived in eastern Christendom under Byzantine authority, while western Christendom was a distant third in the number of Jewish residents.[50] During the Middle Ages Muslim societies proved more tolerant of Judaism than did Christianity. Moreover, Islamic civilization retained "a secular aspect in its general culture that was totally absent in Latin Christendom."[51]

The Jewish "Other" in Western Christendom

As it gained adherents Christianity distinguished itself from both the Islamic and Judaic Other. Church doctrine held that God had rejected the Jews because of their failure to embrace Jesus as the new messiah. Condemnation of the Jewish Other heightened Christian convictions that they were God's chosen people. Many blamed Jews for the crucifixion even though the Romans had executed Christ. Despite such popular prejudices Church pronouncements and policy proclaimed Jews could live peaceably in Christian society as long as they refrained from blasphemy against the sacred teachings and spaces of the faith. The official policy of tolerance notwithstanding, Jewish rights and religious freedom encountered persistent opposition.

The religious wars of the Crusades frequently targeted Jews as well as Muslims. Launched by the Pope in 1096, the Crusades continued off and on for about 200 years. In 1099 the Crusaders succeeded in capturing Jerusalem from Muslims, slaughtering some 30,000 Muslims who had sought refuge at the al Aqsa Mosque in the process. At the same time the Crusaders herded some 6,000 Jews into a synagogue where they were burned to death. By the time the Crusades ended, Muslim forces had regained control of the Levant including Jerusalem and its holy sites.[52]

Zealots attacked communities of Jews throughout Christendom, often confronting them with a choice of conversion to Christianity or death. Individuals and mobs rather than Crusader armies often carried out attacks on the Jewish "enemy within." In France and other parts of Europe Christians often targeted Jews on the Easter holiday, which brought to mind the crucifixion that much of the public blamed on the Jews.[53]

Discrimination marginalized Jews, barring them from engaging in regular occupations thus prompting many to take up money lending and currency exchange. Most faiths including Judaism forbid or discouraged lending money at interest, but a minority of Jews with limited occupational opportunities took up banking and moneylending. Many communities barred Jews from owning land to farm or joining guilds hence their options were limited. On the other hand, many Jews were well equipped to engage in trade and commerce, as they had achieved higher rates of literacy than majority populations and many had experience with trade under both Islamic and Christian rule as a result of being subjected to forced migrations.

Popular resentment rooted in the stereotype of Jews as money hungry usurers provoked retribution even though rulers in medieval Europe often encouraged Jewish banking and commercial activity. These rulers protected Jews because their economic activity facilitated the wellbeing of the rulers' domains and personal wealth. By the thirteenth century moneylending "had become absolutely central to the Jewish economy."[54]

In addition to the widespread stereotypes of moneylending and Christ killing, a myth arose that Jews sacrificed Christians as part of the Passover celebration. By the 1200s widespread prejudice against Jews had led to the requirement that they wear badges or distinctive clothing and/or live in, segregated communities in order to distinguish them from the majority population. Where tolerated, synagogues could not outstrip local churches in size or splendor. Attacks on rabbis and synagogues and periodic book burnings plagued Jews. A campaign launched in Paris in 1242 resulted in thousands of volumes of Judaic texts being burned.

In the mid-fourteenth century, as the bubonic plague swept across Europe, traumatized people often blamed the Jews. Unaware that rats transmitted the plague to humans, many people attributed the "black death" to God's wrath over the perfidy of heretics and Jews. Throughout Europe mobs attacked synagogues and Jewish communities, robbing and killing Jews while sometimes sparing the children in lieu of baptism and conversion.[55]

In fifteenth-century Spain, home to the largest Jewish population in world, an eruption of anti-Semitism resulted in mass expulsions. In 1492 the monarchs Ferdinand and Isabella issued an edict declaring that Jews had done "great damage" and were "a detriment to our holy Catholic faith." Therefore they "resolved that all Jews and Jewesses" be expelled and "never allowed to return" to Spain.[56] Under the Spanish Inquisition, which targeted heretics and Jews, hundreds if not thousands were murdered before they could be expelled.

The Protestant Reformation in Europe fueled anti-Semitism. In 1542 Martin Luther, the architect of the ecclesiastical reform movement, urged the expulsion from central Europe of "this damned, rejected race of Jews." The Protestant reform leader advocated burning down Jewish homes and synagogues. By this time most Jews had been driven out of Western Europe and those who remained forcibly adhered to dress codes and lived in Jewish ghettos.[57]

Forced into exile, most Jews moved to Eastern Europe or the Muslim Near East. In the mid-fifteenth century the Ottoman Turks captured the Byzantine capital of Constantinople, renamed it Istanbul, and offered toleration for people of other faiths, called *dhimmi*. The Ottoman Empire allowed Jews as well as Christians and other minorities to practice their faith in return for paying taxes levied only against them. The initial tolerance of the Ottoman Empire gave way to dress codes and other forms of discrimination, as Islamic religious conservatism reemerged toward the end of the 16th century.

Many Jews migrated to Poland, where some found refuge while others were attacked and expelled. The demographic shift to the east created a new Ashkenazi territory, derived from the medieval Hebrew term for Germany. A vernacular Judeo-German language, Yiddish evolved in Eastern Europe. In the Balkans Ashkenazi encountered Sephardic Jews, those who had been expelled from Spain and Portugal. Another enclave of early modern European Jewish life was northern Italy where Jews were required typically to live in a walled ghetto yet were free to come and go during the day.[58]

As the European Enlightenment unfolded, Jews benefited from growing levels of toleration, especially in England. In many respects Great Britain became the first modern Jewish community in the world.[59] The French Revolution ushered in profound changes throughout Europe and the world, including emphasis on religious freedom and equality under the law. In 1790-91 Jews in France became the first in Europe to receive emancipation removing all restrictions on where they could live and work.[60] Enlightenment rationalism had eroded some of the historic isolation, discrimination and attacks on Jews, yet anti-Semitism continued and, in some cases, accelerated in concert with the rise of nationalism. By the nineteenth century modern "science" increasingly viewed Jews as a separate "race," a designation that anchored anti-Semitism. Within the powerful *volkish* thrust inherent in German national identity, many viewed Jews as an oriental desert race of wanderers who could never assimilate as "true Germans." Generations later Adolf Hitler and other leaders of Nazi Germany seized upon these and other stereotypes to isolate, vilify, and ultimately attempt to destroy the Jewish "race."

As a result of the late-eighteenth century partition of Poland, a million Jews came under Russian imperial authority, where they were un-welcome. Unlike the liberalizing Western societies, autocratic Russia did not consider emancipating the Jews. The Russian Empire confined the newly absorbed Jews to the "pale of settlement," which stretched from the Baltic Sea south to the Black Sea across a great swath of Eastern Europe. In 1881 the assassination of Tsar Alexander II fueled an already entrenched anti-Semitism, as a Jewish woman was one of the conspirators in the regicide. Jews were targeted in the ensuing *pogrom*, the Russian term for a sudden, violent assault. Hundreds of thousands of Jews departed Russian territory for Germany, France, Britain and the United States.[61]

The Russian pogrom reflected a "sharp rise in anti-Semitism in the late 1800s."[62] Scientific racism combined with refueled stereotypes of Jews as Christ killers, usurers, and enemies within spurred anti-Semitism throughout the modern world. Although Jews were a tiny minority in France, the famous Dreyfus Affair underscored deeply entrenched anti-Semitism. In 1894 French authorities accused Captain Alfred Dreyfus, the first Jew to become an officer on the French general staff, with selling military secrets to Germany. Dreyfus, whose father had been a wealthy industrialist, was found guilty of treason and exiled to Devil's Island off the coast of South America. Public outcry over charges of anti-Semitism forced a retrial in which Dreyfus was again convicted, but in 1906 he received a full pardon and was declared innocent.[63]

The Great War (1914-18) spread death and destruction across Europe, a climate that proved conducive to revivified anti-Semitism. Beginning in the early 1900s thousands of anti-Semitic pamphlets, books and articles, many originating in Russia, trumpeted a Jewish plot to take over the world. At the root of the chimerical conspiracy were wealthy Jewish financial elites notably the Rothschild family, which had originated in Germany and amassed great wealth through banking and finance. European Jews did their best to prove their loyalty to the European nations as they "eagerly participated in the war effort, both on the battlefield and on the home front."[64] The Jewish conspiracy theory proliferated with the publication and distribution in multiple languages of *The Protocols of the Elders of Zion*, which originated in Russia but began to circulate widely in the West in the midst of the Dreyfus Affair.

Many Russians, among others, subsequently blamed the Bolshevik Revolution (1917) on the Jewish conspiracy. Karl Marx had been a Jew, as was the prominent Bolshevik internationalist Leon Trotsky, though both had rejected religion. Yet many Russian and European Jews were socialists, including the proponents of revolutionary uprisings in central Europe, Béla Kun and Rosa Luxemburg.[65] Atrocities against Russian Jews spiked during World War I and the ensuing Russian Civil War. The worst occurred in the Ukrainian city of Proskurov in February 1919, as Ukrainian military forces slaughtered some 1,200 Jewish men, women, children and babies in a three-hour paroxysm of violence. From 1917 to 1921 more than 2,000 pogroms were carried out in Eastern Europe, killing an estimated 75,000 Jews while leaving many more injured and homeless.[66]

In light of this history, it is surely understandable why many Jews might conclude that their security could best be served by establishing a homeland of their own. The onset of Nazi Germany and the genocide of the Jews could only propel such sentiments. Horribly persecuted in Europe, the Zionists ultimately exported their trauma to Palestine.

Bibliography

PRIMARY SOURCES

American Israel Public Affairs Committee

Near East Report, 1957-2020

Center for Jewish History, New York City

American Council for Judaism Collection
Isaiah Leo Kenen Papers
Louis Lipsky Papers
Records of the American Jewish Committee
Records of the American Jewish Congress

Dwight D. Eisenhower Presidential Library, Abilene, KS

John Foster Dulles Papers
Dwight D. Eisenhower Papers
Records of the President, White House Central Files
Maxwell M. Rabb Papers

Foreign Relations of the United States (FRUS), US Department of State Publication

FRUS 1945, The Near East and Africa, VIII. Washington: US Government Printing Office (US GPO), 1969.
FRUS, 1946, The Near East and Africa, VII. US GPO, 1969.
FRUS, 1947, The Near East and Africa, V. US GPO, 1971.
FRUS 1948, The Near East, South Asia, and Africa, V, Part 2. US GPO, 1976.
FRUS 1949: The Near, East, South Asia, and Africa, VI: US GPO, 1977.
FRUS 1955-1957, XIV, Arab-Israeli Dispute 1955. US GPO, 1989.
FRUS 1958-1960, Near East Region; Iraq; Iran; Arabian Peninsula, XII. US GPO, 1993.
FRUS, 1961-1963, XVII, Near East, 1961-1962. US GPO, 1994.
FRUS, 1961-1963, XVIII, Near East. US GPO, 1995.
FRUS 1964-1968, XVIII, Arab-Israeli Dispute, 1964-1967. US GPO, 2000.
FRUS 1964-1968, XX, Arab-Israeli Dispute, 1967-1968. US GPO, 2001.
FRUS 1964-1968, XIX, Arab-Israeli Crisis and War, 1967. US GPO, 2004.
FRUS 1969-1976, XXVI, Arab-Israeli Dispute, 1974-1976. US GPO, 2011.

FRUS 1973-1976, XXXVIII, Foundations of Foreign Policy, 1973-1976, Part I. US GPO, 2012.

FRUS, 1977-1980, VIII, Arab-Israeli Dispute, January 1977-August 1978. US GPO, 2013.

FRUS 1969-1976, XXIII, Arab-Israeli Dispute, 1969-1972. US GPO, 2015.

Lyndon Baines Johnson Presidential Library (LBJL), Austin, TX

Krim, Arthur and Mathilde, Reference File
National Security File
Lyndon Baines Johnson Papers
Oral History Interviews
The President's Appointment File
Religion File
White House Central Files

John F. Kennedy Presidential Library, Boston, MA

McGeorge Bundy Personal Papers
Myer Feldman Personal Papers
Hirsh Freed Papers
Oral History Interviews
Papers of President Kennedy
National Security Files
Pre-Presidential Papers

Library of Congress, Washington, DC

Emanuel Celler Papers
Clark M. Clifford Papers
Benjamin V. Cohen Papers
Arthur J. Goldberg Papers
Loy W. Henderson Papers

Jacob Marcus Rader Center of the American Jewish Archives, Cincinnati, OH

Benjamin V. Cohen Papers
B'nai B'rith International Archives
American Jewish Committee Records

Miller Center, University of Virginia

Presidential Telephone Recordings (online): https://millercenter.org/the-presidency/secret-white-house-tapes

Feinberg-Johnson, Feb. 20, 1965
Dirksen-Johnson, June 12, 1967
Goldberg-Johnson July 15, 1967
Rusk-Johnson, Oct. 17, 1968
Clifford-Johnson, Nov. 23, 1968

National Archives and Records Administration, College Park, MD

General Records of the Department of State (Record Group 59)
Middle East Crisis Files, 1967

Harry S. Truman Library Institute, Independence, MO

Dean G. Acheson Papers
Clark Clifford Papers
Edward Jacobson Papers
David K. Niles Papers
Oral History Interviews
President's Secretary's Files
Records of the President, White House Central Files
Harry S. Truman Papers

Western Reserve Historical Society, Cleveland, OH

Abba Hillel Silver Papers

Books Cited

Abisaab, Rula and Malek. *The Shi'ites of Lebanon: Modernism, Communism, and Hizbullah's Islamists.* Syracuse University Press, 2014.

Abrahamian, Ervand. *A History of Modern Iran.* London: Cambridge University Press, 2018

Abunimah, Ali. *The Battle for Justice in Palestine.* Chicago: Haymarket Books, 2014.

Akbarzadeh, Shahram, ed., *Routledge Handbook of Political Islam.* Routledge, 2012.

Akenson, Donald H. *God's Peoples: Covenant Theology in South Africa,* Israel and Ulster. Ithaca: Cornell University Press, 1992.

Anderson Irvine H. *Biblical Interpretation and Middle East Policy.* Gainesville: University Press of Florida, 2005.

Ansary, Tamim. *Destiny Disrupted: A History of the World Through Islamic Eyes.* New York: Public Affairs, 2009

Anziska, Seth. *Preventing Palestine: A Political History from Camp David to Oslo.* Princeton. Princeton University Press, 2018

Aridan, Natan. *Advocating for Israel: Diplomats and Lobbyists from Truman to Nixon.* Lanham: Lexington Books, 2017.

Aruri, Naseer H. *Dishonest Broker: The U.S. Role in Israel and Palestine.* Cambridge, Ma.: South End Press, 2003.

Bacevich, Andrew J. America's *War for the Greater Middle East: A Military History*. New York: Random House, 2016.

Barghouti, Omar. *BDS: Boycott, Divestment, Sanctions: The Global Struggle for Palestinian Rights*. Chicago, IL.: Haymarket Books, 2011

Ben-Zvi, Abraham. *Lyndon B. Johnson and the Politics of Arms Sales to Israel*. London: Frank Cass, 2004

Bergman, Ronen. *Rise and Kill First: The Secret History of Israel's Targeted Assassinations*. New York: Random House, 2018.

Boyer, Paul S. *When Time Shall Be No More: Prophecy Belief in Modern American Culture*. Cambridge, MA: Harvard University Press, 1992.

Ball, George W. Ball and Douglas B. *The Passionate Attachment: America's Involvement with Israel, 1947 to the Present*. New York: W.W. Norton, 1992.

Baskin, Judith R. and Seeskin, Kenneth, eds., *Jewish History, Religion, and Culture*. New York: Cambridge University Press, 2010.

Beattie, Kirk J. *Congress and the Shaping of the Middle East*. New York: Seven Stories Press, 2015.

Beinart, Peter. *The Crisis of Zionism*. New York: Henry Holt and Co., 2012.

Ben-Ami, Shlomo. *Scars of War, Wounds of Peace*. New York: Oxford University Press, 2006.

Blumenthal, Max. *Goliath: Life and Loathing in Greater Israel*. New York: Nation Books, 2013.

Breitman, Richard and Lichtman, Allan J. *FDR and the Jews*. Cambridge: Harvard University Press, 2013.

Brenner, Bjorn. *Gaza Under Hamas: From Islamic Democracy to Islamist Governance*. London: I.B. Tauris, 2017.

Bresheeth-Zabner, Haim. *An Army Like No Other: How the Israel Defense Forces Made a Nation*. London: Verso, 2020.

Brett, Mark G. *Decolonizing God: The Bible and the Tides of Empire*. Sheffield, England: Sheffield Phoenix Press, 2008.

Carenen, Caitlin. *The Fervent Embrace: Liberal Protestants, Evangelicals, and Israel*. New York" New York University Press, 2012.

Cavanagh, Edward and Veracini, Lorenzo, eds., *The Routledge Handbook of Settler Colonialism*. London and New York: Routledge, 2017.

Chamberlin, Paul Thomas. *The Global Offensive: The United States, the Palestine Liberation Organization, and the Making of the Post-Cold War Order*. New York: Oxford University Press, 2012.

Chomsky, Noam. *The Fateful Triangle: The United States, Israel and the Palestinians*. Boston: South End Press, 1983.

Cohen, Avner. *The Worst-Kept Secret: Israel's Bargain with the Bomb*. New York: Columbia University Press, 2010.

Cohen, Naomi W. *The Americanization of Zionism, 1897-1948*. Hanover and London: Brandeis University Press, 2003.

Cole, Juan. *Muhammad: Prophet of Peace Amid the Clash of Empires*. New York: Nation Books, 2018.

Daigle, Craig. *The Limits of Détente: The United States, the Soviet Union, and the Arab-Israeli Conflict, 1969-1973*. New Haven: Yale University Press, 2012.

Davies, Philip R. *In Search of Ancient Israel*. Sheffield, England: JSOT Press, 1992.

Index

Hummel, Daniel G. *Covenant Brothers: Evangelicals, Jews, and US-Israeli Relations.* Philadelphia: University of Pennsylvania Press, 2019.

Jacobs, Matthew F. *Imagining the Middle East: The Building of an American Foreign Policy, 1918-1967.* Chapel Hill: University of North Carolina Press, 2011

Jensehaugen, Jørgen. *Arab-Israeli Diplomacy Under Carter: The US, Israel, and the Palestinians.* New York: I.B. Tauris, 2018.

Johnson, Chalmers. *Blowback: The Costs and Consequences of American Empire.* New York: Henry Holt. 2004.

Judis, John B. *Genesis: Truman, American Jews, and the Origins of the Arab/Israeli Conflict.* New York: Farrar, Straus and Giroux, 2014.

Kaplan, Amy S., *Our American Israel: The Story of an Entangled Alliance.* Cambridge: Harvard University Press, 2018.

Karcher, Carolyn L. ed., *Reclaiming Judaism from Zionism: Stories of Personal Transformation.* Northampton, MA: Olive Branch Press, 2019.

Kenen, Isaiah. *Israel's Defense Line: Her Friends and Foes in Washington.* Buffalo: Prometheus Books, 1981.

Kerr, Malcolm H. *The Arab Cold War: Gamal 'abd al-Nasir and His Rivals, 1958-1970.* New York: Oxford University Press, 1971.

Khalidi, Rashid. *The Hundred Years' War on Palestine: A History of Settler Colonialism and Resistance, 1917-2017.* New York: Metropolitan Books, 2020.

Kimmerling, Baruch. Politicide: Ariel Sharon's War against the Palestinians. London: Verso 2003.

Kenneth Kolander, *America's Israel: The US Congress and American-Israeli Relations, 1967-1975.* University Press of Kentucky, 2020.

Kolsky, Thomas A. *Jews Against Zionism: The American Council for Judaism, 1942-1948.* Philadelphia: Temple University Press, 1990.

Kramer, Gudrun. *A History of Palestine: From the Ottoman Conquest to the Founding of the State of Israel.* Princeton: Princeton University Press, 2008.

Kuzmarov, Jeremy. *Obama's Unending Wars: Fronting the Foreign Policy of the Permanent Warfare State.* Atlanta: Clarity Press, 2019.

Lapidus, Ira M., *A History of Islamic Societies.* New York: Cambridge University Press, 2014, 3d ed.

Laron, Guy. *The Six-Day War: The Breaking of the Middle East.* New Have: Yale University Press, 2017.

Lesch, David W. and Haas, Mark L. *The Middle East and the United States: History, Politics, and Ideologies.* New York: Routledge, 2018, sixth ed.

Lim, Audrea, ed., *The Case for Sanctions Against Israel.* London: Verso, 2012.

Louis, William Roger. *The British Empire in the Middle East, 1945-1951: Arab Nationalism, the United States, and Postwar Imperialism.* London: Oxford University Press, 1984.

_____ and Shlaim, Avi, eds., *The 1967 Arab-Israeli War: Origins and Consequences.* New York: Cambridge University Press, 2012.

Lustick, Ian S. *Paradigm Lost: From Two-State Solution to One-State Reality.* Philadelphia: University of Pennsylvania Press, 2019.

Maddock, Shane J. *Nuclear Apartheid: The Quest for American Atomic Supremacy from World War II to the Present.* Chapel Hill: University of North Carolina Press, 2010.

Index

Maira, Sunania. *Boycott! The Academy and Justice for Palestine*. Berkeley: University of California Press, 2018.

Mart, Michelle. *Eye on Israel: How America Came to View the Jewish State as an Ally*. Albany: State University of New York Press, 2006.

Masalha, Nur. *Imperial Israel and the Palestinians: The Politics of Expansion*. London: Pluto Press, 2000.

_____. *The Zionist Bible: Biblical Precedent, Colonialism, and the Erasure of Memory*. Berne: Acumen, 2013.

Mearsheimer, John and Walt, Stephen. *The Israel Lobby and US Foreign Policy*. New York: Farrar, Straus and Giroux, 2007.

Miller, Aaron David. *The Much Too Promised Land: America's Elusive Search for Arab-Israeli Peace*. New York: Bantam Books, 2008.

Morris, Benny. *Israel's Border Wars, 1949-1956: Arab Infiltration, Israeli Retaliation, and the Countdown to the Suez War*. New York: Oxford University Press, 1993.

Nelson, Cary and Braum, Gabriel N. *The Case Against Academic Boycotts of Israel*. Detroit: Wayne State University Press, 2015.

Niesiolowski-Spano, Lukasz. *Origin Myths and Holy Places in the Old Testament*. London: Equinox Publishing, 2011.

Novick, Peter. *The Holocaust in American Life*. Boston: Houghton Mifflin, 1999.

Olive, Ronald J. *Capturing Jonathan Pollard*. Annapolis, MD: Naval Institute Press, 2006.

Oren, Michael B. *Power, Faith, and Fantasy: America in the Middle East 1776-Present*. New York: W.W. Norton, 2007.

Pappé, Ilan. *The Ethnic Cleansing of Palestine*. Oxford: One-World Publications, 2006.

_____. *The Biggest Prison on Earth: A History of the Occupied Territories*. London: Oneworld, 2017.

Pedahzur, Ami. *The Triumph of Israel's Radical Right*. New York: Oxford University Press, 2012.

Pfeffer, Anshel. *Bibi: The Turbulent Life and Times of Benjamin Netanyahu*. New York: Basic Books, 2018.

Pitkanen, Pekka. "Ancient Israel and Settler Colonialism," *Settler Colonial Studies* 4, (2013): 64-81.

Polakow-Suransky, Sasha. *The Unspoken Alliance: Israel's Secret Relationship with Apartheid South Africa*. New York: Vintage Books, 2011.

Preston, Andrew. *Sword of the spirit, Shield of Faith: Religion in American War and Diplomacy*. New York: Anchor Books, 2012.

Prior, Michael. *The Bible and Colonialism: A Moral Critique*. Sheffield, England: Sheffield Academic Press, 1997.

Quigley, John. *The Six-Day War and Israeli Self-Defense: Questioning the Legal Basis for Preventative War*. New York: Cambridge University Press, 2013.

Rabinovich, Itmar. *The Road Not Taken: Early Arab-Israeli Negotiations*. New York: Oxford University Press, 1991.

Robinson, Shira. *Citizen Strangers: Palestinians and the Birth of Israel's Settler State*. Palo Alto, CA: Stanford University Press, 2013.

Radosh, Allis and Radosh, Ronald. *A Safe Haven: Harry S. Truman and the Founding of Israel*. New York: Harper 2009.

Raider, Mark A. *The Emergence of American Zionism*. New York: New York
University Press, 1998.

Raphael, Marc Lee. *Abba Hillel Silver: A Profile in American Judaism*. New York:
Holmes and Meier, 1989.

Raz, Avi. *The Bride and the Dowry: Israel, Jordan, and the Palestinians in
The Aftermath of the June 1967 War*. New Haven: Yale University Press, 2012.

Rogan, Eugene. *The Arabs*. London: Penguin Books, 2012.

Rogerson, J.W. and Lieu, Judith M. *The Oxford Handbook of Biblical Studies*. New
York: Oxford University Press, 2006.

Romer, Thomas. *The Invention of God*. Cambridge, MA.: Harvard University Press,
2015.

Rubenberg, Cheryl A. *Israel and the American National Interest: A Critical
Examination*. Urbana and Chicago: University of Illinois Press, 1986.

Sand, Shlomo. *The Invention of the Jewish People*. New York: Verso Books, 2010.

Sasson, Theodore. *The New American Zionism*. New York: New York University
Press, 2014.

Sayward, Amy L. *The United Nations in International History*. London: Bloomsbury
Publishing, 2017.

Scahill, Jeremy. *Dirty Wars: The World is a Battlefield*. New York: Nation Books,
2013.

Schueller, Malani Johar. *US Orientalisms: Race, Nation, and Gender in Literature*. Ann
Arbor: University of Michigan Press, 1998.

Segev, Tom. *1967: Israel, the War, and the Year that Transformed the Middle East*.
New York: Metropolitan Books, 2005.

Shaim, Avi. *The Iron Wall: Israel and the Arab World*. New York: W.W. Norton,
2014.

Siniver, Asaf. *Abba Eban: A Biography*. New York; Overlook Duckworth, 2015.

Slater, Robert. *Warrior Statesman: The Life of Moshe Dayan*. New York: St. Martin's
Press, 1991.

Smith, Charles D. *Palestine and the Arab-Israeli Conflict: A History with Documents*.
Boston: Bedford St. Martins, 9th ed., 2017.

Smith, Grant F. *Big Israel—How the Israel Lobby Moves America*. Washington:
Institute for Research: Middle Eastern Policy (IRmep), 2016.

_____, *Foreign Agents*. Washington: Institute for Research: Middle East
Policy, 2007

_____, *The Israel Lobby Enters State Government: Rise of the Virginia Israel
Advisory Board*. Washington: Institute for Research: Middle East Policy, 2019.

Snyder, Timothy, *Bloodlands: Europe Between Hitler and Stalin*. New York: Basic
Books, 2010.

Spector, Stephen. *Evangelicals and Israel: The Story of American Christian Zionism*.
New York: Oxford University Press, 2009.

Stocker, James R. *Spheres of Intervention: US Foreign Policy and the Collapse of Lebanon,
1967-1976*. Ithaca: Cornell University Press, 2016.

Strieff, Daniel *Jimmy Carter and the Middle East: The Politics of Presidential Diplomacy*.
New York: Palgrave-Macmillan, 2015.

Index

Tal, Alon. *Pollution in a Promised Land: An Environmental History of Israel.* Berkeley: University of California Press, 2002.

Terry, Janice J. *US Foreign Policy in the Middle East: The Role of Lobbies and Special Interest Groups.* London: Pluto Press, 2005.

Thompson, Thomas L. *Early History of the Israelite People: From the Written and Archeological Sources.* Leiden: E.J. Brill, 1992.

Tillman, Seth P. *The United States in the Middle East: Interests and Obstacles.* Bloomington: Indian University Press, 1982.

Tivnan, Edward. *The Lobby: Jewish Political Power and American Foreign Policy.* New York: Touchstone, 1987.

Truman, Harry S. *Memoirs: Years of Trial and Hope.* Garden City, N.J.: Doubleday, 1955-56

Tyler, Patrick, *Fortress Israel: The inside Story of the Military Elite who Run the Country—and Why They Can't Make Peace.* New York: Farrar, Strauss, and Giroux, 2012.

Veracini, Lorenzo. *Settler Colonialism: A Theoretical Overview.* New York: Palgrave Macmillan, 2010.

_____, *Israel and Settler Society.* London: Pluto Press, 2006.

Wagner, Donald E. and Davis, Walter T. eds., *Zionism and the Quest for Justice on the Holy Land.* Eugene, R: Pickwick Publications, 2014.

Walther, Karine V. *Sacred Interests: The United States and the Islamic World, 1881-1921.* Chapel Hill: University of North Carolina Press, 2015.

Waxman, Dov. *Trouble in the Tribe: The American Jewish Conflict over Israel.* Princeton: Princeton University Press, 2016.

Whitelam, Keith W. *The Invention of Ancient Israel: The Silencing of Palestinian History.* London and New York: Routledge.

Wilford, Hugh. *America's Great Game: The CIA's Secret Arabists and the Shaping of the Modern Middle East.* New York: Basic Books, 2013.

Woods, Randall Bennett. *Fulbright: A Biography.* New York: Cambridge University Press, 1995.

Yaqub, Salim. *Imperfect Strangers: Americans, Arabs and US-Middle East Relations in the 1970s.* Ithaca, New York: Cornell University Press, 2016.

Yergin, Daniel. *The Prize: The Epic Quest for Oil, Money and Power.* New York: Simon and Schuster, 2008; 1991.

Zertal, Idith and Eldar, Akiva. *Lords of the Land: The War Over Israel's Settlements in the Occupied Territories, 1967-2007.* New York: Nation Books, 2007.

Notes

Introduction

[1] Saree Makdisi, "Kill, Kill and Kill," *Washington Report on Middle East Affairs* (June/July 2018): 8-9.

[2] Walter L. Hixson, "From Right to Return to Right to Starve and Kill," *Washington Report on Middle East Affairs* (August/September 2019): 15-16.

[3] "Open-Fire Policy," May 14, 2018, B'Tselem (The Israeli Information Center for Human Rights in the Occupied Territories); https://www.btselem.org/press_releases/20180514_appalling_indifference_to _human_life_at_gaza_fence.

[4] Walter L. Hixson, *Israel's Armor: The Israel Lobby in the First Generation of the Palestine Conflict.* New York Cambridge University Press, 2019; Theodore Sasson, *The New American Zionism.* New York: New York University Press, 2014; Janice J. Terry, *US Foreign Policy in the Middle East: The Role of Lobbies and Special Interest Groups.* London: Pluto Press, 2005; the following works were foundational but are now outdated: J.J. Goldberg, *Jewish Power: Inside the American Jewish Establishment.* Reading, MA: Addison-Wesley, 1996; George W. Ball and Douglas B. Ball, *The Passionate Attachment: America's Involvement with Israel, 1947 to the Present.* New York: W.W. Norton, 1992; Edward Tivnan, *The Lobby: Jewish Political Power and American Foreign Policy.* New York: Touchstone, 1987; Cheryl A. Rubenberg, *Israel and the American National Interest: A Critical Examination.* Urbana and Chicago: University of Illinois Press, 1986; Paul Findley, *They Dare to Speak Out: People and Institutions Confront Israel's Lobby.* Westport, CT: Lawrence Hill and Co., 1985; and Seth P. Tillman, *The United States in the Middle East: Interests and Obstacles.* Bloomington: Indian University Press, 1982.

[5] Grant F. Smith, *Foreign Agents: The American Israel Public Affairs Committee from the 1963 Fulbright Hearings to the 2005 Espionage Scandal.* Washington: IRmep, 2007; Smith, *Big Israel: How the Israel Lobby Moves America.* Washington: IRmep, 2016; Smith, *The Israel Lobby Enters Sate Government* (2019). See https://www.irmep.org/.

[6] John Mearsheimer and Stephen Walt, *The Israel Lobby and US Foreign Policy.* New York: Farrar, Straus and Giroux, 2007; see the discussion in Hixson, *Israel's Armor,* 7-9.

[7] See the discussion in Conclusions.

[8] Grant F. Smith, "Censorship, Entanglement and Corruption: The Israel Lobby 2021 Agenda," Webinar available at Institute for Research: Middle Eastern

Policy (IRmep); https://www.youtube.com/watch?v=Gw0E5E4-6sQ&feature=youtu.be.

9 Mor Loushy, "The Kings of Capitol Hill" [documentary film], Stop Press! Productions, 2020.

10 Kirk J. Beattie, *Congress and the Shaping of the Middle East.* New York: Seven Stories Press, 2015: 14.

11 IRmep Country Polls Fielded by Google Consumer Surveys, March 2016; cited in Grant F. Smith, "Most Americans Believe Palestinians Occupy Israeli Land--Israel-AIPAC Claims of 'Disputed Lands' Are Working," *Antiwar.com*, Mar. 25, 2016. https://original.antiwar.com/smith-grant/2016/03/24/most-americans-believe-palestinians-occupy-israeli-land/.

12 Smith, "Censorship, Entanglement and Corruption: The Israel Lobby 2021 Agenda." YouTube webinar https://youtu.be/Gw0E5E4-6sQ

13 For an overview of the concept, see Walter L. Hixson, *American Settler Colonialism: A History.* New York: Palgrave Macmillan, 2013: 1-22; and Edward Cavanagh and Lorenzo Veracini, eds., *The Routledge Handbook of the History of Settler Colonialism.* London and New York: Routledge, 2017; see also Shira Robinson, *Citizen Strangers: Palestinians and the Birth of Israel's Liberal Settler State.* Palo Alto: Stanford University Press, 2013; Lorenzo Veracini, *Israel and Settler Society.* London: Pluto Press, 2006; and Caroline Elkins and Susan Pedersen, eds., *Settler Colonialism in the Twentieth Century.* New York: Routledge, 2005.

14 Karine V. Walther, *Sacred Interests: The United States and the Islamic World, 1821-1921.* Chapel Hill: University of North Carolina Press, 2015: 274-75.

15 Amy S. Kaplan, *Our American Israel: The Story of an Entangled Alliance.* Cambridge, MA: Harvard University Press, 2018: 20.

16 Eugene Rogan, *The Arabs.* London: Penguin Books, 2012: 196-201.

17 Hixson, *Israel's Armor*, 21-23.

18 Ben-Gurion letter to his son, Oct. 5, 1937. Archived online by Jewish Voice for Peace. https://jewishvoiceforpeace.org/the-ben-gurion-letter/; see also "JPS Responds to CAMERA's Call for Accuracy: Ben-Gurion and the Arab Transfer Reviewed work(s)," *Journal of Palestine Studies* 41, No. 2 (Winter 2012): 245-250.

19 Timothy Snyder, *Bloodlands: Europe Between Hitler and Stalin.* New York: Basic Books 2010.

20 Patrick Tyler, *Fortress Israel: The Inside Story of the Military Elite who Run the Country—and Why They Can't Make Peace.* New York: Farrar, Strauss, and Giroux, 2012; Haim Bresheeth-Zabner, An Army Like No Other: How the Israel Defense Forces Made a Nation. London: Verso, 2020.

21 Amy L. Sayward, *The United Nations in International History.* London: Bloomsbury Publishing, 2017: 149-217.

22 Hixson, *Israel's Armor*, 3.

23 Kenen interview by Alvin Goldstein, July 11, 1973, Isaiah Leo Kenen Papers, Center for Jewish History, New York, Box 14.

24 Feinberg quoted in "Looking Back and Looking Forward in 1965," Annotations: The NEH Preservation Project. https://www.wnyc.org/story/looking-back-and-looking-forward-1965/.

25 "Abba Eban," *New World Encyclopedia* https://www.newworldencyclopedia.org/entry/Abba_Eban

26 Quoted in Avi Shlaim, *Israel and Palestine: Reappraisals, Revisions, Refutations.* London: Verso, 2009: 115.

27 Amnon Cavari, "Six Decades of Public Affection," in Robert O. Freedman, ed., *Israel and the United States: Six Decades of US-Israeli Relations.* Boulder, CO: Westview Press, 2012: 100-05.

28 Arnon Degani, "From Republic to Empire: Israel and the Palestinians after 1948," in Cavanagh and Veracini, eds., *Routledge Handbook of History of Settler Colonialism,* 355.

29 Israel constitutes "the most important element of liberal Jewish identity and mobilization in the United States," according to Yossi Shain and Neil Rogashevsky. "If American Jews sought to "check their Zionism at the door," they would risk "checking their Judaism as well." Quoted in "Between JDate and J Street: US Foreign Policy and the Liberal Jewish Dilemma in America," in Josh DeWind and Renata Segura, eds., *Diaspora Lobbies and the US Government.* New York: New York University Press, 2014: 66. Peter Beinart referenced this conundrum in the title of his influential book, *The Crisis of Zionism.* New York: Henry Holt and Co., 2012; Dov Waxman, argues persuasively, however, that the uncompromisingly pro-Israeli Jewish establishment "is more right-wing and religious than the majority of American Jews." Waxman, *Trouble in the Tribe: The American Jewish Conflict over Israel.* Princeton: Princeton University Press, 2016: 177. See also my discussion at the end of Chapter 9.

30 See, for example, the searing account by Andrew Bacevich, *America's War for the Greater Middle East: A Military History* (New York: Random House, 2016). Bacevich chronicles the abject failure of US policy but like most authors does not examine in depth the critical role of the special relationship and the Israel lobby. Neither does an otherwise useful anthology edited by David W. Lesch and Mark L. Haas, *The Middle East and the United States: History, Politics, and Ideologies.* New York: Routledge, 2018, sixth ed.

Chapter 1 The Rise of American Zionism

1 "American Jewish Conference. 1943-1944," AJA, Box 1; "The Zionist Position: A Statement Submitted to the Delegates to the American Jewish Conference," Aug. 29, 1943, Abba Hillel Silver Papers, Western Reserve Historical Society (WRHS), Cleveland, Series III, 1916-1945, Box 2; Marc Lee Raphael. *Abba Hillel Silver: A Profile in American Judaism.* New York: Holmes and Meier, 1989: 85-89.

2 "Declaration Adopted by the Biltmore Conference," No. 8, May 11, 1942, Jewish Virtual Library. https://www.jewishvirtuallibrary.org/the-biltmore-conference-1942.

3 Brandeis to James Arthur Balfour, Feb. 3, 1920; Brandeis to Lord Curzon, Feb. 3, 1920, both in Benjamin V. Cohen Papers, Jacob Rader Marcus Center of the American Jewish Archives (AJA), Cincinnati, OH, Box 1; Irvine H. Anderson. *Biblical Interpretation and Middle East Policy*. Gainesville: University Press of Florida, 2005: 61; Matthew F. Jacobs, *Imagining the Middle East: The Building of an American Foreign Policy, 1918-1967*. Chapel Hill: University of North Carolina Press, 2011: 190-92; John B. Judis. *Genesis: Truman, American Jews, and the Origins of the Arab/Israeli Conflict*. New York: Farrar, Straus and Giroux, 2014: 144-63.

4 Brandeis to James Arthur Balfour, Feb. 3, 1920; Brandeis to Lord Curzon, Feb. 3, 1920, both in Benjamin V. Cohen Papers, Jacob Rader Marcus Center of the American Jewish Archives (AJA), Cincinnati, OH, Box 1.

5 David A. Gerber, ed., *Anti-Semitism in American History*. Champaign-Urbana: University of Illinois Press, 1986.

6 Michelle Mart, *Eye on Israel: How America Came to View the Jewish State as an Ally*. Albany: State University of New York Press, 2006: x.

7 Phyllis Goldstein, *A Convenient Hatred: The History of Anti-Semitism*. Brookline, MA: Facing History and Ourselves, 2012: 251-53; "Anti-Defamation League, 1913-1995," B'nai B'rith International Archives, AJA, Boxes C1-1 to C1-6,.

8 Kaplan, *Our American Israel*, 24, 30, 39.

9 Hixson, *Israel's Armor*, 28; see also Mark A. Raider, *The Emergence of American Zionism*. New York: New York University Press, 1998; and Naomi W. Cohen, *The Americanization of Zionism, 1897-1948*. Hanover and London: Brandeis University Press, 2003.

10 AJC Statement, Oct. 27, 1943, AJC Records, AJA, Box B8; "Statement of the American Jewish Conference on the Withdrawal of the American Jewish Committee," Nov. 7, 1943, Series III, 1916-1945, Abba Hillel Silver Papers, Western Reserve Historical Society, Cleveland, OH, Box 2.

11 Lessing J. Rosenwald (ACJ) to Harry Truman, Oct. 1, 1946, Official File 204, Papers of Harry S. Truman, Harry S. Truman Library Institute, Independence, Mo., (HSTL), Box 914; see also Thomas A. Kolsky, *Jews Against Zionism: The American Council for Judaism, 1942-1948*. Philadelphia: Temple University Press, 1990.

12 Andrew Preston, *Sword of the Spirit, Shield of Faith: Religion in American War and Diplomacy*. New York: Anchor Books, 2012: 25

13 Michael B. Oren, *Power, Faith, and Fantasy: America in the Middle East 1776-Present*. New York: W.W. Norton, 2007: 84; Peter Grose, *Israel in the Mind of America*. New York: Schocken Books, 1983: 3-22; Paul S. Boyer, *When Time Shall Be No More: Prophecy Belief in Modern American Culture*. Cambridge, MA: Harvard University Press, 1992: 74-75.

14 Walther, *Sacred Interests*, 5-6; 33-67; 157-237; see also Malini Johar Schueller. *US Orientalisms: Race, Nation, and Gender in Literature*. Ann Arbor: University of Michigan Press, 1998.

15 Amnon Cavari, "Six Decades of Public Affection: Trends in American Public Attitudes Toward Israel," in Robert O. Freedman, ed., *Israel and the United States: Six Decades of US-Israeli Relations*. Boulder, CO.: Westview Press, 2012: 114-15; Anderson, *Biblical Interpretation and Middle East Policy*, 19.

[16] Anderson, *Biblical Interpretation and Middle East Policy*, 108, 32-50, 29; see also Daniel G. Hummel, *Covenant Brothers: Evangelicals, Jews, and US-Israeli Relations*. Philadelphia: University of Pennsylvania Press, 2019: 1-76; and Stephen Spector, *Evangelicals and Israel: The Story of American Christian Zionism*. New York: Oxford University Press, 2009: 1-75.

[17] Kaplan, *Our American Israel*, 19.

[18] Caitlin Carenen, *The Fervent Embrace: Liberal Protestants, Evangelicals, and Israel*. New York: New York University Press, 2012: 20-27.

[19] Richard Breitman and Allan Lichtman, *FDR and the Jews*. Cambridge: Harvard University Press, 2013: 94.

[20] Carenen, *The Fervent Embrace*, 25.

[21] *New York Times*, Mar. 28, 1939; Smith, *Foreign Agents*, 15.

[22] "Declaration Adopted by the Biltmore Conference."

[23] AZEC Executive Committee minutes, Feb. 24, 1947, Silver Papers, Series I, Roll 4; American Jewish Conference, Minutes of Meeting of the Interim Committee, Sept. 18, 1947, Kenen Papers (KP), Box 3; Report of the Interim Committee to the Fourth Session American Jewish Conference, Nov. 20, 1947, KP, Box 4.

[24] Carenen, *Fervent Embrace*, 25.

[25] Mark A. Raider, et al, ed., *Abba Hillel Silver and American Zionism*. London: Frank Cass, 1997: 116; AZEC documents, Silver Papers, WRHS, Box 8.

[26] Doreen Bierbrier, ""The American Zionist Emergency Council: An Analysis of a Pressure Group," *American Jewish Historical Quarterly* LX (September 1970): 87-93.

[27] Maurice Bisgyer to Kenen, Nov. 1, 1943, KP, Box 3; for Kenen's early work promoting Zionism in Cleveland, see KP, Box 8; Isaiah Leo Kenen, *Israel's Defense Line: Her Friends and Foes in Washington*. Buffalo: Prometheus books, 1981: 14.

[28] Kenen to Delegates of the American Jewish Conference, Feb. 24, 1944, Silver Papers, Series III, 1916-1945, Box 1.

[29] Kenen, *Israel's Defense Line*, 18; Netanyahu to Silver, July 6, 1944, Silver Papers, Series I, Box 6.

[30] Gudrun Kramer, *A History of Palestine: From the Ottoman Conquest to the Founding of the State of Israel*. Princeton: Princeton university Press, 2008: 307-09; Judis, Genesis, 216.

[31] Breitman and Lichtman, *FDR and the Jews*, 251; Hixson, *Israel's Armor*, 37.

[32] DOS Memorandum for the President, May 28, 1945; Joseph Grew to Truman, May 1, 1945; Loy Henderson to Secretary, Aug. 31, 1945, all in President's Secretary's Files, Harry S Truman Library Institute (HSTL), Box 161; Loy Henderson to Dean Rusk, Nov. 20, 1977, The Papers of Loy Henderson, LOC, Box 11.

[33] *FRUS 1945, VIII*, 770-71, Docs. 867N.01/8-1845 and 867N.01/10-1845, 722.

[34] Truman to Ibn Saud, Oct. 28, 1946, President's Secretary's Files, HSTL, Box 162.

[35] *FRUS, 1946, The Near East and Africa, VII.* Washington: U.S. Government Printing Office, 1969, 604-05, Doc. 867N.01/5-1046, 714-17, Doc. 867N.01/10-1546; see also Department of State *Bulletin,* May 26, 1946, 917.

[36] "Telephone Conversation with Henry Monsky," Feb. 10, 1947, KP, Box 3.

[37] Wise to Truman, Oct. 7, 1946, President's Secretary's Files, Box 161; Jewish Agency to Truman, May 2, 1946, Official File 204, HSTL, Box 914.

[38] *FRUS, 1947, The Near East and Africa,* V. Washington: GPO, 1971: 1056-57, Doc. 867N.01/2-2547; 1074-77, Doc. 867N.01/4-2347; 1094-96, Doc. 867N.01/5-2947; *FRUS, 1946, VII,* 618, Doc. 867N.01/6-546; on British policy in Palestine, see William Roger Louis, *The British Empire in the Middle East, 1945-1951: Arab Nationalism, the United States, and Postwar Imperialism.* London: Oxford University Press, 1984: 381-572.

[39] *FRUS, 1946, VII,* 604-05, Doc. 867N.01/5-1046, 714-17, Doc. 867N.01/10-1546; see also Department of State *Bulletin,* May 26, 1946, 917; *FRUS, 1947,* V, Doc. 867N.01/1-1747, 1011-14.

[40] Hixson, *Israel's Armor,* 44.

[41] Harry S. Truman, *Memoirs: Years of Trial and Hope.* Garden City, N.J.: Doubleday, 1955-56: 158.

[42] Oren, Power, Faith, and Fantasy, 492.

[43] Hixson, *Israel's Armor,* 45.

[44] George Wadsworth to Herschel Johnson, Sept. 18, 1947, President's Secretary's Files, HSTL, Box 161.

[45] Frank Goldman, "Behind the Scenes of the UN Decision," *The National Jewish Monthly* (January 1948): 163, Official File 204, HSTL, Box 916; Weizmann to Truman, Dec. 9, 1947, Official File 204, Box 915.

[46] Hixson, *Israel's Armor,* 46.

[47] *FRUS 1948, The Near East, South Asia, and Africa, V, Part 2.* Washington: US Government Printing Office, 1976: 739, Doc. 501.BB Palestine/3-1848' 840-41, Doc. 867N.01/4-2248; 877-79, Doc. 501.BB Palestine/4-3048.

[48] St. Louis Council, American Jewish Congress to Truman, Feb. 26, 1948, Official File 204, Box 916; Weizmann to Truman, Apr. 9, 1948, Official File 204, Box 916.

[49] "Memorandum of Conference on Palestine," March 24, 1948, Clark M. Clifford Papers, HSTL, Box 13.

[50] Hixson, *Israel's Armor,* 52.

[51] Jacobson to Truman, Feb. 21, 1948; Truman to Jacobson, Feb. 27, 1948, both in Official File 204, Box 916; Film, "Decision: The Conflicts of Harry S. Truman," Episode Six, "At War with the Experts," HST Associates, 1964, HSTL.

[52] Ilan Pappé, *The Ethnic Cleansing of Palestine.* Oxford: One-World Publications, 2006.

[53] Truman de facto recognition statement, May 14, 1948, Official File 204, Box 917; *FRUS 1948,* V, Part 2: 1005, Doc. 867N.01/5-1748; Peter L. Hahn, *Caught in the Middle East: The US Policy Toward the Arab-Israeli Conflict 1945-1961.* Chapel Hill: University of North Carolina Press, 2004: 50.

[54] Radosh, Allis and Radosh, Ronald. *A Safe Haven: Harry S. Truman and the Founding of Israel.* New York: Harper 2009: 47.

[55] Anderson, *Biblical Interpretation and Middle East Policy*, 75.

[56] Austin to Marshall, May 19, 1948, President's Secretary's Files, Box 161; Hahn, *Caught in the Middle East*, 69.

[57] Hixson, *Israel's Armor*, 57.

[58] *Ibid.*, 58-59.

[59] Nur Masalha, Imperial Israel and the Palestinians: *The Politics of Expansion.* London: Pluto Press, 2000, 8; Kramer, History of Palestine, 320.

[60] Hixson, *Israel's Armor*, 71-72.

[61] *FRUS 1949: The Near, East, South Asia, and Africa*, VI: Washington: US Government Printing Office, 1977: 1322-23, Doc. 867N.01/5-449; 1530-31, Resolution 303; 1551-56, Doc. 501.BB Palestine/12-2049.

[62] *Ibid.*, 1537.

[63] Hixson, *Israel's Armor*, 61.

[64] Avi Shlaim, *The Iron Wall: Israel and the Arab World.* New York: W.W. Norton, 2014: 53; see also Itmar Rabinovich, *The Road Not Taken: Early Arab-Israeli Negotiations.* New York: Oxford University Press, 1991.

[65] Asaf Siniver, *Abba Eban: A Biography.* New York; Overlook Duckworth, 2015: 174-75.

[66] Address by Lipsky, ZOA annual convention, June 17, 1951, KP, Box 5.

[67] Natan Aridan, *Advocating for Israel: Diplomats and Lobbyists from Truman to Nixon.* Lanham: Lexington Books, 2017: 19, 35-36.

[68] "Memorandum Presented to the President of the United States," Nov. 15, 1950, KP, Box 1.

[69] Hixson, *Israel's Armor*, 75-76.

[70] NSC 47/5, Mar. 14, 1951, Department of State, Office of the Historian. https://history.state.gov/historicaldocuments/frus1951v05/d20; Hixson, *Israel's Armor*, 77.

[71] Hahn, Caught in the Middle East, 80.

[72] Kenen to Rabbi Martin Douglas, Oct. 24, 1951, KP, Box 1.

[73] Acheson, Memorandum of Conversation with Ben-Gurion and Eban, May 8, 1951; Acheson, Memorandum of Conversation with Feinberg and John Waldo, July 17, 1951, both in Acheson Papers—Secretary of State File, HSTL; Kenen, *Israel's Defense Line*, 80-86.

[74] Hixson, *Israel's Armor*, 79-80.

[75] Eric R. Crouse, *American Christians Support for Israel: Standing with the Chosen People, 1948 to 1975.* Lanham, Md., Lexington Books 2015: 55; Radosh and Radosh, A Safe Haven, 344-46; Preston, Sword of the Spirit, 437.

[76] Kenen to Lipsky, Oct. 24, 1951, KP, Box 5.

[77] Hixson, *Israel's Armor*, 83-84.

Chapter 2 Taming Two Presidents

[1] Dulles, "Memorandum of Conversation with Nixon," Oct. 18, 1955, Dulles Papers, Subject Series, Dwight D. Eisenhower Presidential Library, Abilene, Ks., Box 11; Dulles, "Memorandum of Conversation with Jacob K. Javits," Jan. 27, 1953, Dulles Papers, Chronological Series, Box 1.

[2] Kenen to Lipsky, Mar. 24, 1953, KP, Box 5; Dean Alfange, et al to Dear Friend, Apr. 2, 1953, KP, Box 2.

[3] *FRUS, 1952-1954, The Near and Middle East, IX.* Washington: US Government Printing Office, 1986: 1418-23, S/PRS Files, Lot 77 D 22, 1370, Doc. 120.1580/11-1753; Shlaim, *Iron Wall,* 94-95.

[4] Hixson, *Israel's Armor,* 92-93.

[5] ACPC letter, Karl Behr to Dear Friends, Oct. 27, 1953; Abstract of Meeting of Jewish Representatives with Secretary of State Dulles," Oct. 26, 1953, both in KP, Box 9; *FRUS, 1952-1954, IX,* 1386. Doc. 784A.5 MSP/10/2653.

[6] Hixson, *Israel's Armor,* 93.

[7] Benny Morris, *Israel's Border Wars, 1949-1956: Arab Infiltration, Israeli Retaliation, and the Countdown to the Suez War.* New York: Oxford University Press, 1993.

[8] Shlaim, *Iron Wall,* 95-98; Hixson, *Israel's Armor,* 90-94.

[9] Kenen to Lipsky, Nov. 23, 1953, KP, Box 5; Doug Rossinow, "'The Edge of the Abyss: The Origins of the Israel Lobby, 1949-1954," *Modern American History* 1 (March 2018): 23-43.

[10] Hugh Wilford, *America's Great Game: The CIA's Secret Arabists and the Shaping of the Modern Middle East.* New York: Basic Books, 2013: 118-31.

[11] Hixson, *Israel's Armor,* 99.

[12] Dulles to Lipsky, Aug. 2, 1954, JFD Chronological Series, Box 9.

[13] Dulles to Herbert Hoover, Jr, Nov. 1, 1955;" Dulles," Telephone Call to Mr. Nixon," Aug. 13, 1954, both in JFD Personnel Series, Box 1.

[14] The first 400 pages of *FRUS 1955-1957, XIV, Arab-Israeli Dispute 1955* (Washington: US Government Printing Office, 1989) focus on Project Alpha.

[15] Hixon, *Israel's Armor,* 100.

[16] *FRUS 1952-1954, IX,* 1528-29, Doc. 806.

[17] "Telephone Call from Mr. Dean," Oct. 18, 1954, Dulles Papers, Telephone Conversation Series, Box 13.

[18] "Memorandum of Conversation with Ambassador Eban of Israel," Oct. 26, 1954, Dulles Papers, Subject Series Box 11.

[19] AZCPA press release, Oct. 30, 1954, KP, Box 2.

[20] See the more complete discussion in Hixson, *Israel's Armor,* 102-21; see also Leonard Weiss, "The Lavon Affair: How a False-Flag Operation Led to War and the Israeli Bomb," *Bulletin of Atomic Scientists* (Nov. 4, 2016); https://doi.org/10.1177/0096340213493259.

[21] On the Sinai War, see Motti Golani, *Israel in Search of a War: The Sinai Campaign, 1955-1956.* Brighton: Sussex Academic Press, 1998.

[22] Aridan, Advocating for Israel, 140-41.

23 Hahn, *Caught in Middle East*, 211; Rabbi Jerome Unger to Local Committees of AZC, Feb. 8, 1957; "Congressional Reaction to Sanctions and Withdrawal from Gaza and Gulf of Aqaba," undated, both in KP, Box 15.

24 "The American Israel Public Affairs Committee from 1955 Until 1968," KP, Box 20.

25 Ibid; Kenen to Larry Laskey, Dec. 6 1957, KP, Box 13.

26 *FRUS 1955-1957, XVI*, 1230-31, Doc. 627; 1341-44, Doc. 671; 107, Doc.45; Hahn, Caught in Middle East, 215; Kenen, *Israel's Defense Line*, 136.

27 *FRUS 1958-1960*, Near East Region; Iraq; Iran; Arabian Peninsula, XII. Washington: US Government Printing Office, 1993: 98, Doc. 30.

28 Ibid., 832, Doc. 415.

29 See the discussion and citations in Walter L. Hixson, *The Myth of American Diplomacy: National Identity and US Foreign Policy*. New Haven: Yale University Press, 2008: 183-84; see also, Preston, *Sword of the Spirit*, 440-41.

30 Kaplan, *Our American Israel*, 72, 83, 90; Michelle Mart, *Eye on Israel: How America Came to View the Jewish State as an Ally*: Albany: State University of New York Press, 2006: 173.

31 Mart, *Eye on Israel*, 176.

32 Kaplan, *Our American Israel*, 76, 93.

33 "Dear Friends," Mar. 27, 1959; Kenen to Rep. Laurence Curtis, May 7, 1959; Kenen, "ACZPA letter, Confidential—Not for Publication," May 7, 1959, all in KP, Box 2.

34 Kenen, "Memorandum for Rabbi Philip S. Bernstein," Aug. 29, 1957, KP, Box 7.

35 Kenen to Laskey, Dec. 6, 1957; Kenen to Laskey, Jan. 2, 1958; Kenen to Laskey, Jan. 9, 1958, all in KP, Box 13; Kenen, "ACZPA letter, Confidential—Not for Publication," May 7, 1959, KP, Box 2; Hixson, *Israel's Armor*, 113.

36 "Arab Blacklist," *NER VI* (June 19, 1962): 49; "Nasser Rebuffed US Peace Bid," *NER VI* (Sept. 25, 1962): 77; "Wheat, Cotton and MIGS," *NER VI* (Nov. 20, 1962): 94

37 "The American Israel Public Affairs Committee from 1955 Until 1968"; Kenen to Marver Bernstein, Nov. 8, 1960, KP, Box 11.

38 "The American Israel Public Affairs Committee from 1955 Until 1968."

39 J.W. Fulbright to The President, Sept. 29, 1962, Kennedy Papers, White House Central Files, Subject File, Israel, John F. Kennedy Presidential Library, Boston, Box 60.

40 Kenen to Bernstein, June 19, 1961, KP, Box 7.

41 "DOJ Orders the AZC to Register as a Foreign Agent: Documents," The Israel Lobby Archive, Institute for Research: Middle Eastern Policy. https://www.israellobby.org/AZCDOJ/

42 See analysis and transcripts of the Fulbright hearings in Smith *Foreign Agents*, 19-65. http://www.israellobby.org/JA-AZC/default.asp

43 "1951-1964 Lobbying Disclosures, AZC, AZCPA, AIPAC," Israel Lobby Archive, Institute for Research: Middle Eastern Policy. https://www.israellobby.org/AZCPA/

44 Ibid.

[45] Feldman, "Memorandum for the President," April 26, 1963, "Israel, 1963," Myer Feldman Personal Papers, JFK Library, Boston, Box 55.

[46] Randall Bennett Woods, *Fulbright: A Biography*. New York: Cambridge University Press, 1995: 309-11.

[47] "No Sensations," *NER, VII* (August 13, 1963): 70-71.

[48] Woods, *Fulbright*, 670-72.

[49] Kenen to Philip Bernstein, January 1961, KP, Box 7.

[50] Myer Feldman, recorded interview by John Stewart, August 26, 1967, 557-61, JFK OHP, JFK Library.

[51] "Remarks by Myer Feldman at meeting of the American Israel Public Affairs Committee and the Jewish Community Council of Greater Washington," May 5, 1963, Feldman Papers, Box 29; Feldman interview by John F. Stewart, Dec. 11, 1966, 474-75, JFK OHP.

[52] *FRUS, 1961-1963, XVIII, Near East*. Washington: US Government Printing Office, 1995: 59-61, Docs. 20-1; 526-27, Doc. 244.

[53] Memorandum for President, "Your Meeting with Israel Prime Minister Ben-Gurion," May 25, 1961; State Department, "Talking Outline for Subjects to be Raised by the President," both in President's Office Files; Israel, General, 1961-1963, Papers of President Kennedy, JFK Library, Box 119A.

[54] "Palestine: Refugees: General, 1962: August-September," Kennedy Papers, National Security File; see also Hixson, *Israel's Armor*, 130-33.

[55] Feldman Memorandum to President, Aug. 10, 1962, Kennedy Papers, Box 118A; William Brubeck to Robert Komer and Myer Feldman, Sept. 22, 1962, Kennedy Papers, Box 119.

[56] FRUS, 1961-1963, XVIII, 67, Doc. 25.

[57] Ben-Gurion to JFK, Aug. 20, 1962, President's Office Files, Israel, Security, 1961-1963; Ben-Gurion to Avraham Harman, Sept. 17, 1962, both in Kennedy Papers, Box 119A.

[58] *FRUS, 1961-1963, XVIII*, 96, Doc. 41; 151-52, Doc. 64; Feldman, "Memorandum for the President," Nov. 27, 1962; Feldman, "The Johnson Plan," Sept. 25, 1962, both in Feldman Papers, Box 55; Phillips Talbot interview by Dennis J. Obrien, New York, Aug. 13, 1970, JFK OHI, 26-27.

[59] Hixson, *Israel's Armor*, 141-45.

[60] Avner Cohen, *The Worst-Kept Secret: Israel's Bargain with the Bomb*. New York: Columbia University Press, 2010.

[61] *FRUS, 1961-1963, XVII, Near East, 1961-1962*. Washington: US Government Printing Office, 1994: 24-5, Doc. 3; 36, Doc. 15.

[62] *Ibid.*, 9, Doc. 5; 14, Doc. 7.

[63] *FRUS 1961-63 XVII*, 283, Doc. 120.

[64] *Ibid.*, 283, Doc. 120; FRUS 1961-1963, XVIII, 659-60, Doc. 303.

[65] *FRUS, 1961-1963, XVIII*, 659-60, Doc. 303; 127, Doc. 55; 612-14, Doc. 283.

[66] *Ibid.*, 525, Doc. 243; 1-2, Docs. 1-2; 651, Doc. 300.

[67] Kenen, "Analysis of American Policy in the Middle East Since 1960," undated, KP, Box 8; "The American Israel Public Affairs Committee from 1955 Until 1968."

[68] "The Implications for Israel of the Arab Unity Proclamation of April 17" [1963], Kennedy Papers, Box 119.

[69] The classic work is by Malcolm H. Kerr, *The Arab Cold War: Gamal 'abd al-Nasir and His Rivals, 1958-1970.* New York: Oxford University Press, 1971.

[70] Robert Strong, "Objectives of Israel and American Zionists in 1963-64," May 7, 1963, Kennedy Papers, Box 119.

[71] Gruening, *Congressional Record, Senate,* May 12, 1963, Feldman Papers, Box 56; Kenen to Executive, National and Local Committees, Nov. 8, 1963, KP, Box 10.

[72] Leonard Farbstein press release, "Israel, 1963," Feldman Papers, Box 55; *FRUS, 1961-1963, XVIII,* 2-5, Doc. 2.

[73] *FRUS, 1961-1963, XVIII,* 590, Doc. 273; 720-22, Doc. 332; 536, Doc. 248; 780-81, Doc. 360; 667, Doc. 308; JFK to Levi Eshkol, Oct. 2, 1963, Kennedy Papers, Box 119A; JFK to Emanuel Celler, Jan. 15, 1963, Feldman Papers, Box 56.

[74] *FRUS, 1961-1963, XVIII,* 528-29, Doc. 244.

[75] Hixson, *Israel's Armor,* 127-28.

Chapter 3 Enabling Israeli Aggression

[1] Olivia Sohns, "The Future Foretold: Lyndon Baines Johnson's Congressional Support for Israel," *Diplomacy & Statecraft* 28 (2017): 60.

[2] Kenen, *Israel's Defense Line,* 134-37; Woods, *Fulbright,* 311.

[3] Hixson, *Israel's Armor,* 147-49.

[4] Walter L. Hixson, "LBJ Tops Trump in History's Recount," *Washington Report on Middle East Affairs* (January-February 2021); https://www.wrmea.org/2021-january-february/january-february-2021-table-of-contents.html.

[5] President Johnson Retains Mike Feldman," *Steel and Garnet* (January 1964), "Girard College," Feldman Papers, Box 34; *FRUS 1964-1968, XVIII, Arab-Israeli Dispute, 1964-1967.* Washington: USGPO, 2000: Doc. 65; Hixson, *Israel's Armor,* 149.

[6] *FRUS, 1964-1968, XVIII,* 152-59, Doc. 65; "Comments on Memorandum of Conversation on June 1 Between President Johnson and Prime Minister Eshkol," June 1964, Feldman Papers, Box 58.

[7] *FRUS, 1964-1968, XVIII,* 152-59, Doc. 65; *NER,* X (Aug. 9, 1966): 61.

[8] "Democratic Plank on Near East," *NER VIII* (Aug. 25, 1964): 69-71; "Disappointing GOP Plank," *NER VIII* (July 14, 1964): 57.

[9] *FRUS 1964-1968, XVIII,* 17-23, Doc. 9; 43, Doc. 18; 100, Doc. 41; Benjamin Read to McGeorge Bundy, Nov. 5, 1963, Kennedy Papers, Box 119A.

[10] FRUS 1964-1968, XVIII, 100, Doc. 41.

[11] Feldman, "Issues Affecting Jewish Community in New York State," undated; Feldman, "Memorandum for the President, Meeting with Secretary McNamara," Dec. 6, 1963, both in Feldman Papers, Box 56; Feldman, Memorandum for the President, "Tanks for Israel," May 11, 1964, "Israel, 1963," Feldman Papers, Box 55.

[12] *FRUS 1964-1968, XVIII,* 313, Doc. 140; 343-46, Doc. 157.

[13] Feinberg-Johnson Telephone Conversation, Feb. 20, 1965, Tape 6861, 6502.04, PNO 10, The Miller Center (University of Virginia); https://millercenter.org/the-presidency/secret-white-house-tapes.

[14] *FRUS 1964-1968, XVIII*, 232-34, Doc. 102; 407, Doc. 190.

[15] *Ibid.*, 393, Doc. 182; 548, Doc. 268.

[16] Hixson, *Israel's Armor*, 155; David Rodman, "Armored Breakthrough: The 1965 American Sale of Tanks to Israel," *Middle East Review of International Affairs* 8 (2004). Rubin Center Research in International Affairs. *http://www.rubincenter.org/2004/06/rodman-2004-06-01/*

[17] *FRUS 1964-1968, XVIII*, 21, Doc. 9; Charles D. Smith, "The United States and the 1967 War," in William Roger Louis and Avi Shlaim, eds., *The 1967 Arab-Israeli War: Origins and Consequences*. New York: Cambridge University Press, 2012: 167.

[18] Marvin Watson to LBJ, Sept. 28, 1966, Lyndon Baines Johnson Papers, Lyndon Baines Johnson Presidential Library (LBJL), Austin, TX, Box 6.

[19] "Regrettable and Unnecessary," *NER X* (Sept. 20, 1966): 74-75.

[20] "US Help for Israel, 1964-1966"; Rostow to Johnson, Dec. 19, 1966, NSF, Country File, Israel, Johnson Papers, Box 140; "Perceptive Understanding," *NER X* (July 12, 1966): 53.

[21] Hixson, *Israel's Armor*, 159-60; *FRUS 1964-1968*, XVIII, 549-53, Docs. 269-71.

[22] *FRUS 1964-1968*, XVIII, 667, Doc. 338.

[23] *FRUS, 1964-1968, XVIII*, 658-700, Docs. 333-56; Shlaim, *Iron Wall*, 248-49; Hixson, *Israel's Armor*, 163-64.

[24] "Unjust and Unwise," *NER X* (Nov. 19, 1966): 93-94.

[25] FRUS, 1964-1968, XVIII, 717, Doc. 366.

[26] *Ibid.*, 723, Doc. 369.

[27] *Ibid.*, 774-78, Docs. 395-97; 812-19, Docs. 414-16.

[28] *Ibid.*, 755-780, Docs. 386-99; Smith, "United States and 1967 War," 169; Segev, *1967*, 302.

[29] "Israel at 18: Partner in Progress," *A Supplement to the NER* (May 1966), B-4.

[30] Clea Lutz Bunch, "Strike at Samu: Jordan, Israel, the United States, and the Origins of the Six-Day War," *Diplomatic History* 32 (January 2008): 55-76.

[31] Shlaim, The Iron Wall, 250.

[32] FRUS, 1964-1968, XVIII, 789-90, Doc. 402; Shlaim, The Iron Wall, 250.

[33] Johnson, May 23 statement, The President's Appointment File [Diary backup], Johnson Papers, Box 67; John Quigley, *The Six-Day War and Israeli Self-Defense: Questioning the Legal Basis of Preventative War*. New York: Cambridge University Press, 2013: 51.

[34] *FRUS 1964-1968, XIX, Arab-Israeli Crisis and War, 1967*. Washington: US Government Printing Office, 2004: 80-81, Doc. 49; Rusk to Johnson, May 22, 1967, NSF, NSC Histories, May 12-June 19, 1967, LBJL, Box 17; Johnson, May 23 Statement.

35 Embassy Amman to Secretary of State and White House, May 26, 1967, NSF, NSC Histories, May 12-June 19, 1967, LBJL, Box 17; "Statement by President Nasser to Arab Trade Unionists."
http://www.sixdaywar.co.uk/historical_documents.htm.

36 Rostow to LBJ, May 24, 1967, NSF "Memos to the President Walt Rostow, Box 16, 2 of 2; Children's letters from Hebrew schools, petitions, statements from synagogues, rabbis, and Jewish Community Centers nationwide in National Security—Defense (Ex ND 19/CO 1-6) June 22, 1967, Johnson Papers, Box 194.

37 Barbour, Embassy Tel Aviv to Secretary of State, May 23, 1967, NSF, NSC Histories, May 12-June 19, 67, LBJL, Box 17.

38 FRUS 1964-1968 XIX, 127, Doc. 72; 142-43, Doc. 77.

39 Ibid., 143, Doc. 77.

40 FRUS 1964-1968 XIX, 146-158, Docs. 78-83; 206-07, Doc. 112.

41 Ibid., Doc. 124.

42 Hixson, Israel's Armor, 184; Rostow to LBJ, May 31, 1967, NSF, NSC Histories, May 12-June 19, 1967, LBJL, Box 18.

43 Hixson, Israel's Armor, 180; Robert Slater, Warrior Statesman: The Life of Moshe Dayan. New York: St. Martin's Press, 1991.

44 FRUS 1964-1968 XIX, 210-11, Doc. 114.

45 Hixson, Israel's Armor, 178-207. See also Guy Laron, The Six-Day War: The Breaking of the Middle East. New Haven: Yale University Press, 2017.

46 See the discussion and references in Hixson, Israel's Armor, 199-204.

47 FRUS 1964-1968 XIX, 311, Doc. 164.

48 Ibid., Doc. 167.

49 Kenen, "War Notes," 1967, KP, Box 11.

50 Ibid; Kenen, Israel's Defense Line, 207; Jerome Bakst to Arnold Foster, June 26, 1967, "Israel 1967-1973," Anti-Defamation League 1913-1995, BBIA, Box 1a-8.

51 Kenen, "War Notes," June 1967, KP, Box 11.

52 FRUS, 1964-1968, XIX, 354-55, Doc. 198.

53 Tom Segev, 1967: Israel, the War, and the Year that Transformed the Middle East. New York: Metropolitan Books, 2005:302; FRUS, 1964-1968, XIX, 341-42, Doc. 190.

54 Hixson, Israel's Armor, 193-95; see also Segev, 1967, 116-19, 347.

55 Johnson-Everett Dirksen Telephone Conversation, June 12, 1967, Tape WH6706.02 PNO 2, Miller Center.

56 Hixson, Israel's Armor, 210.

57 "For Rights and Security," NER XI (June 13, 1967): 45-46; Kenen, "War Notes."

58 FRUS 1964-1968, XIX, 436, 566-68, Docs. 264, 325.

59 Hixson, Israel's Armor, 211.

60 FRUS 1964-1968 XIX, 616-18, Doc. 344.

61 Goldberg-Johnson Telephone Conversation, July 15, 1967, Tape 12003 WH6707.01 PNO 2, Miller Center.

[62] Avi Raz, *The Bride and the Dowry: Israel, Jordan, and the Palestinians in the Aftermath of the June 1967 War*. New Haven: Yale University Press, 2012: 136.

[63] *FRUS 1964-1968, XIX*, 685, Doc. 375; 719, Doc. 391.

[64] "Meeting on August 27 [1967] Between Minister Evron and Myer Feldman," Feldman Papers, Box 56.

[65] *FRUS 1964-1968, XIX*, 739-40, Doc. 399.

[66] *Ibid.*, 566-68, Doc. 325.

[67] "Arms to Jordan?" *NER* XI (July 25, 1967): 57-5; "Stand Pat for Peace—Nothing Less," *NER* XI (August 8, 1967) 61.

[68] Eugene Rogan, *The Arabs*. London: Penguin Books, 2012: 430.

[69] *FRUS 1964-1968, XIX*, 773, Doc. 414; 984-85, Doc. 501.

[70] Shlaim, *Iron Wall*, 277.

[71] Shlomo Ben-Ami, *Scars of War, Wounds of Peace*. New York: Oxford University Press, 2006: 125-27.

[72] "New Arab Diplomatic Offensive," *NER XI* (Sept. 19, 67): 73

[73] Resolution 242, *FRUS 1964-1968, XIX*, 1062-63, Doc. 542.

[74] "Can There Be Peace?" *A Supplement to the Near East Report* (January 1968): A-14-16.

[75] Quigley, Six-Day War and Israeli Self-Defense, 171-72.

[76] *FRUS 1964-1968, XX, Arab-Israeli Dispute, 1967-1968*. Washington: US Government Printing Office, 2001: 436, Doc. 220.

[77] Raz, *Bride and Dowry*, 4.

[78] Ben-Ami, *Scars of War,* 116.

[79] Nev Gordon, *Israel's Occupation*. Berkeley: University of California Pres, 2008.

[80] *FRUS 1964-1968 XIX*, 480-81, Doc. 288; 770-74, Doc. 414; 781, Doc. 418; "The Arms Race in the Near East."

[81] *FRUS 1964-1968 XIX*, 788-89, Doc. 420; 842, Doc. 445; Walt Rostow to LBJ, Sept. 22, 1967 PLBJ, NSF, Country File, Israel, LBJL, Box 140.

[82] *FRUS 1964-1968, XX*, 189-91, Doc. 91; 194-95, Doc. 94; Memo of Conversation Averell Harriman, Feb. 13, 1968, NSF, Country File, Israel, LBJL, Box 141.

[83] Saunders to Rostow, Dec. 29, 1967, PLBJ, NSF, Country File, Israel, LBJL, Box 141; Rostow to LBJ, Dec. 17, 1967, NSF, Country File, Israel, LBJL, Box 143; DOS Telegram, Jan. 9, 1968, Central Foreign Policy Files, Political and Defense, Department of State Central Files, Record Group 59 (RG 59), National Archives, College Park, Md., Box 2225; *FRUS 1964-1968, XIX*, 894-95, Doc. 468.

[84] Salim Yaqub, *Imperfect Strangers: Americans, Arabs and US-Middle East Relations in the 1970s*. Ithaca, New York: Cornell University Press, 2016: 1.

[85] Wiggins, US Mission UN to Secretary of State, October 1968, NSF, Agency File, LBJL, Box 70.

[86] *FRUS 1964-1968, XX*, 194-95., Doc. 94; Parker Hart to Rusk, Oct. 15, 1968, Central Foreign Policy Files, 1967-1969, Political and Defense, RG 59, Box 1558.

[87] Shane J. Maddock, *Nuclear Apartheid: The Quest for American Atomic Supremacy from World War II to the Present*. Chapel Hill: University of North Carolina Press, 2010: 279-84.

[88] *FRUS 1964-1968, XX,* 482-83, Doc. 246.

[89] Rostow to Johnson, Oct. 25, 1968, NSF, Country File, Israel, LBJL, Box 142; *FRUS 1964-1968, XX,* 507, Doc. 256; 573, Doc. 290.

[90] Johnson-Rusk Telephone Conversation, Oct. 17, 1968, Tape 13559 WH6810.05 PNO 10, Miller Center.

[91] *FRUS 1964-1968, XX,* 585-86, Doc. 299.

[92] *Ibid.,* 689, Doc. 348; Johnson-Clifford Telephone Conversation, Nov. 23, 1968, Tape 13761 WH6811.08 PNO 1, Miller Center.

[93] *FRUS 1964-1968, XX,* 585-86, Doc. 299.

[94] Diplomat Alfred Atherton to Parker T. Hart, Jan. 8, 1969, Central Foreign Policy Files, Political and Defense, RG 59, Box 2224; Abraham Ben-Zvi, *Lyndon B. Johnson and the Politics of Arms Sales to Israel.* London: Frank Cass, 2004: 11-23.

[95] Hixson, *Israel's Armor,* 149.

Chapter 4 Cementing the Occupation

[1] *FRUS* 1969-1976, XXIII, Doc. 54.

[2] Cohen, *Worst-Kept Secret;* see also Cohen and William Burr, "Israel Crosses the Threshold," April 28, 2006, The National Security Archive, George Washington University. http://nsarchive.gwu.edu/NSAEBB/NSAEBB189/.

[3] Yaqub, *Imperfect Strangers,* 26, 146-49.

[4] "Voices for Peace" *NER* XIII, Apr. 30, 1969: 34-35.

[5] *FRUS* 1969-1976, XXIII, Arab-Israeli Dispute, 1969-1972. Washington: US Government Printing Office, 2015: Doc. 67.

[6] "Statements by the President," *NER* XIV, Feb. 4, 1970: 54.

[7] "Congress speaks Out on U.S. Policy," *NER Special Survey,* May 1970: 82-114.

[8] "Convergence of U.S.-Israel Interests," *NER* XIV Dec. 30, 1970: 198.

[9] *FRUS* 1969-1976, XXIII, Doc. 190.

[10] *Ibid.,* Doc. 232, 233.

[11] "Decision to Resume Sales of F-4's to Israel Reported," *New York Times,* Dec. 31, 1971.

[12] Craig Daigle, The Limits of Détente: The United States, the Soviet Union, and the Arab-Israeli Conflict, 1969-1973. New Haven: Yale University Press, 2012: 258.

[13] *FRUS 1973-1976, XXXVIII, Foundation of Foreign Policy,* 1973-1976, *Part I.* Washington: US Government Printing Office, 2012: Doc. 11.

[14] CIA, "The Russian Ouster—Causes and Consequences," Aug. 22, 1972, accessed online: https://www.cia.gov/library/readingroom/docs/CIA-RDP85T00875R002000120009-4.pdf

[15] Daigle, *Limits of Détente,* 294-98

[16] Yaqub, Imperfect Strangers, 111-42.

[17] *Ibid.,* 132-34.

[18] Daniel Yergin, *The Prize: The Epic Quest for Oil, Money and Power.* New York: Simon and Schuster, 2008; 1991): 570-94.

[19] *FRUS 1969-1976, XXVI, Arab-Israeli Dispute, 1974-1976.* Washington: US Government Printing Office, 2011: Doc. 189.

[20] *Ibid.,* Doc. 36.

[21] *Ibid.,* Doc. 162.

[22] Daigle, *Limits of Détente,* 335-36.

[23] Paul Thomas Chamberlin, *The Global Offensive: The United States, the Palestine Liberation Organization, and the Making of the Post-Cold War Order.* New York: Oxford University Press, 2012.

[24] FRUS, 1969-1976, XXVI, Doc. 23

[25] Chamberlin, *Global Offensive,* 245.

[26] Gerald R. Ford, *A Time to Heal: The Autobiography of Gerald R. Ford.* Norwalk, Ct.: Easton Press, 1987: 247.

[27] "A Confusion of Interests" *NER* XIX April 16, 1975: 65.

[28] FRUS, 1969-1976, XXVI, Docs. 156, 162.

[29] Kenneth Kolander, *America's Israel: The US Congress and American-Israeli Relations, 1967-1975.* University Press of Kentucky, 2020; "Senate Leaders Stand Firm with Israel" *NER* XIX Apr. 30, 1975: 79; "Congressmen Speak Out for Israel" *NER* XIX May 7, 1975: 82.

[30] FRUS 1969-1976, XXVI, Docs. 171, 176.

[31] Kolander, *America's Israel.*

[32] "The Spirit of 76" *NER* XIX (May 28, 1975): 93; Yaqub, *Imperfect Strangers,* 169-71.

[33] Shlaim, *Iron Wall,* 340-46.

[34] Tony Shaw and Giora Goodman, "Hollywood's Raid on Entebbe: Behind the Scenes of the United States-Israel Alliance," *Diplomatic History* 42 (September 2018): 590-612.

[35] Peter Novick, *The Holocaust in American Life.* Boston: Houghton Mifflin, 1999: 15, 200-01; 211-12.

[36] Norman Finkelstein, *The Holocaust Industry.* London: Verso Books, 2003; 2001: 47.

[37] *Ibid.,* 73.

[38] *Ibid.,* 50.

[39] *FRUS,* 1977-1980, VIII, Arab-Israeli Dispute, January 1977-August 1978. Washington: US Government Printing Office, 2013: Doc. 165; on the settler movement see Idith Zertal and Akiva Eldar, *Lords of the Land: The War Over Israel's Settlements in the Occupied Territories, 1967-2007.* New York: Nation Books, 2007.

[40] Seth Anziska, *Preventing Palestine: A Political History from Camp David to Oslo.* Princeton: Princeton University Press, 2018: 176.

[41] *Ibid.,* 60-61.

[42] Sasson, *New American Zionism,* 26; Tivnan, *The Lobby,* 98-134.

[43] FRUS, 1977-1980, VIII, Doc. 38.

[44] *NER* XXI (June 22, 1977): 101; *FRUS, 1977-1980, VIII,* Doc. 38.

[45] FRUS, 1977-1980, VIII, Doc. 49.

[46] *Ibid.,* Doc. 165.

[47] Ibid.

48 "US and Soviets Set Mutual Guidelines for Mideast Peace," *New York Times*, Oct. 1, 1977.

49 Anziska, *Preventing Palestine*, 89-90; *NER* XXI (Oct. 5, 1977): 165.

50 FRUS, 1977-1980, VIII, Doc. 124.

51 Two recent comprehensive studies of Carter's Middle East diplomacy essentially share this conclusion. See Daniel Strieff, *Jimmy Carter and the Middle East: The Politics of Presidential Diplomacy*. New York: Palgrave-Macmillan, 2015 and Jørgen Jensehaugen, *Arab-Israeli Diplomacy Under Carter: The US, Israel, and the Palestinians*. New York: I.B. Tauris, 2018.

52 Anziska, *Preventing Palestine*, 117-38.

53 FRUS, 1977-1980, Vol. IX, Arab-Israeli Dispute, August 1978-December 1980. Washington: US Government Printing Office, 2014: Doc. 165.

54 Anziska, *Preventing Palestine*, 153.

55 "A Tale of Two Platforms" *NER* XXIV (Aug. 22, 1980): 157.

56 *Ibid.*, 168.

57 "The Jewish Vote in the 1980 Election," *NER* XXIV (Nov. 14, 1980): 210; "Broad Christian Support for Israel" *NER* XXIV (Nov. 21, 1980): 215.

58 Hummel, *Covenant Brothers*, 2.

59 *Ibid.*, 1, 138.

60 *Ibid.*, 89, 103-04.

61 Neil Rubin, "The Relationship Between American Evangelical Christians and the State of Israel," in Robert O. Freedman, ed., *Israel and the United States: Six Decades of US-Israeli Relations*. Boulder, CO.: Westview Press, 2012: 237.

62 Hummel, Covenant Brothers, 160.

63 Gary M. Burge, "Evangelicals and Christian Zionism," in Donald E. Wagner and Walter T. Davis, eds., *Zionism and the Quest for Justice on the Holy Land*. Eugene, R: Pickwick Publications, 2014: 176.

64 Hummel, *Covenant Brothers*, 160.

65 *Ibid.*, 169-70.

66 Rubin, "Relationship Between American Evangelical Christians and Israel," 240.

Chapter 5 Beating Back Challenges

1 Anziska, *Preventing Palestine*, 162; "Jerusalem and the Settlements," *NER* XXIV (March 26, 1980): 60.

2 Anziska, Preventing Palestine, 167.

3 "Israel Had 'Reason for Concern,'" *NER* XXV (June 26, 1981): 126.

4 "A Loss and a Look to the Future," *NER* (Oct. 28, 1981): 199-200.

5 "Secretary Haig's Leadership," *NER* XXVI (Jan. 22, 1982): 13.

6 Avi Shlaim, *Israel and Palestine: Reappraisals, Revisions, Refutations*. London: Verso, 2009: xiii; see also Baruch Kimmerling, *Politicide: Ariel Sharon's War against the Palestinians*. London: Verso 2003.

7 Anziska, *Preventing Palestine*, 201; Patrick Tyler, *Fortress Israel: The Inside Story of the Military Elite Who Rule the Country—and Why They Can't Make Peace*. New York: Farrar, Struss, and Giroux, 2012: 301-02.

[8] James R. Stocker, *Spheres of Intervention: US Foreign Policy and the Collapse of Lebanon, 1967-1976*. Ithaca: Cornell University Press, 2016; David Hirst. *Beware of Small States: Lebanon, Battleground of the Middle East*. New York: Nation Books, 2010.

[9] Ronen Bergman, *Rise and Kill First: The Secret History of Israel's Targeted Assassinations*. New York: Random House, 2018: 232.

[10] Shlaim, *Iron Wall*, 426-31; Hirst, *Beware of Small States*, 155-60.

[11] Shlaim, *Iron Wall*, 447-48; 429-32.

[12] Anziska, *Preventing Palestine*, 211-12.

[13] *Ibid.*, 183; Ronald Reagan, *An American Life*. New York: Simon and Schuster, 1990: 433.

[14] Anziska, *Preventing Palestine*, 211-13, 250.

[15] "Israel's Service to American National Interest," *NER* XXVI June 18, 1982: 121.

[16] "The Casualties" *NER* XXVI, July 9, 1982: 137; Anziska, *Preventing Palestine*, 221-24.

[17] Anziska, *Preventing Palestine*, 226; Hirst, Beware of Small States, 194.

[18] "Undermining America's Interests," *NER* XXVII (April 8, 1983): 57.

[19] Rula and Malek Abisaab, *The Shi'ites of Lebanon: Modernism, Communism, and Hizbullah's Islamists*. Syracuse University Press, 2014.

[20] Shlaim, *Iron Wall*, 447-48.

[21] "Pro-Israel Congress Adjourns" *NER* XXVII (Nov. 25, 1983): 207; "A Good First Step," *NER* XXVII (Dec. 2, 1983): 209; "Reagan Tilts toward Israel," *NER* XXVII (Dec. 23, 1983): 221.

[22] "The Reagan Record" *NER* XXVIII (Aug. 24, 1984): 141.

[23] "A Ringing Endorsement" *NER* XVIII (Nov. 5, 1984): 181; "The 98th Congress," *NER* XVIII, Nov. 19, 1984: 189; "Where Praise is Due," *NER* XXXI (Dec. 28, 1987): 209.

[24] "The Arms Sale" *NER* XXIX (Oct. 7, 1984): 159; "Jordan Arms Sale Shelved," *NER* XXX (Feb. 10, 1986): 22; "Fig Leaf Hunting," *NER* XXXI (June 15, 1987): 85; "Arms Sales Intermission" *NER* XXXI, (June 22, 1987): 99.

[25] Tyler, *Fortress Israel*, 324-26.

[26] "Iranian Mirage" *NER* XXX (Nov. 17, 1986): 181.

[27] Film, "The Occupation of the American Mind," directed by Loretta Alpern and Jeremy Earp, 2016. https://www.youtube.com/watch?v=dP0-YohJR-g.

[28] Dov Waxman, "The Pro-Israel Lobby in the United States: Past, Present, and Future," in Freedman, ed., *Israel and the United States,* 201.

[29] Waxman, "Pro-Israel Lobby in the United States," 88.

[30] "The Kings of Capitol Hill [film]," directed by Mor Loushy, Stop Press! Productions, 2020.

[31] Lucille Barnes, "Senator Simon Recalls AIPAC Request That He Run Against Charles Percy," *Washington Report on Middle East Affairs* (March 1999): 60.

[32] Hummel, *Covenant Brothers*, 179-80.

[33] Waxman, "Pro-Israel Lobby in the United States," 87.

[34] Smith, *Foreign Agents*, 115.

[35] "Israel and the News Media"; "Special Survey: *NER* at 25" (December 1982): 197-200; "The *Washington Post's* Frontal War against Israel," *NER* XXV (March 27): 1981: 50.

[36] Gordon, *Israel's Occupation*, 131.

[37] Ilan Pappe, *The Biggest Prison on Earth: A History of the Occupied Territories*. London: One World, 2017: 169.

[38] Gordon, *Israel's Occupation*, 167.

[39] Mitchell Kaidy, "CAMERA and FLAME: Pressuring U.S. Media," *Washington Report on Middle East Affairs* (July/August 1993): 29.

[40] Ibid.

[41] Ibid.

[42] "Aid Wins by Record Margin," *NER* XXXIV (July 10, 1989): 114; "Israel Stands Tall on the Hill," *NER* XXXIV (Nov. 5, 1990): 207.

[43] John Judis, "On the Homefront: The Gulf War's Strangest Bedfellows," *Washington Post*, June 23, 1991.
https://www.washingtonpost.com/archive/opinions/1991/06/23/on-the-home-front-the-gulf-wars-strangest-bedfellows/b2b9195f-0d4a-4a3b-a18f-b8982156f351/

[44] "Heard on the Hill," *NER* XXXV (March 11, 1991): 37.

[45] *New York Times*, Dec. 7, 1987.

[46] "Soviet Jews, By the Numbers" *NER* XXXVI (Jan. 13, 1992): 5.

[47] "Jim Baker 1989 AIPAC speech," C-SPAN video.
https://www.c-span.org/video/?c4532888/jim-baker-1989-aipac-speech

[48] "US Credibility Shaken" *NER* XXXV (June 3, 1991): 93.

[49] "Settlements—A Side Show" *NER* XXXV (April 29, 1991): 74.

[50] "Behind the Peace Process," *NER* XXXV (June 17, 1991): 101.

[51] How 'lonely little' George H.W. Bush Changed the US-Israel Relationship," *The Times of Israel*, Dec. 2, 2018.
https://www.timesofisrael.com/how-lonely-little-george-h-w-bush-changed-the-us-israel-relationship/.

[52] "Bush Urges Delay on Aid for Israel; Threatens a Veto," *New York Times*, Sept. 13, 1991.

[53] *Ibid*; "Members Blast Baker on Guarantees" *NER Special Supplement* (March 2, 1992): 38.

[54] "Jews Grow 'Hawkish'" *NER*, XXXV (Oct. 14, 1991): 173; "American, Pro-Israel and Proud," *NER*, XXXVI (April 13, 1992): 65.

[55] "A Pro-Israel Platform" *NER*, XXXVI (July 13, 1992): 133; "A Pro-Israel Platform," *NER*, XXXVI (Aug. 24, 1992): 157.

[56] "Charge of Antisemitism 'Abhorrent,' Baker Says," *Washington Post*, April 2, 1992.
https://www.washingtonpost.com/archive/politics/1992/04/02/charge-of-antisemitism-abhorrent-baker-says/741d6a59-6d27-4c4c-8e13-b653d02941df/

[57] "How 'lonely little' George H.W. Bush Changed the US-Israel Relationship."

[58] "Clinton and Gore: A Pro-Israel Team," *NER* Special Supplement (Jan. 18, 1993).

59 "Bush's Opposition to Israel in '91 Hurt His Bid for Second term, and Skewed US Foreign Policy Right," *Mondoweiss*, Dec. 6, 2018. https://mondoweiss.net/2018/12/opposition-foreign-policy/

Chapter 6 Fending Off Peace

1 Roby Nathanson and Ron Mandelbaum, "Aid and Trade: Economic Relations between the United States and Israel, 1948-2010," in Freedman, ed., *Israel and the United States:* 124-42.

2 "Jewish Lobbyist Ousted for Slurs," *New York Times*, June 29, 1993.

3 Waxman, *Trouble in the Tribe*, 159.

4 AIPAC Is Indispensable," *NER*, XXXVII (Aug. 23, 1993): 149.

5 *Ibid.*; "Rabin: I'm a Friend of AIPAC," *NER* XXXVII (July 26, 1993): 131; "AIPAC'S Statement on the Peace Process" *NER* XXXVII (Sept. 6, 1993): 151; "US, Israel: Moving the Peace Process Forward," *NER* XXXVII (Oct. 4, 1993): 175; Waxman, *Trouble in the Tribe*, 160.

6 See the discussion in Waxman, *Trouble in the Tribe*, 147-73.

7 American Jews Continue to support Israeli Government's Peace Initiative," *NER*, XXXVIII (Sept. 19, 1994): 168; "AIPAC 1994 Policy Statement," *NER*, XXXVIII (March 21, 1994): 51.

8 Connie Bruck, "Friends of Israel," *The New Yorker* (September 1, 2014). https://www.newyorker.com/magazine/2014/09/01/friends-israel

9 Khaled Elgindy, *Blind Spot: America and the Palestinians, from Balfour to Trump.* Washington: Brookings Institution Press, 2019: 137-41.

10 Ali Abunimah, *The Battle for Justice in Palestine*. Chicago: Haymarket Books, 2014: 78.

11 Elgindy, Blind Spot, 142.

12 Noura Erakat, *Justice for Some: Law and the Question of Palestine*. Stanford: Stanford University Press, 2019: 159-64; see also

13 Shlaim, *Iron Wall*, 546-48.

14 "House Sends Letter to Clinton: Keep Jerusalem United," *NER* XXXVIII (Oct. 17, 1994): 191.

15 Bruck, "Friends of Israel."

16 Ibid.

17 "Jerusalem Embassy Act Approved," *NER* XXXIX (Nov. 6, 1995): 136.

18 "Jerusalem Embassy Act of 1995." https://www.congress.gov/104/plaws/publ45/PLAW-104publ45.pdf

19 Hummel, Covenant Brothers, 200-201.

20 Shlaim, *Iron Wall*, 542-43.

21 Anziska, *Preventing Palestine*, 286.

22 Hummel, *Covenant Brothers*: 199.

23 Pappe, *Biggest Prison on Earth*, 192-97.

24 Rogan, *The Arabs*, 544.

25 Bjorn Brenner, *Gaza Under Hamas: From Islamic Democracy to Islamist Governance.* London: I.B. Tauris, 2017.

26 Shlaim, Iron Wall, 474; Pappe, Biggest Prison on Earth, 192.

27 Mohammed M. Hafez and Marc-André Walther, "Hamas: Between Pragmatism and Radicalism," in Akbarzadeh, ed., *Routledge Handbook of Political Islam*, 67.

28 See the discussion in Hixson *Israel's Armor*, 238.

29 "Kohr: AIPAC Established Relationships with All New Members of Congress," *NER* XL (Nov. 18, 1996): 109.

30 "AIPAC Ranks Second in *Fortune's* 'Clout in the Capital' Survey," *NER* XLI (Dec. 1, 1997): 105.

31 Shlaim, *Iron Wall*, 626.

32 Bruck, "Friends of Israel"; "Netanyahu in 2001: 'America is a Thing You Can Move Very Easily,'" *The Huffington Post*, May 25, 2011. https://www.huffpost.com/entry/netanyahu-in-2001-america_n_649427.

33 Anshel Pfeffer, *Bibi: The Turbulent Life and Times of Benjamin Netanyahu*. New York: Basic Books, 2018: 240-41.

34 Bruck, "Friends of Israel."

35 "West Bank Settlements: Hype and Reality," *NER* XXXIX (Sept. 23, 1996): 95.

36 "US Stands with Israel at the UN," *NER* XLII (Feb. 22, 1998): 13.

37 Smith, *Palestine and the Arab-Israeli Conflict*, 457-59.

38 "Falwell to Mobilize Support for Israel," *New York Times*, Jan. 21, 1998; Rubin, "Relationship Between American Evangelical Christians and State of Israel," 246.

39 "No to Pressure on Israel," *NER* XLII (Mar. 23, 1998): 21; "Members Criticize US 'Ultimatum,'" *NER* XLII (May 18, 1998): 42.

40 *NER* XLII (Nov. 16, 1998): 101.

41 "AIPAC Speaks Out on Peace," *NER* XLI (Aug. 25, 1997): 77.

42 Ami Pedahzur, *The Triumph of Israel's Radical Right*. New York: Oxford, 2012: 149.

43 Rashid Khalidi, "Dennis Ross: 'More Israeli Than the Israelis,'" *Washington Report on Middle East Affairs* (January/February 2012): 18-19.

44 Aaron David Miller, *The Much Too Promised Land: America's Elusive Search for Arab-Israeli Peace*. New York: Bantam Books, 2008: 123.

45 Ben-Ami, *Defending the Holy Land*, 464-68; Shlaim, *Iron Wall*, 681-89.

46 "Balking at the Brink of Peace," *NER* XLIV (Nov. 13, 2000): 87.

47 Ben-Ami, *Defending the Holy Land*, 469-70; Kimmerling, *Politicide*.

48 *The Guardian*, Sept. 28, 2000.

49 Degani, "From Republic to Empire: Israel and the Palestinians after 1948," in Cavanagh and Veracini, eds., *Routledge Handbook of History of Settler Colonialism*, 362.

50 Gordon, *Israel's Occupation*, 143.

51 Beverley Milton-Edwards, "Perpetual Struggle: The Significance of the Arab-Israeli Conflict for Islamists," in Shahram Akbarzadeh, ed., *Routledge Handbook of Political Islam*. New York: Routledge, 2012: 242, 247.

52 Gordon, *Israel's Occupation*, xvii.

53 Shlaim, *Iron Wall*, 751-56.

54 "Defensive Barriers," *NER* XLVI (July 15, 2002): 57; "Kangaroo Case," *NER* XLVIII (Feb. 9, 2004): 11.

55 "Historic AIPAC Policy Conference," *NER* XLIV (May 29, 2000): 41-43.

56 "Gore Chooses Sen Lieberman as Running Mate," *Los Angeles Times*, Aug. 8, 2000. https://www.latimes.com/archives/la-xpm-2000-aug-08-mn-635-story.html

57 Elgindy, *Blind Spot*, 167-76.

58 "Violent Betrayal," *NER* XLV (Feb. 19, 2001): 14; "Heard on the Hill," *NER*, XLV (March 19, 2001): 24.

59 "Show of Solidarity," *NER* XLV (April 2, 2001): 25; "Relations Review," *NER* XLV (Apr. 16, 2001): 29; "Eye to Eye," *NER* XLV (May 14, 2001): 37.

60 "Powell's Plea," *NER* XLV (May 28, 2001): 41.

61 "Setting it Straight," *NER* XLV (June 11, 2001): 46.

62 Kapan, *Our American Israel*, 8.

63 "Off the Mark," *NER* XLV (Oct. 8, 2001): 75.

64 Chalmers Johnson, *Blowback: The Costs and Consequences of American Empire*. New York: Henry Holt. 2004; Hixson, chapter 10, Myth, *Myth of American Diplomacy*, 277-304.

65 "Quiet Cooperation," *NER* XLV (Oct. 22, 2001): 78. "Solid Support," *NER* XLV (Nov. 5, 2001): 82.

66 The *NER* cited a poll showing 52 percent of Americans sympathized more with Israel whereas only 10 percent more with Palestinians. "Backing Israel," *NER* XLVI (Apr. 8, 2002): 25; "Circle of Terror," *NER* XLVI (July 29, 2002): 61.

67 Akbarzadeh, ed., *Routledge Handbook of Political Islam*.

68 Rogan, *The Arabs*, 610.

69 Shlaim, *Iron Wall*, 747.

70 Shlaim, Iron Wall, 710-50; see also Kimmerling, *Politicide: Sharon's War Against the Palestinians*.

71 "Pro-Israel Demonstration Draws Tens of Thousands to Washington," *Los Angeles Times*, Apr. 16, 2002. https://www.latimes.com/archives/la-xpm-2002-apr-16-mn-38141-story.html.

72 "Thousands Rally for Israel," April 16, 2002, *Washington Post*; "Speakers Stick to Consensus Theme at National Solidarity Rally for Israel," Jewish Telegraphic Agency, Apr. 16, 2002. https://www.jta.org/2002/04/16/archive/speakers-stick-to-consensus-theme-at-national-solidarity-rally-for-israel.

73 "Thousands Rally for Israel"; "Speakers Stick to Consensus Theme at National Solidarity Rally."

74 Rubin, "Relationship Between American Evangelical Christians and Israel," 233.

75 "True Friends," *NER* XLVI (May 6, 2002): 33; "*NER* Interviews: David Ivry," *NER* XLVI (Jan. 28, 2002): 7.

76 *New York Times*, Feb. 5, 2004.

77 "Principled Stance," *NER* XLVII (Apr. 28, 2003): 3; "Heard on the Hill," *NER* XLVII (May 12, 2003): 35; "Continental Divide," *NER* XLVII (June 23, 2003): 48.

78 "Tolerating Terror," *NER* XLVI (June 3, 2002): 43; "Arafat Under Fire," *NER* XLVIII (Aug. 16, 2004): 59.

[79] Bergman, *Rise and Kill First*: 561-63.

[80] "A Clean Break" [1996], Encyclopedia of the Middle East; http://www.mideastweb.org/Middle-East-Encyclopedia/clean_break.htm.

[81] Mearsheimer and Walt, *Israel Lobby*, 231-43.

[82] "A Just War," *NER* XLVII (Mar. 31, 2003): 21; "*NER* Interviews Dr. Kenneth Pollack," *NER* XLVI (Sept. 23, 2002): 7; "*NER* Interviews Dr. Amatzia Baram," *NER* XLVI (Oct. 7, 2002): 80.

[83] Elgindy, *Blind Spot*, 178.

[84] *Ibid.*, 178-79.

[85] "Overwhelming Support," *NER* XLVIII (June 28, 2004): 467; "Historic Agreement Forged," *NER* XLVIII (Apr. 26, 2004): 34.

[86] Elgindy, *Blind Spot*, 179.

[87] "The Ties that Bind," *NER* XLVIII (June 1, 2004): 37.

[88] Robert O. Freedman, "George W. Bush, Barack Obama, and the Arab-Israeli Conflict from 2001 to 2011," in Freedman, ed., *Israel and the United States*: 48.

[89] "Not So Gentle Rhetoric from the Gentleman from South Carolina," Jewish Telegraph Agency, May 24, 2004. https://www.jta.org/2004/05/24/archive/not-so-gentle-rhetoric-from-the-gentleman-from-south-carolina.

Chapter 7 AIPAC in Command

[1] Hirst, *Beware of Small States*, 258-61.

[2] Lara Deeb, "Hizbullah in Lebanon," in Akbarzadeh, ed., *Routledge Handbook of Political Islam*: 78.

[3] Hirst, *Beware of Small States*, 328-74; 396-401.

[4] Tyler, *Fortress Israel*, 470.

[5] "AIPAC Applauds Passage of Congressional Resolutions Backing Israel," AIPAC Press Release, July 20, 2006. https://web.archive.org/web/20070701023955/http://www.aipac.org/PDFdocs/Press/Hizballah_Hamas_HouseResolutionpassage.pdf.

[6] "AIPAC Applauds Passage of Congressional Resolutions Backing Israel," July 20, 2006. http://www.aipac.org/PDFdocs/Press/Hizballah_Hamas_HouseResolutionpassage.pdf

[7] Hirst, *Beware of Small States*, 375-97.

[8] Deeb, "Hizbullah in Lebanon," 81; see also Abisaabs, *Shi'ites of Lebanon*.

[9] Max Blumenthal, *Goliath: Life and Loathing in Greater Israel*. New York: Nation Books, 2013: 11.

[10] Bergman, Rise and Kill First, 131.

[11] Erakat, *Justice for Some*, 209-10.

[12] "Landmark address," *NER* XLVIII (Jan. 12, 2004): 2.

[13] Sasson, New American Zionism, 39, 60.

[14] Aaron D. Pina, "Palestinian Elections," Congressional Research Service, Feb. 9, 2006. https://fas.org/sgp/crs/mideast/RL33269.pdf; Elgindy, *Blind Spot*, 186.

[15] Elgindy, *Blind Spot*, 188; Abunimah, *Battle for Justice in Palestine*, 83.

[16] Marc Andrei-Walther, "Hamas: Between Pragmatism and Radicalism," in Akbarzadeh, *Routledge Handbook of Political Islam*: 71, 62.

[17] Brenner, *Gaza Under Hamas*, 198.

[18] Hafez and Walther, "Hamas: Between Pragmatism and Radicalism," 62-63.

[19] Abunimah, *Battle for Justice in Palestine*: 75-83.

[20] Elgindy, *Blind Spot*, 181-90.

[21] "Standards Upheld," *NER* LI (Apr. 11, 2007): 25.

[22] Elgindy, *Blind Spot*, 187-97.

[23] Norman G. Finkelstein, *Gaza: An Inquest Into its Martyrdom*. Berkeley: University of California Press, 2018: 58-61.

[24] *Ibid.*, 68-73.

[25] *Ibid.*, 105.

[26] *Ibid.*, 130.

[27] "*NER* Interviews Howard A. Kohr," *NER* XLVIII (Dec. 20, 2004): 97.

[28] "Congressional Commitment," *NER* XLVII (July 30, 2003): 62.

[29] "Summer of solidarity," *NER* XLVII Sept. 8, 2003: 69.

[30] "Pro-Israel Group Lobbies for US Aid, Funds Congressional Trips," *Wall Street Journal*, Feb. 14, 2019. https://www.wsj.com/articles/pro-israel-group-lobbies-for-u-s-aid-funds-congressional-trips-11550174834.

[31] Connie Bruck, "Friends of Israel," *The New Yorker* (Aug. 25, 2014).

[32] Bruck, "Friends of Israel."

[33] Bruck, "Friends of Israel."

[34] "Join AIPAC's Congressional Club," AIPAC online. https://www.aipac.org/take-action/congressional-club.

[35] Beattie, *Congress and the Shaping of the Middle East*, 92, 251, 395-409.

[36] Rubin, "Relationship Between Evangelical Christians and Israel," 234.

[37] Hummel, *Covenant Brothers*, 23, 202.

[38] *Ibid.*, 186, 205.

[39] Rubin, "Relationship Between Evangelical Christians and Israel," 236-37.

[40] "*NER* Interviews David Brog," *NER* LI (Feb. 5, 2007): 6.

[41] Rubin, "Relationship Between Evangelical Christians and Israel," 233; Hummel, *Covenant Brothers*, 13, 206.

[42] Hummel, Covenant Brothers, 238.

[43] "Light and Shadows in US-Israeli Military Ties, 1948-2010," in Freedman, ed., *Israel and the United States, 143-64*.

[44] "Lessons Learned," *NER* LII (May 16-31, 2008): 28.

[45] "Joint Defense," *NER* LI (Aug. 16-Sept. 15, 2007): 59)

[46] "Securely United," *NER* LI (Sept. 16-30, 2007): 63.

[47] "Historic Victory," *NER* LII (Nov. 1-Dec. 31, 2008): 71.

[48] "US to Give $900 Million in Gaza Aid, Officials Say," *New York Times*, Feb. 23, 2009.

[49] "The President's Speech in Cairo," The White House, President Barack Obama. https://obamawhitehouse.archives.gov/issues/foreign-policy/presidents-speech-cairo-a-new-beginning

[50] Bernard Avishai, "Netanyahu and the Republicans," *The New Yorker*, Feb. 4, 2015 https://www.newyorker.com/news/news-desk/netanyahu-republicans

[51] AIPAC-Backed Letter Gets 329 House Signatures," Jewish Telegraphic Agency, May 28, 2009. https://www.jta.org/2009/05/28/politics/aipac-backed-letter-gets-329-house-signatures

[52] Josh Ruebner, "Obama's Legacy on Israel/Palestine," *Institute for Palestine Studies* 46 (2016/17). https://www.palestine-studies.org/jps/fulltext/207365.

[53] "Netanyahu Declares Ten-Month Settlement Freeze," *Haaretz*, Nov. 25, 2009. https://www.haaretz.com/1.5122924.

[54] "So Much for a Friendly Biden Visit to Israel," *Foreign Policy Passport*, Mar. 9, 2010. https://foreignpolicy.com/2010/03/09/so-much-for-a-friendly-biden-visit-to-israel/

[55] "House Letter Reaffirming US-Israel Bonds," Mar. 25, 2010, Jewish Virtual Library. https://www.jewishvirtuallibrary.org/house-letter-reaffirming-u-s-israel-bonds-march-2010

[56] "Lawmakers Reaffirm US-Israel Alliance," *NER* (Apr. 23, 2010), AIPAC online.

[57] "House Leaders to Obama: Pledge to Use Veto in UN," *NER* (Feb. 3, 2011), AIPAC online.

[58] Ruebner, "Obama's Legacy on Israel/Palestine."

[59] Finkelstein, *Gaza Martyrdom*, 197.

[60] *Ibid.*, 141-76; Blumenthal, *Goliath*, 102-05.

[61] "Congress Stands up for Israel" (June 11, 2010); "Congress Affirms Israel's Right to Self-Defense" (July 12, 2010), both in *NER*, AIPAC online.

[62] Bruck, "Friends of Israel;" "Netanyahu Campaign Video Boast of 'lecturing' Obama in the Oval Office," *The Times of Israel*, Mar. 28, 2019. https://www.timesofisrael.com/netanyahu-campaign-video-boasts-of-lecturing-obama-in-the-oval-office/.

[63] Bruck, "Friends of Israel."

[64] "Congress Opposes Palestinian Statehood, Calls on PA to Return to Talks," *NER* (July 18, 2011), AIPAC online.

[65] "Remarks by the President at the AIPAC Policy Conference 2011," May 22, 2011, the White House. https://obamawhitehouse.archives.gov/the-press-office/2011/05/22/remarks-president-aipac-policy-conference-2011

[66] Ruebner, "Obama's Legacy on Israel/Palestine."

[67] "112th Congress Expected to be Most Pro-Israel Ever," *NER* (Nov. 19, 2010), AIPAC online.

[68] Philip Weiss, "The Root cause of the Conflict is the Israel Lobby," *Mondoweiss*, Nov. 26, 2019; https://mondoweiss.net/2019/11/the-root-cause-of-the-conflict-is-the-israel-lobby/.

[69] Nathan Thrall, "How the Battle Over Israel and Anti-Semitism is Fracturing American Politics," *New York Times Magazine*, Mar. 28, 2019; https://www.nytimes.com/2019/03/28/magazine/battle-over-bds-israel-palestinians-antisemitism.html.

[70] "US Presidential Election: Jewish Voting Record," Jewish Virtual Library. https://www.jewishvirtuallibrary.org/jewish-voting-record-in-u-s-presidential-elections

[71] Ruebner, "Obama's Legacy on Israel/Palestine."

[72] Netanyahu Apologizes to Turkish PM for Israeli Role in Gaza Flotilla Raid," *The Guardian*, Mar. 22, 2013.

[73] Elgindy, *Blind Spot*, 229-30.

[74] *Ibid.*, 232.

[75] "Kerry: 'Jewish state' demand 'a mistake,'" *The Times of Israel*, Mar. 14, 2004; https://www.timesofisrael.com/kerry-jewish-state-demand-a-mistake/; "Israel Risks Becoming Apartheid State if Peace Talks Fail, Says John Kerry," *The Guardian*, April 28, 2014.

[76] Finkelstein, *Gaza*, 201-37.

[77] "Obama Calls for Ceasefire as Kerry Announces Aid to Gaza," July 21, 2014, MSNBC. http://www.msnbc.com/msnbc/obama-gaza-cease-fire-kerry-announces-aid-israel-hamas.

[78] "The Occupation of the American Mind," directed by Loretta Alpern and Jeremy Earp, 2016. https://www.occupationmovie.org/

[79] "US Leadership stands with Israel, Calls for Demilitarization of Gaza," *NER* (Aug. 1, 2014): AIPAC online.

[80] Finkelstein, Gaza: Inquest into Martyrdom, 320-22.

[81] "Occupation of the American Mind."

[82] Bruck, "Friends of Israel."

[83] "US Senate Unanimously Approves Resolution Giving Full Support of Israel on Gaza," *Haaretz*, July 20, 2014. https://www.haaretz.com/u-s-senate-unanimously-approves-resolution-giving-full-support-of-israel-on-gaza-1.5256107.

[84] "Congress Approves More Money for Israel's Iron Dome," CNN, Aug. 27, 2014. https://www.cnn.com/2014/08/01/politics/congress-israel-iron-dome/index.html

[85] Bruck, "Friends of Israel."

[86] Mor Loushy, "The Kings of Capitol Hill," Stop Press! Productions, 2020; see also Walter L. Hixson, "Former AIPAC Insiders Condemn Lobby in New Israeli Documentary," *Washington Report on Middle East Affairs* (Jan./Feb. 2021).

Chapter 8 Demonizing Iran, Cashing in on Trump

[1] Ervand Abrahamian, *A History of Modern Iran*. New York: Cambridge University Press, 2018: 190-202.

[2] *New York Times*, Feb. 12, 2002; Abrahamian, *History of Modern Iran*, 187-202.

[3] Virtually any and every edition of the *NER* in the twenty-first century contains articles and sometimes special editions reflecting hostility to the Islamic movements and regimes. See AIPAC online.

4 John Walsh, "Why Is the Peace Movement Silent About AIPAC?" *Counterpunch*, April 17, 2007 https://www.counterpunch.org/2007/04/17/why-is-the-peace-movement-silent-about-aipac/; Mearsheimer and Walt, *Israel Lobby*, 301.

5 Cause for Concern," *NER* XLVII (July 28, 2003): 55; "Going Nuclear," *NER* XLVII (Sept. 8, 2003): 65; "IAEA's Free Pass to Iran," *NER* XLVIII (Sept. 27, 2004): 69.

6 "Bipartisan Commitment," *NER* LII (Sept. 16-30, 2008):15; "Editorial: Implementation is Essential," *NER* (July 12, 2010), AIPAC online.

7 "The Central Bank of Iran: The 'Lifeblood' of the Iranian Financial System," *NER* (Dec. 21, 2011), AIPAC online; "Sanctions Bite as Iran's Nuclear Program Continues," *NER* (March 26, 2012), AIPAC online.

8 "Editorial: A Nuclear Iran Threatens America," *NER* (Apr. 24, 2012), AIPAC online.

9 *Ibid.*, xix.

10 "Netanyahu's Bomb Diagram Succeeds—But Not in the way the PM Wanted," *The Guardian*, Sept. 27, 2012. https://www.theguardian.com/world/2012/sep/27/binyamin-netanyahu-cartoon-bomb-un.

11 Bergman, *Rise and Kill First*, xix-xxii.

12 "Mohsen Fakhrizadeh: Iran Scientist 'killed by remote-controlled weapon,'" BBC News, Dec. 1, 2020. https://www.bbc.com/news/world-middle-east-55128970.

13 "Alleged Assassination Plots Involving Foreign leaders," Senate Select Committee Interim Report (94th Congress), November 1975. https://www.cia.gov/library/readingroom/docs/CIA-RDP83-01042R000200090002-0.pdf.

14 Erakat, *Justice for Some*, 187-93.

15 Jeremy Scahill, Dirty Wars: The World is a Battlefield. New York: Nation Books, 2013: 244-363; see also Jeremy Kuzmarov, Obama's Unending Wars: Fronting the Foreign Policy of the Permanent Warfare State. Atlanta: Clarity Press, 2019.

16 "US Kills Iran General Qassem Suleimani in Strike Ordered by Trump, The Guardian, Jan. 3, 2020. https://www.theguardian.com/world/2020/jan/03/baghdad-airport-iraq-attack-deaths-iran-us-tensions.

17 Erakat, *Justice for Some*, 192-94.

18 Gary M. Burge, "Evangelicals and Christian Zionism," in Donald E. Wagner and Walter T. Davis, eds., *Zionism and the Quest for Justice in the Holy Land*. Eugene, OR: Pickwick Publications, 2014: 180.

19 "Key Lawmakers Urge Increased Pressure on Iran," *NER* (Dec. 6, 2013), AIPAC online.

20 "Israel PM Netanyahu Criticizes Iran 'Deal of the Century,'" BBC News, Nov. 8, 2013. https://www.bbc.com/news/av/world-middle-east-24866004/israel-pm-netanyahu-criticises-iran-deal-of-the-century.

[21] Trita Parsi, "Should the United States Back Out of Middle East to End Endless Wars?" *Washington Report on Middle East Affairs* (March/April 2020): 34. https://www.wrmea.org/2020-march-april/should-u.s.-back-out-of-middle-east-to-end-endless-wars.html.

[22] "How Netanyahu's Speech to Congress has Jeopardized US-Israel Relations," *The Guardian*, Feb. 24, 2015. https://www.theguardian.com/world/2015/feb/24/obama-binyamin-netanyahu-congress-speech-boehner-leaks.

[23] Bruck, "Friends of Israel."

[24] "Israeli Prime Minister Benjamin Netanyahu Addresses Joint Meeting of Congress," *NER* (March 26, 2015), AIPAC online.

[25] "PM Netanyahu's Speech at AIPAC," Mar. 2, 2015. https://www.youtube.com/watch?v=45lyp8EeBNs.

[26] Netanyahu address to the US Congress, March 3, 2015. https://www.youtube.com/watch?v=wRf1cdw4IAY.

[27] "Editorial—Iran's Aggression Merits Sanctions, Not Concessions," *NER* (April 2016); "Defeating ISIS Requires Simultaneously Countering Iran," *NER* (January 2016), both AIPAC online.

[28] Gideon Levy, "With Iran Deal, Israel Turns a Day of Celebration into a Day of Mourning," *Haaretz*, July 15, 2015. https://www.haaretz.com/opinion/.premium-israel-s-artificial-day-of-mourning-1.5305545

[29] Grant F. Smith, "The Jonathan Pollard Exception: Israeli Espionage Against the US is Rarely Prosecuted," Antiwar.com. https://original.antiwar.com/smith-grant/2020/12/02/the-jonathan-pollard-exception/.

[30] Ronald J. Olive, *Capturing Jonathan Pollard*. Annapolis, MD: Naval Institute Press, 2006: 237-38.

[31] "H.R. 938--United States-Israel Strategic Partnership Act of 2014" (113th Congress, 2013-14). https://www.congress.gov/bill/113th-congress/house-bill/938.

[32] "AIPAC, Our Agenda: 'Strengthen US-Israel Strategic Cooperation,'" https://www.aipac.org/learn/legislative-agenda/agenda-display?agendaid=%7BD9F4B5E3-4883-4800-97FB-7D5655789AAA%7D.

[33] "US Finalizes Deal to Give Israel $38 Billion in Military Aid," *New York Times*, Sept. 13, 2016.

[34] "Testimony—AIPAC CEO Howard Kohr's Congressional Testimony [House Appropriations Subcommittee on State, Foreign Operations and Related Programs] on Security Assistance to Israel," *NER* (April 2016): AIPAC online.

[35] Jeff Halper, *War Against the People: Israel, the Palestinians and Global Pacification*. London: Pluto Press, 2015; Jonathan Cook, "Israeli Spyware Technology Tested on Palestinians," *Washington Report on Middle East Affairs* (January/February 2020): 8-11.

[36] Kohr testimony, *NER* (April 2016).

[37] "UNSC Resolution 2334 Undermines Peace," *NER* (January 2017), AIPAC online.

[38] Thrall, "Battle over Israel Fracturing American Politics."

[39] "Mike Pompeo's Quid Pro Quo for Sheldon Adelson," *Mondoweiss*, Dec. 5, 2019; https://mondoweiss.net/2019/12/mike-pompeos-quid-pro-quo-for-sheldon-adelson/.

[40] Nathan Guttman, "Evangelicals, Right-wingers Prove Dominance Over AIPAC in Senate Vote," *Forward*, Aug. 7, 2017.

[41] Taylor Force Act (H.R. 1164): 115th Congress. https://www.congress.gov/bill/115th-congress/house-bill/1164.

[42] Walter L. Hixson, "From Right to Return to Right to Starve and Kill," *Washington Report on Middle East Affairs* (August/September 2019): 15-16.

[43] Eric S. Margolis, "A Big Step for a Greater Israel," *Washington Report on Middle East Affairs* (January/February 2019): 33-34.

[44] "US Chides Likud Campaign for 'Promoting Hatred' Against Arab Israelis," *The Times of Israel*, Mar. 12, 2020; https://www.timesofisrael.com/us-chides-likud-campaign-for-promoting-hatred-against-arab-israelis.

[45] Abunimah, *Battle for Justice in Palestine*, 36.

[46] Walter L. Hixson, "Occupation of the *Atlantic* Mind," *Washington Report on Middle East Affairs* (June/July 2019): 26-27.

[47] "Trump Administration Says Israel's West Bank Settlements Do Not Violate International Law," *Washington Post*, Nov. 19, 2019.

[48] "Peace to Prosperity: A Vision to Improve the Lives of the Palestinian and Israeli People." https://www.whitehouse.gov/wp-content/uploads/2020/01/Peace-to-Prosperity-0120.pdf.

[49] "'Take a Cold shower' and Don't 'Screw Up'—Kushner Shamefully Blames Palestinians," *Mondoweiss*, Feb. 3, 2020; https://mondoweiss.net/2020/02/take-a-cold-shower-and-dont-screw-up-kushner-shamefully-blames-palestinians/.

[50] Christopher M. Davidson, *Shadow Wars: The Secret Struggle for the Middle East.* London: Oneworld Publications, 2016.

[51] Andrew J. Bacevich, America's War for the Greater Middle East: A Military History. New York: Random House, 2016.

Chapter 9 Resistance to Israeli Apartheid

[1] "Congresswoman McCollum Introduces First-Ever legislation in Support of Palestinian Human Rights." Jewish Voice for Peace, Nov 14, 2017. https://jewishvoiceforpeace.org/congresswoman-mccollum-introduces-first-ever-legislation-support-palestinian-human-rights/

[2] "What Lessons Can Activists Take Away from the Promoting Human Rights by Ending Israeli Military Detention of Palestinian Children Act?" *Washington Report for Middle East Affairs* conference, Mar. 22, 2019. https://www.wrmea.org/2019-may/what-lessons-can-activists-take-away-from-the-promoting-human-rights-by-ending-israeli-military-detention-of-palestinian-children-act.html.

[3] "McCollum Introduces Legislation to Promote Human Rights for Palestinian Children;" "Children in Israeli Military Detention: Observations and Recommendations," UNICEF (February 2013). https://www.unicef.org/oPt/UNICEF_oPt_Children_in_Israeli_Military_Detention_Observations_and_Recommendations_-_6_March_2013.pdf

[4] "McCollum Introduces Legislation to Promote Human Rights for Palestinian Children."

[5] Brad Parker, "I Was Meant to Talk about Palestinian Kids at the UN. Israel Forced Me Out," +972 The Magazine, Feb. 24, 2020; https://www.972mag.com/palestinian-children-security-council/.

[6] Sunania Maira, Boycott! The Academy and Justice for Palestine. Berkeley: University of California Press, 2018: 4.

[7] Audrea Lim, ed., The Case for Sanctions Against Israel. London: Verso, 2012: 55.

[8] Sasha Polakow-Suransky, The Unspoken Alliance: Israel's Secret Relationship with Apartheid South Africa. New York: Vintage Books, 2011: 107, 62, 150.

[9] "Tutu: Israel's Humiliation of Palestinians 'Familiar to Black South Africans,'" Haaretz, Mar. 10, 2014. https://www.haaretz.com/israel-s-treatment-of-palestinians-like-apartheid-1.5331392.

[10] "The United Nations: Israeli Response to 'Zionism is Racism' Resolution, Nov. 10, 1975, Jewish Virtual Library. https://www.jewishvirtuallibrary.org/israeli-statement-in-response-to-quot-zionism-is-racism-quot-resolution-november-1975.

[11] Mearsheimer and Walt, The Israel Lobby, 193.

[12] Abunimah, Battle for Justice in Palestine, 24-25.

[13] Emma Green, "Israel's New Law Inflames the Core Tension of its Identity," The Atlantic, July 21, 2018. https://www.theatlantic.com/international/archive/2018/07/israel-nation-state-law/565712/

[14] Gideon Levy, "A Law that Tells the Truth About Israel," Washington Report on Middle East Affairs (October 2018): 8-10; https://www.wrmea.org/israel-palestine/israels-new-nation-state-law-zionism-uber-alles.html.

[15] Nathan Thrall, "How the Battle Over Israel and Anti-Semitism is Fracturing American Politics," New York Times Magazine, Mar. 28, 2019. https://www.nytimes.com/2019/03/28/magazine/battle-over-bds-israel-palestinians-antisemitism.html.

[16] Abunimah, Battle for Justice in Palestine, 33.

[17] Thrall, "Battle Over Israel and Anti-Semitism Fracturing American Politics."

[18] Abunimah, Battle for Justice in Palestine, 35.

[19] Noam Chomsky, The Fateful Triangle: The United States, Israel and the Palestinians. Boston: South End Press, 1983.

[20] Terry, US Foreign Policy in the Middle East: Role of Lobbies and Special Interest Groups; Goldberg, Jewish Power; Ball and Ball, The Passionate Attachment; Tivnan, The Lobby; Rubenberg, Israel and the National Interest; Findley, They Dare to Speak Out; and Tillman, United States in the Middle East: Interests and Obstacles.

21 Peter Kirstein, "The Tenure Denial of Norman Finkelstein," *Academe* blog, June 8, 2012. https://academeblog.org/2012/06/08/the-tenure-denial-of-norman-finkelstein/

22 See the discussion in Hixson, *Israel's Armor*, 6-10; Chomsky, *Fateful Triangle*; Mearsheimer and Walt, *The Israel Lobby*.

23 *Washington Report on Middle East Affairs.* https://www.wrmea.org/.

24 *"The Electronic Intifada."* https://electronicintifada.net/.

25 Antiwar.com https://www.antiwar.com/.

26 *"Informed Comment."* https://www.juancole.com/; David Burt and Alison Griswold, "Professor Denied Appointment at Yale Sues CIA and FBI," *Yale Daily News*, July 16, 2001. https://yaledailynews.com/blog/2011/07/16/professor-denied-appointment-at-yale-sues-cia-and-fbi/.

27 *Institute for Research: Middle Eastern Policy.* https://www.irmep.org/; IRmep Conferences: https://www.irmep.org/conferences/default.asp.

28 Mondoweiss.net https://mondoweiss.net/.

29 "BDS: Freedom, Justice, Equality." https://bdsmovement.net/; see also Omar Barghouti, *BDS: Boycott, Divestment, Sanctions: The Global Struggle for Palestinian Rights.* Chicago, IL.: Haymarket Books, 2011; Lim, ed., *Case for Sanctions Against Israel.*

30 "PACBI Guidelines for the International Cultural Boycott of Israel." https://bdsmovement.net/pacbi/cultural-boycott-guidelines.

31 Rubin, "Relationship Between Evangelical Christians and Israel," 243-44; "Major Churches Divest," https://bdsmovement.net/impact/major-churches-divest.

32 "PACBI—A List of Artists Who Respect the BDS Call." http://www.pacbi.org/etemplate.php?id=1992.

33 "Is BDS Anti-Semitic?" *New York Times*, July 27, 2019. https://www.nytimes.com/2019/07/27/world/middleeast/bds-israel-boycott-antisemitic.html.

34 "Rachel Corrie Foundation for Peace and Justice." https://rachelcorriefoundation.org/.

35 Ashley Dawson and Bill V. Mullen, eds., *Against Apartheid: The Case for Boycotting Israeli Universities.* Chicago: Haymarket Books, 2015.

36 "PACBI Guidelines for the International Cultural Boycott of Israel." https://bdsmovement.net/pacbi/cultural-boycott-guidelines.

37 "Noam Chomsky Opposes Cultural Boycott of Israel," Up Front, Al Jazeera English, Feb. 1, 2016. https://www.youtube.com/watch?v=UbA0pUK808I.

38 Jordan Michael Smith, "An Unpopular Man [Finkelstein]," *The New Republic*, July 7, 2015. https://newrepublic.com/article/122257/unpopular-man-norman-finkelstein-comes-out-against-bds-movement.

39 Abunimah, *Battle for Justice in Palestine*: 125-27.

40 "Is BDS Anti-Semitic?"

41 Walter L. Hixson, *American Settler Colonialism: A History.* New York: Palgrave Macmillan, 2013: 195.

42 "Palestinian Civil Society Call for BDS," July 9, 2005. https://bdsmovement.net/call.

[43] Waxman, *Trouble in the Tribe*: 6-8.

[44] Sasson, *New American Zionism*, 87-88; Israel constitutes "the most important element of liberal Jewish identity and mobilization in the United States," according to Yossi Shain and Neil Rogashevsky. "If American Jews sought to "check their Zionism at the door," they would risk "checking their Judaism as well." Quoted in "Between JDate and J Street: US Foreign Policy and the Liberal Jewish Dilemma in America," in Josh DeWind and Renata Segura, eds., *Diaspora Lobbies and the US Government*. New York: New York University Press, 2014: 66.

[45] Carolyn L. Karcher, ed., *Reclaiming Judaism from Zionism: Stories of Personal Transformation*. Northampton, MA: Olive Branch Press, 2019: vii.

[46] Waxman, *Trouble in the Tribe*, 181-82; see also Sasson, New American Zionism.

[47] Waxman, *Trouble in the Tribe*, 175-86.

[48] *Ibid.*, 182; Goldberg, *Jewish Power*, 363.

[49] Waxman, *Trouble in the Tribe*, 184, 177.

[50] *Ibid.*, 185, 209.

[51] *Ibid.*, 120.

[52] Peter Beinart, *The Crisis of Zionism*. New York: Henry Holt and Co., 2012.

[53] Waxman, Trouble in the Tribe, 191-92.

[54] "Israeli and American Jews: Twin Portraits from Pew Research Center Surveys," Jan. 24, 2017. https://www.pewforum.org/essay/american-and-israeli-jews-twin-portraits-from-pew-research-center-surveys/.

[55] Waxman, *Trouble in the Tribe*, 54.

[56] Waxman, "Pro-Israel Lobby in United States," 91; J Street, "Boycott, Divestment and Sanctions (BDS)"; https://jstreet.org/policy/boycott-divestment-and-sanctions-bds/#.XYYw55NKhN0.

[57] Waxman, *Trouble in the Tribe*, 165-71.

[58] "Jewish Coalition Rejects Lobbying Group's Bid to Join," *New York Times*, April 30, 2014. https://www.nytimes.com/2014/05/01/us/jewish-coalition-rejects-lobbying-groups-bid-to-join.html.

[59] "J Street Saddened and Disturbed by Passage of Israel's Nation-State Law," July 19, 2018 press release. https://jstreet.org/press-releases/j-street-saddened-and-disturbed-by-passage-of-israels-nation-state-law/#.X-H-CS2cb5k.

[60] J Street Forum, PBS NewsHour, Oct. 28, 2019. https://www.youtube.com/watch?v=WFOo2Vzj0Ps.

[61] "Pro-Israel Democratic Super-PAC to Air Attack Ads Against Bernie Sanders," *New York Times*, Jan. 29, 2020.

[62] "House Vote on Two-State Solution Shows Congress More Divided Than Ever over Israel," *Mondoweiss*, Dec. 9, 2019. https://mondoweiss.net/2019/12/house-vote-on-two-state-solution-shows-congress-more-divided-than-ever-over-israel/.

[63] Americans for Peace Now, "About Us: Mission Statement"; https://peacenow.org/page.php?id=679#.XYYzI5NKhN1.

[64] "Boycott, Divestment and Sanctions (BDS), J Street statement, undated. https://jstreet.org/policy/boycott-divestment-and-sanctions-bds/#.X8-

Kmy1h2u4; https://peacenow.org/page.php?name=bds-name-and-shame-them#.X8-LTS1h2u5.

[65] Rabbi Alissa Wise, interview by Katie Miranda, Mar. 30, 2019. https://www.youtube.com/watch?v=Mtys-s0y8os&feature=youtu.be.

[66] "Jewish Voice for Peace: Mission." https://jewishvoiceforpeace.org/mission/

[67] Wise interview by Miranda; Josh Nathan-Kazis, "Jewish Voice for Peace Activists Disrupt Bibi at GA," *Forward*, Nov. 8, 2010. https://forward.com/news/132952/jewish-voice-for-peace-activists-interrupt-bibi-at/.

[68] "About Deadly Exchange." https://deadlyexchange.org/about-deadly-exchange/.

[69] Wise interview by Miranda; "About Deadly Exchange."

[70] "IfNotNow." https://ifnotnowmovement.org/about-us/.

[71] Waxman, *Trouble in the Tribe*, 189.

Chapter 10 Repressing Free Speech

[1] Executive Summary, "The Palestine Exception to Free Speech: A Movement Under Attack in the US," Center for Constitutional Rights, Sept. 30, 2015; https://ccrjustice.org/the-palestine-exception.

[2] Ali Abuminah, "Israel's New Strategy: 'sabotage' and "attack' the Global Justice Movement," *Electronic Intifada*, Feb. 16, 2010. https://electronicintifada.net/content/israels-new-strategy-sabotage-and-attack-global-justice-movement/8683.

[3] Maira, *Boycott!* 85-92.

[4] Executive Summary, "The Palestine Exception to Free Speech."

[5] Abunimah, Battle for Justice in Palestine: 137-44; Maira, Boycott! 100.

[6] Alon Tal, Pollution in a Promised Land: An Environmental History of Israel. Berkeley: University of California Press, 2002.

[7] Asa Winstanley, "BDS Is Winning, Admits Top Israeli 'Sabotage' Strategist," *The Electronic Intifada*, Apr. 21, 2017. https://electronicintifada.net/blogs/asa-winstanley/bds-winning-admits-top-israeli-sabotage-strategist.

[8] "Taking Back the Campus," *NER* XLVII (Oct. 20, 2003): 83.

[9] "Repositioning the Campus," *NER* XLIX (Aug. 1, 2005): 60.

[10] "Campus Leaders Experience Israel," *NER* (AIPAC online), July 23, 2010.

[11] "AIPAC'S Top Campus Awards Presented at Policy Conference," *NER* (AIPAC online), March 26, 2012.

[12] "Over 500 Attend AIPAC High School Summit," *NER* (AIPAC online), Oct. 25, 2010.

[13] Maira, *Boycott!* 56-57.

[14] David Lloyd and Malani Johar Schuller, "The Israeli State of Exception and the Case for Academic Boycott," *AAUP Journal of Academic Freedom* 4 (2013). https://www.aaup.org/reports-publications/journal-academic-freedom/volume-4

[15] Cary Nelson and Gabriel N. Braum, *The Case Against Academic Boycotts of Israel.* Detroit: Wayne State University Press, 2015; Emma Petit, "'Ousted' from Academe, Steven Salaita Says He's Driving a School Bus to Make Ends Meet," Feb. 19, 2019, *Chronicle of Higher Education.* https://www.chronicle.com/article/Ousted-From-Academe/245732.

[16] Sasson, New American Zionism, 49-50.

[17] Batya Ungar-Sargon, "How the Israel Lobby Captured Hillel," *Foreign Policy* (online), Nov. 23, 2015; https://foreignpolicy.com/2015/11/23/how-the-israel-lobby-captured-hillel-international-college-campus/.

[18] "Open Hillel." http://www.openhillel.org/about

[19] "Leader of Christian Zionists Named Head of Adelson Campus Anti-BDS Group," *Forward,* July 8, 2015; https://forward.com/news/311662/leader-of-christian-zionists-named-head-of-adelson-campus-anti-bds-group/.

[20] Canary Mission.org; https://canarymission.org/.

[21] "Censored Film Names Adam Millstein as Canary Mission Funder," *The Electronic Intifada,* Aug. 27, 2018; https://electronicintifada.net/content/censored-film-names-adam-milstein-canary-mission-funder/25356; To access the film, search: "Watch the Film the Israel Lobby Didn't Want You to See."

[22] David Greenberg, et al, "The Blacklist in the Coal Mine," *Tablet,* Oct. 26, 2016; https://www.tabletmag.com/sections/news/articles/the-blacklist-in-the-coal-mine-canary-missions-fear-mongering-agenda-college-campuses

[23] "2019 Year-in-Review: Movement for Palestinian Rights Thrives Despite Censorship," Palestine Legal. https://palestinelegal.org/2019-report.

[24] Walter L. Hixson, "The Zionist Campaign Against Free Speech on Campus," *Washington Report on Middle East Affairs* (August/September 2020): 34-35.

[25] Ibid.

[26] "Awad, et al, vs. Fordham University," Center for Constitutional Rights. https://ccrjustice.org/home/what-we-do/our-cases/awad-et-al-v-fordham-university; "Fordham University Students Win Landmark Fight to Establish University Club," Aug. 6, 2019, Palestine Legal. https://palestinelegal.org/news/2019/8/6/fordham-university-students-win-landmark-fight-to-establish-palestine-club.

[27] Hixson, Hixson, "Zionist Campaign Against Free Speech on Campus."

[28] Ibid.

[29] "President Bollinger Condemns Anti-Semitism in a Statement Before the Senate Plenary," Mar. 6, 2020, Columbia university, Office of the President. https://president.columbia.edu/news/president-bollinger-condemns-anti-semitism-statement-senate-plenary.

[30] Hixson, "Zionist Campaign Against Free Speech on Campus"; Academic Engagement Network. https://academicengagement.org/.

[31] "Success! Bard College Clears Students Investigated for Protesting Anti-Palestinian Racism," Mar. 9, 2020, Palestine Legal. https://palestinelegal.org/news/2020/3/9/success-bard-clears-students-investigated-for-protesting-anti-palestinian-racism.

[32] "Tufts Students for Justice in Palestine Attacked by University President During Covid-19 Crisis," Apr. 29, 2020, Palestine Legal. https://palestinelegal.org/news/2020/4/29/tufts-sjp-attacked-by-university-president-during-covid-19-crisis; Hixson, "Zionist Campaign Against Free Speech on Campus."

[33] Waxman, *Trouble in the Tribe*, 89.

[34] "House members are Again Pushing a Bill that Would Censor Palestine Advocacy on College Campuses," *Mondoweiss*, Aug. 6, 2019. https://mondoweiss.net/2019/08/palestine-advocacy-campuses/.

[35] "Boycott, Divestment and Sanctions (BDS), J Street statement, undated. https://jstreet.org/policy/boycott-divestment-and-sanctions-bds/#.X8-Kmy1h2u4; https://peacenow.org/page.php?name=bds-name-and-shame-them#.X8-LTS1h2u5.

[36] Barry Trachtenberg, "Challenging the Anti-Semitism Awareness Act: Pushing Back Against Jewish Exceptionalist Politics," *Washington Report on Middle East Affairs* (May 2018): 25-28.

[37] Thrall, "Battle Over Israel and Anti-Semitism Fracturing American Politics."

[38] "US Orders Duke and UNC to Recast Tone in Mideast Studies," *New York Times*, Sept. 19, 2019.

[39] "Legislation," Palestine Legal. https://legislation.palestinelegal.org.

[40] Maria LaHood, "Recent legislation that Threatens First Amendment Rights of Palestinian Solidarity Activists and the Legal Challenges Thereto," *Washington Report on Middle East Affairs* (May 2017). https://www.wrmea.org/017-may/recent-legislation-that-threatens-first-amendment-rights-of-palestinian-solidarity-activists-and-the-legal-challenges-thereto.html

[41] "Is BDS Anti-Semitic?" *New York Times*, July 27, 2019; https://www.nytimes.com/2019/07/27/world/middleeast/bds-israel-boycott-antisemitic.html; Asa Winstanley, "Israel's Growing Strategic Threat to our Freedom of Speech," *Middle East Monitor*, Nov. 27, 2020"; https://www.middleeastmonitor.com/20201127-israels-growing-strategic-threat-to-our-freedom-of-speech/.

[42] "Zoom, Facebook and YouTube Censor SF State Palestine Class," Palestine Legal, Nov. 14, 2020; https://palestinelegal.org/news/2020/9/23/zoom-censors-palestine-class-threatened-to-revoke-zoom-account-for-entire-cal-state-system-over-webinar; Nora Barrows Friedman, "Zoom Censors Events about Zoom Censorship," *Electronic Intifada*, Nov. 13, 2020; https://electronicintifada.net/content/zoom-censors-events-about-zoom-censorship/31696.

[43] Katherine Franke, "The Pro-Israel Push to Purge US Campus Critics," *New York Review of Books Daily*, Dec. 12, 2018; https://www.nybooks.com/daily/2018/12/12/the-pro-israel-push-to-purge-us-campus-critics/.

[44] Gideon Levy, "In U.S. Media, Israel is Untouchable," *Washington Report on Middle East Affairs* (January/February 2019): 14-15.

[45] "Omar: 'I unequivocally apologize' after backlash over New Israel Tweets," CNN .com, Feb. 12, 2019. https://www.cnn.com/2019/02/11/politics/ilhan-omar-aipac-backlash/index.html.

[46] Tim Farron, "Why do Evangelicals Support Trump? They're Giving Christianity a Bad Name," *The Guardian*, June 5, 2019. https://www.theguardian.com/commentisfree/2019/jun/05/us-evangelical-christians-trump-bad-name.

[47] "Republicans and Democrats Grown Even Further Apart in View of Israel, Palestinians," Pew Research Center, Jan. 23, 2018. https://www.people-press.org/2018/01/23/republicans-and-democrats-grow-even-further-apart-in-views-of-israel-palestinians/.

[48] "Mike Pence Slams Ilhan Omar at AIPAC," *Haaretz*, Mar. 25, 2019. https://www.haaretz.com/us-news/mike-pence-slams-ilhan-omar-at-aipac-full-transcript-1.7059025.

[49] Noa Landau, "Israel Presented Tlaib with a Cruel Dilemma: Her Principles or Her Family," *Washington Report on Middle East Affairs* (October 2019): 8-9.

[50] Thrall, "Battle Over Israel and Anti-Semitism Fracturing American Politics."

[51] Josh Ruebner, "Palestinian Americans Sidelined During DNC Platform Debate," *Mondoweiss*, July 30, 2020. https://mondoweiss.net/2020/07/palestinian-americans-sidelined-during-dnc-platform-debate/.

[52] Ali Harb, "How AIPAC Is Losing Bipartisan Support in Washington," *Middle East Eye*, Feb. 14, 2020; https://www.middleeasteye.net/big-story/how-aipac-losing-bipartisan-support-washington.

[53] Alex Kane, "'They've Incited Hate: The Democratic Congresswoman Taking on AIPAC," *+972 Magazine*, Feb. 14, 2020; https://www.972mag.com/betty-mccollum-aipac-palestinian-rights/.

[54] Ian S. Lustick, *Paradigm Lost: From Two-State Solution to One-State Reality.* Philadelphia: University of Pennsylvania Press, 2019.

[55] "AIPAC Tells US Lawmakers it Won't Push Back If They Criticize Annexation," *The Times of Israel*, June 11, 2020. https://www.timesofisrael.com/in-first-aipac-gives-us-lawmakers-green-light-to-criticize-israel-on-annexation/.

[56] Alex Kane, "Democratic Lobby Group Defends Israel's Demolition of Palestinian Hamlet," Dec. 16, 2020, *+972 Magazine*. https://www.972mag.com/democrats-israel-lobby-demolition/.

[57] *New York Times,* Mar. 28, 2019.

[58] J Street, "2020 Election Report," https://jstreet.org/2020-election-report/#.X8uw5i1h1N0.

[59] "Billionaire Casino Boss Sheldon Adelson Splashes the Cash in Bid to Help Trump," *The Guardian*, Oct. 30, 2020; https://www.theguardian.com/us-news/2020/oct/31/sheldon-adelson-trump-republicans-election.

[60] *New York Times*, Aug. 20, 2019.

[61] "How Did Jews Vote? Polls Offer Imperfect Take, Though Big Picture is Clear," *The Times of Israel*," Dec. 5, 2020. https://www.timesofisrael.com/how-did-us-jews-vote-polls-offer-imperfect-take-though-big-picture-is-clear/; "Jewish Voters Play a Role in Deciding the 2020 Election," *Jewish Journal*, Dec. 5, 2020; https://jewishjournal.org/2020/11/12/jewish-voters-play-a-role-in-deciding-the-2020-election/.

[62] "Mazel Tov, Trump. You've Revived the Jewish Left," *New York Times*, Aug. 24, 2019.

[63] "Evangelicals Stick with Trump, See Upside Even if He Loses," Associated Press, Nov. 7, 2020. https://apnews.com/article/election-2020-joe-biden-donald-trump-race-and-ethnicity-elections-7433585aae55ea0cadd9ea5f0eb00a62.

Chapter 11 Conclusions

[1] Michael Arria, "Why the Democratic Party Platform Matters," *Mondoweiss*, July 31, 2020. https://mondoweiss.net/2020/07/why-the-democratic-party-platform-matters/.

[2] "Engel Bragged, 'I Sit Down with AIPAC on Every Piece of Legislation' Coming out of the Foreign Affairs Committee," *Mondoweiss*, June 25, 2020. https://mondoweiss.net/2020/06/engel-bragged-of-sitting-down-with-aipac-on-every-piece-of-legislation-that-comes-out-of-foreign-affairs/.

[3] Eric Alterman, "In New York, Zionism and Liberalism faced Off—and Liberalism Won," *Nation*, July 1, 2020. https://www.thenation.com/article/politics/eliot-engel-israel/.

[4] "Ilhan Omar Wins Primary in Minnesota Over Well-Funded Rival," The Wall Street Journal, Aug. 12, 2020; https://www.wsj.com/articles/ilhan-omar-faces-well-funded-rival-in-democratic-primary-in-minnesota-11597152277.

[5] Philip Weiss, "Beinart's 'earthquake'—Why so Powerful? Why Now?" *Mondoweiss*, July 22, 2020. https://mondoweiss.net/2020/07/beinarts-earthquake-why-so-powerful-why-now/.

[6] Philip Weiss, "Finkelstein, a Victim of the Israel Lobby, Denies That It Has Power," *Mondoweiss*, Feb. 23, 2008; https://mondoweiss.net/2008/02/last-fall-norma/; "Noam Chomsky and Omar Baddar Debate the Israel Lobby," May 3, 2012; https://www.youtube.com/watch?v=REdxS1rbsmk.

[7] Khalidi, Hundred Years' War on Palestine, 233.

[8] "US Foreign Aid to Israel," Congressional Research Service, Nov. 16, 2020. https://fas.org/sgp/crs/mideast/RL33222.pdf.

[9] George Altshuler, "AIPAC Plans Considerable Growth, D.C. Zoning Documents Show," *Washington Jewish Week*, Dec. 9, 2016. https://washingtonjewishweek.com/35176/aipac-plans-considerable-growth-d-c-zoning-documents-show/news/local-news/.

¹⁰ Michael Neibauer, "Citing Rapid Growth, Leading pro-Israel Lobby Pitches Major D.C. HQ Expansion," *Washington Business Journal*, Oct. 29, 2015. https://www.bizjournals.com/washington/breaking_ground/2015/10/citing-rapid-growth-leading-pro-israel-lobby.html; in December 2020 AIPAC's page on "Linked In" cited 492 AIPAC employees. https://www.linkedin.com/company/aipac.

¹¹ "Pro-Israel Group Lobbies for U.S. Aid, Funds Congressional Trips," *The Wall Street Journal*, Feb. 14, 2019. https://www.wsj.com/articles/pro-israel-group-lobbies-for-u-s-aid-funds-congressional-trips-11550174834.

¹² Grant F. Smith, *The Israel Lobby Enters State Government: Rise of the Virginia Israel Advisory Board.* Washington: Institute for Research: Middle East Policy, 2019.

¹³ Grant F. Smith, *Big Israel.* Washington: IRmep, 2016: 317.

¹⁴ Mor Loushy, "The Kings of Capitol Hill" [documentary film], Stop Press! Productions, 2020.

¹⁵ Asa Winstanley, "The Black Lives Matter Movement's Stand with Palestinians Has a History," *Middle East Monitor*, July 1, 2020. https://www.middleeastmonitor.com/20200701-the-black-lives-matter-movements-stand-with-palestinians-has-a-history/.

Appendix

¹ "Danny Danon's Bible speech Goes Viral," Israelnationalnews.com (May 16, 2019). http://www.israelnationalnews.com/News/News.aspx/263262.

² Nur Masalha, *The Zionist Bible: Biblical Precedent, Colonialism, and the Erasure of Memory.* Berne: Acumen, 2013: 125.

³ Raz, *Bride and Dowry*, 140, 184; "Myths and Facts—The Background to the Arab-Israel War" *NER Special Supplement* (August 1967): B-4.

⁴ Nathan Thrall, "How the Battle Over Israel and Anti-Semitism is Fracturing American Politics," *New York Times Magazine*, Mar. 28, 2019.

⁵ "Chapter 5: Connection with and Attitudes Toward Israel," Pew Research Center, Oct. 1, 2013. https://www.pewforum.org/2013/10/01/chapter-5-connection-with-and-attitudes-towards-israel/.

⁶ Donald H. Akenson, *God's Peoples: Covenant Theology in South Africa, Israel and Ulster.* Ithaca: Cornell University Press, 1992: 349, 155, 9-10.

⁷ Michael Prior, *The Bible and Colonialism: A Moral Critique.* Sheffield, England: Sheffield Academic Press, 1997: 291; Emanuel Pfoh, "From the Search for Ancient Israel to the History of Ancient Palestine," in Hjelm and Thompson, *History, Archaeology and the Bible after 'Historicity,'* 149; Pappé, "Bible in the Service of Zionism," 207.

⁸ Biblical studies are a complex and evolving arena of inquiry. For an overview see the anthology by J.W. Rogerson and Judith M. Lieu, *The Oxford Handbook of Biblical Studies.* New York: Oxford University Press, 2006.

⁹ Thomas L. Thompson, *Early History of the Israelite People: From the Written and Archeological Sources.* Leiden: E.J. Brill, 1992: 2.

[10] Keith W. Whitelam, *The Invention of Ancient Israel: The Silencing of Palestinian History*. London and New York: Routledge, 1996: 2-3; see also Philip R. Davies, *In Search of Ancient Israel*. Sheffield, England: JSOT Press, 1992.

[11] "Minimalists," also referenced as the "Copenhagen School," include Thompson and Davies cited above as well as Niels Peter Lemche. Denied tenure at Marquette University, Thompson resumed his academic career at the University of Copenhagen.

[12] Thomas Romer, *The Invention of God*. Cambridge, MA.: Harvard University Press, 2015: 3.

[13] Pfoh, "From Search for Ancient Israel to History of Palestine," 146-47; Lukasz Niesiolowski-Spano, *Origin Myths and Holy Places in the Old Testament*. London: Equinox Publishing, 2011: 250.

[14] Pfoh, "From Search for Ancient Israel to History of Palestine," 149; see also Mark G. Brett, *Decolonizing God: The Bible and the Tides of Empire*. Sheffield, England: Sheffield Phoenix Press, 2008.

[15] Prior, *Bible and Colonialism*, 248; Shlomo Sand, *The Invention of the Jewish People*. New York: Verso Books, 2010: 118-22.

[16] Israel Finkelstein and Neil A. Silberman, *The Bible Unearthed: Archaeology's New Vision of Ancient Israel and the Origin of its Sacred Texts*. New York: Touchstone, 2001: 61-63.

[17] Romer, *Invention of God*, 52.

[18] Finkelstein and Silberman, *Bible Unearthed*, 81-82, 118.

[19] Romer, *Invention of God*, 106.

[20] Marc Zvi Brettler, "The Hebrew Bible and the Early History of Israel," in Judith R. Baskin and Kenneth Seeskin, eds., *Jewish History, Religion, and Culture*. New York: Cambridge University Press, 2010: 16.

[21] Masalha, *Zionist Bible*, 246.

[22] Romer, *Invention of God*, 9-12.

[23] Prior, *Bible and Colonialism*, 251; Romer, *Invention of God*, 13.

[24] William F. Albright, *From Stone Age to Christianity: Monotheism and the Historical Process*. Baltimore: Johns Hopkins University Press, 1957; 1946: 280-81.

[25] Pekka Pitkanen, "Ancient Israel and Settler Colonialism," *Settler Colonial Studies* 4, (2013): 64-81; Pitkanen review of Nur Masalha, *The Zionist Bible* in *Settler Colonial Studies* 5 (2015), 398-99; on genocidal discourses in Deuteronomy, see Brett, *Decolonizing God*, 79-93.

[26] Brettler, "Hebrew Bible and Early History of Israel," 20-22.

[27] Ibid., 29.

[28] Prior, *Bible and Colonialism*, 289.

[29] Finkelstein and Silberman, *Bible Unearthed*, 44.

[30] Romer, *Invention of God*, 20.

[31] Ibid., 160.

[32] Exodus 20: 3; Deuteronomy 17: 2, *Holy Bible*.

[33] Romer, *Invention of God*, 101.

[34] Finkelstein and Silberman, *Bible Unearthed*, 44.

[35] Alan F. Segal, "The Second Temple Period," in Baskin and Seeskin, eds., *Jewish History, Religion, and Culture*, 34-38.

[36] Romer, *Invention of God*, 5.

[37] Segal, "Second Temple Period," 40.

[38] Phyllis Goldstein, *A Convenient Hatred: The History of Antisemitism*. Brookline, MA.: Facing History and Ourselves, 2012, 31.

[39] Ibid., 12, 17.

[40] Gudrun Kramer, *A History of Palestine: From the Ottoman Conquest to the Founding of the State of Israel*. Princeton: Princeton University Press, 2008: 13-14.

[41] Segal, "Second Temple Period," 60-61.

[42] Goldstein, *Convenient Hatred*, 20-21.

[43] Bart D. Ehrman, *Jesus: Apocalyptic Prophet of the New Millennium*. New York: Oxford University Press, 1999.

[44] Goldstein, *Convenient Hatred*, 33.

[45] Segal, "Second Temple Period," 65.

[46] Ira M. Lapidus, *A History of Islamic Societies*. New York: Cambridge University Press, 2014, 3d ed.: 33-36.

[47] Tamim Ansary, *Destiny Disrupted: A History of the World Through Islamic Eyes*. New York: Public Affairs, 2009: 17-20; Lapidus, *History of Islamic Societies*, 40.

[48] Juan Cole, *Muhammad: Prophet of Peace amid the Clash of Empires*. New York: Nation Books, 2018.

[49] Lapidus, *History of Islamic Societies*, 38-41.

[50] Norman A. Stillman, The Jewish Experience in the Muslim World," in Baskin and Seeskin, eds., *Jewish History, Religion, and Culture*, 87-88.

[51] Ibid., 90.

[52] Robert Chazan, "Jewish Life in Western Christendom," in Baskin and Seeskin, eds., *Jewish History, Religion, and Culture*, 113-39.

[53] Goldstein, *Convenient Hatred*, 63-73.

[54] Chazan, "Jewish Life in Western Christendom," 130-31.

[55] Goldstein, *Convenient Hatred*, 75-107.

[56] *Ibid.*, 107.

[57] *Ibid.*, 123-24.

[58] *Ibid.*, 137-55.

[59] *Ibid.*, 170; Chazan, "Jewish Life in Western Christendom," 123, 138.

[60] Marsha L. Rozenblit, "European Jewry, 1800-1933," in Baskin and Seeskin, eds., *Jewish History, Religion, and Culture*, 170-75.

[61] *Ibid.*, 175-205.

[62] Goldstein, *Convenient Hatred*, 207.

[63] Rozenblit, "European Jewry, 1800-1933," 192-94.

[64] *Ibid.*, 198.

[65] *Ibid.*, 198.

[66] Goldstein, *Convenient Hatred*, 243-45.

Index

235

Index

Index

Index

Index

Index

Made in United States
North Haven, CT
30 November 2021